T5-BCI-874

INNOVATION IN ELECTRONIC MAIL

INNOVATION IN ELECTRONIC MAIL

Towards Open Information Networks - Perspectives on Innovation Policy

Peter H.M. VERVEST

1987

NORTH-HOLLAND - AMSTERDAM · NEW YORK · OXFORD · TOKYO

384.34
V57i

© PETER VERVEST – 1986

All rights reserved. No part of this publication may be reproduced, stored in a retrieval system, or transmitted, in any form or by any means, electronic, mechanical, photocopying, recording or otherwise, without the prior permission of the copyright owner.

ISBN 0 444 70153 2

Publishers
ELSEVIER SCIENCE PUBLISHERS B.V.
P.O. BOX 1991
1000 BZ AMSTERDAM
THE NETHERLANDS

Sole distributors for the U.S.A. and Canada
ELSEVIER SCIENCE PUBLISHING COMPANY, INC?
52 VANDERBILT AVENUE
NEW YORK, N.Y. 10017
U.S.A.

PRINTED IN THE NETHERLANDS

Peter Vervest – born in Eindhoven, on 22nd of May 1955 – studied law and management sciences at the universities of Utrecht and Delft in the Netherlands. Since 1979 he has been working with Philips Telecommunications in Hilversum, where he has been Product Manager of 'New Telecommunication Services' specializing in the field of electronic mail. In 1984 he was appointed Application Manager at Philips International Home Interactive Systems in Eindhoven. In 1983 he was elected to the faculty of the Technical Department of the Erasmus University Graduate School of Management in Rotterdam. In 1986 he was awarded the doctor's degree in technical sciences cum laude from the Technische Hogeschool Delft.

Dr. Vervest has lectured throughout Europe and has written a number of reports and papers on the subject of electronic mail. His publications include 'Electronic Mail and Message Handling', a book which has been well received in Europe and the United States of America and has been translated into Japanese. His research also includes a detail study of industrial buying of word processing equipment, which was presented to the European Academy for Advanced Research in Marketing in 1980.

UNIVERSITY LIBRARIES
CARNEGIE-MELLON UNIVERSITY
PITTSBURGH, PENNSYLVANIA 15213

to Kathelijne
and my parents

FOREWORD

The development of human civilisation is parallelled by a development in communication and information technology. When our early predecessors became hunters, they were forced to develop speech in order to be able to hunt in groups. Later, the large, ancient agricultural empires required written language and courier services for their administration. The industrial revolution required faster and more extensive systems for communication, and the 19th century assigned much of its creativity and entrepreneurship towards meeting this challenge. Out of this struggle emerged services such as the regular mail, telegraph, telephone and later telex. As we enter another stage of the evolution of our civilisation, with information playing the prime role, many argue that new means of communication will again be required. Electronic mail is a cluster of technologies that will meet this challenge, together with information systems, the mass media and their derivatives.

This study explores the development of electronic mail from the aspect of innovation theory. It assesses the social and technological driving forces involved, present and future technologies, the bottlenecks limiting further use and development, and the competition between the new systems. In addition, it scans the possibilities and conditions for co-operation. After discussing the developments in telecommunications and electronic mail, and innovation theory, a definition of electronic mail is given which forms the basis for the remainder of the book. Next the bottlenecks hindering the further development and applications are discussed, followed by an in-depth analysis of the standardisation and public policy aspects. The book closes with a discussion about open information networks.

This book is aimed at two groups of readers. Those active in the field of telecommunication will find a well documented and highly original view about the developments and decisions required for the further proliferation of electronic mail technology.Those interested in innovation theory will find a case about a highly complex subject, complex both from the point of view of the multitude of mutually competing new technologies, as well as from the point of view of a highly diffused and complex selection environment. It is the logical continuation of the path entered by Nelson and Winter, and followed by authors such as Dosi. In this book, the author has managed to extend the economic theory of innovation to include complex technological trajectories and complex selection environments, and at the same time arriving at practical conclusions and recommendations for practitioners in industry and government.

Foreword by J.G. Wissema

The concepts behind this book were developed as a result of research made at the Management of Technology Section of Rotterdam Business School. As such, it served as a Ph.D. thesis for the Delft University of Technology (Technische Hogeschool Delft), the Netherlands. During the same period, the author held several commercial and development functions with Philips Telecommunications Industry, as well as Philips Home Interactive Systems. I would like to thank all those who contributed to this investigation. This includes the sponsors, Philips Home Interactive Systems, the Department of Economic Affairs, the Dutch PTT, and the Department of Education and Sciences. There was academic support from the universities of Rotterdam, Delft, Eindhoven and Brighton (United Kingdom). Many members of industry and research institutions in the United States of America, Japan and Europe were questioned regarding their opinions on certain aspects during study tours. The International Communications Association rendered assistance in a questionnaire distributed among their members. The PhD committee and the project's liaison group also gave many valuable suggestions. MBA students and secretaries rendered research and administrative assistance.

This book is a truly inter-disciplinary investigation which concerns itself with the introduction of new technology. It is hoped that it will provide a role in assisting industry, government and students in their study of similar innovation processes in the future.

Johan G. Wissema
Professor of Technology Management
Erasmus University Rotterdam, the Netherlands

CONTENTS

FIGURES AND TABLES

ABBREVIATIONS

ANSI	American National Standards Institute
AICF	Access, Interworking and Conversion Facilities
AMF	Administrative and Management Facilities
AT&T	American Telephone & Telegraph company
CAD	Computer-Aided Design
CAE	Computer-Aided Engineering
CAM	Computer-Aided Manufacturing
CAPTAIN	Character And Pattern Telephone Access Information Network
CASE	Common Application Service Element
CBMS	Computer Based Message System
CCITT	International Telegraph and Telephone Consultative Committee
CE	Communication Entity
CEN	Comité Européen de Normalisation
CENELEC	Comité Européen de Normalisation Electronique
CER	Receiving Communication Entity
CEPT	Conference of European Post and Telecommunications Administrations
CES	Sending Communication Entity
CSPDN	Circuit Switched Public Data Network
DP	Draft Proposal
DCA	Document Content Architecture
DCE	Data Circuit-terminating Equipment
DIA	Document Interchange Architecture
DIS	Draft International Standard
DS	Document Storage
DTE	Data Terminal Equipment
EC	European Community
ECMA	European Computer Manufacturers Association
EMS	Electronic Mail System
ESPRIT	European Strategic Program for R&D on Information Technology
FCC	Federal Communications Commission
ICA	International Communications Association
IEEE	Institute of Electrical and Electronics Engineers
IFIP	International Federation for Information Processing
INTUG	International Telecommunications User Group
IPM	Interpersonal Messaging
IS	International Standard
ISDN	Integrated Services Digital Network
ISO	International Organisation for Standardisation
ITSTC	Steering Committee for Information Technology
JMPT	Japanese Ministry of Post and Telecommunications
JTPC	Joint Technical Programs Committee (IEC – ISO)
LAN	Local Area Network
MAP	Manufacturers Automation Protocol
MD	Management Domain

MH	Message Handling
MHS	Message Handling System
MITI	Ministry of International Trade and Industry of Japan
MPF	Message Processing Facilities
MTA	Message Transfer Agent
MTAE	Message Transfer Agent Entity
MTF	Message Transfer Facilities
MTL	Message Transfer Layer
NAPLPS	North American Presentation Level Protocol Syntax
NBS	National Bureau of Standards
NTIA	National Telecommunications and Information Agency
NTT	Nippon Telegraph & Telephone Public Corporation
OA	Office Automation
ODA	Office Document Architecture
ODIF	Office Document Interchange Format
OSI	Open Systems Interconnection
OTA	US Congress Office of Technology Assessment
PABX	Private Automatic Branch Exchange
PC	Personal Computer
PSPDN	Packet Switched Public Data Network
PSTN	Public Switched Telephone Network
RACE	R&D in Advanced Communications in Europe
RTS	Reliable Transfer Service
SAP	Service Access Point
SASE	Specific Application Service Element
SDE	Submission/Delivery Entity
SNA	Systems Network Architecture
SOGITS	Senior Officials Group for Information Technology Standardization
SOGT	Senior Officials Group for Telecommunications
SPAG	Standards Promotion and Application Group
TDCC	Transportation Data Co-ordinating Committee
TTXAU	Teletex Access Unit
UA	User Agent
UAE	User Agent Element
UAL	User Agent Layer
UE	User Element
VAN	Value Added Network
WAN	Wide Area Network
WP	Word Processor

PREFACE

New developments in information technology provide both a challenge and a threat to the current practice of management. In the future, information services will govern the processes and structures of modern business; they will have an enormous impact on both our business and our social life. According to McFarlan, McKenney and Pyburn (1983), a new balance will have to be found between local and central power, and a new kind of -corporate- planning is necessary. Moreover, the applications of new information technology may result in profound changes in our modern households.

In order to organize the use of new information technologies, a new paradigm is necessary. Data may be distributed around the world; people or organizations may wish to exchange information, but the availability of such data, or the accessability of information is at present often cumbersome, expensive, ill-timed or even impossible. Taking 'electronic mail' as the point of departure, this study seeks the new way of organizing modern information technology in 'Message Handling Systems'. In corrobaration with 'Open Systems Interconnection' a new paradigm is given to organize the application of new information technology; at the same time it provides new directions for technological developments.

The study was started as a doctor's thesis (which was awarded cum laude by the Technische Hogeschool Delft in June 1986) and supported by many individuals and organizations worldwide. First I wish to thank my promotor, professor Hans Wissema for his enormous enthousiasm and his continued inspiration. A second word of thanks should go to the immediate contributors: 'Philips International BV', 'Philips Telecommunicatie Industrie BV', 'Erasmus Universiteit Rotterdam', 'Staatsbedrijf der Posterijen, Telegrafie en Telefonie', 'Ministerie van Economische Zaken', 'Ministerie van Onderwijs en Wetenschappen'. Their contributions were certainly not limited to finance, but included also organizational and intellectual support. I also wish to thank all the other numerous people who have contributed in one way or another to the formation of this book. My hope is that this work may facilitate, guide, and perhaps give direction, to the optimal use of the new information technology.

Peter H.M. Vervest
Eindhoven, July 1986

INTRODUCTION

The integration of various computer and communications technologies has given a new meaning to the term 'electronic mail'. Since the early days of the telegraph, electronic mail has developed into computer-based message exchange. There has been a rapid development in the supporting technologies, which are neither stable at present nor expected to be stable in the near future (1).

Applications are under development which will greatly extend and diversify the use of electronic mail from person-to-person correspondence as at present to new areas. New applications include different types of group communications such as bulletin boards and conferencing (2). As well as this electronic mail will in future be applied to communications between human beings and computer systems, offering access to remote information as well as different kinds of information transactions with respect to, among other things, financial transfer, ordering, logistics and decision support (3).

At the same time the anticipated users are shifting from the specialised business organizations to virtually anybody with access to a terminal, be it a telephone or a sophisticated computer system. Electronic mail may become as important as postal and telephone services today.

Towards message handling

Why is it that developments in electronic mail hold such a promise for the future? I will argue that the main factor is the use of computers as an intermediate means for human beings to interface with a telecommunication system. Because of rapid developments in terminal equipment, such as communicating personal computers, and because of the ongoing storage of massive amounts of data in computer systems, a new idea becomes conceivable: the development of a worldwide message exchange capability to facilitate interpersonal communications as well as information transfer in the broadest sense of that term.

The current process of innovation in electronic mail started with the invention of the 'electronic mailbox': in the early 1970s a number of researchers, brought together by the US Department of Defense via the Advanced Research Projects Agency Network (ARPANET), designed and developed the first experimental systems to exchange computer resident messages among themselves (4). Each individual user was given a computer mailbox, i.e. a personal working area within a computer system to compose, send, receive and file messages. The electronic mailbox was an important new concept and was totally new at that time as it meant that a computer would act as an 'agent' of the human being and intervene in the communications process.

However, the early electronic mailbox systems, or Computer Based Message System (CBMS), lacked a way to exchange messages between different systems which were connected via a network. The first problem was to effect message exchange independent of the type of public or private telecommunication means being used. Secondly, agreement was necessary between the computer systems themselves with respect to the process of message communications and the type of messages to be exchanged (5).

To resolve these problems international standardization was sought to set common rules as an architecture for 'open systems interconnection'. The International Organization for Standardization (ISO) developed a general Reference Model for Open Systems Interconnection (OSI) as a framework (6). In 1984 the International Telegraph and Telephone Consultative Committee (CCITT) set the Recommendations Series X.400 on Message Handling Systems (MHS) (7). The Open Systems Interconnection / Message Handling Systems (OSI/ MHS) model forms the basis for further agreements on computer-based message exchange. It should be noted that as of today, the interconnection problems have still not been resolved exhaustively.

Systems interconnection, however, cannot be an isolated objective. The purpose is meaningful communications, i.e. the cooperation among distributed systems to perform a common task: this is a pressing issue for the design of future message handling systems since the content of a message need not be irrelevant for the engineering aspects of the system itself (8). As will be explained in this study, message handling is primarily an intermediate function between system application processes on the one hand and system communication processes on the other. 'Meaningful interconnection' is critical for the overall efficiency and effectiveness of message handling.

With this in mind I will adopt the position that OSI/MHS is a new trajectory for technological advance. It will be a way to shield the variety of networks and communication protocols from the application processes (and vice versa) and to effect meaningful relations between systems.

Public service

In addition to common rules for message exchange, the actual interconnect facilities to effect that exchange need to be developed. The availability of these facilities will be particularly important for the process of innovation in electronic mail. It leads to the question of whether these facilities should be offered as a public service, and if so, which role governments have in ensuring the availability and quality of the service.

The rationale for a public telecommunication service is essentially to share facilities among different users on the basis of 'equal' access. This can have both economic and social benefits. First, depending on the pattern of communication, the utility of a telecommunication system increases with the number of users. Second, sharing can be more efficient and cost-effective in the longer term.

The operation of a (public) telecommunication system raises a number of important issues, in particular:

1. what should be the network plan?
2. how should users access the system?
3. how should users address each other?
4. what data transfer services should be offered?
5. how are costs to be allocated to the users?

Let us take the telephone system as an example: the network plan determines which locations are interconnected and how they are numbered. Access to the telephone system is given via the telephone set; via dialling the telephone number, the system establishes a circuit from one telephone location to another. As soon as the circuit has been established, data can be transferred (i.e. normally for voice communications between human beings). Costs are in general allocated to the calling party on the basis of call duration and distance.

Another example is the postal system. There is a network plan of geographic addresses at which mailboxes are located as the access points of the postal system. Users address each other by name, geographical address and postal code. Data to be tranferred can, in principle, be anything that is contained in an envelope, and cost allocation is to the sender on the basis of weight and distance.

Analogies can be seen with transportation systems such as the rail and road systems: there is a network plan; a means to access the system (trains and cars); a way to find the appropriate location (timetables and road-maps); a transfer mechanism (railway and roads); and a method to allocate costs (tickets and taxes).

The operation of a shared telecommunication system requires a strong 'service' orientation on behalf of the system operator. Sharing should offer added-value to the user when compared with private (or closed) systems. Where this added-value lies, is a trade-off between network intelligence and terminal intelligence. Computers increasingly add artificiality to the telecommunication process: terminals become intelligent devices which act as agents of the human beings to serve their communication needs. It is within this context that the computerized terminal will need working areas, as part of the telecommunication system, in order to gather, compile, process, and store data for transfer to computer systems which are able to be connected.

Within this context of 'open' computer systems, public message handling services are important which:

1. enable the access to the intermediate telecommunication systems and the connected user systems, and at the same time verify the compliance with access rules;
2. allow knowledge about the identity and communication capabilities of the connected systems;
3. ensure reliable message transfer between connected systems.

The success of the innovation in electronic mail will greatly depend on the availability of these public services and the way in which they are implemented. However, it does not necessarily mean that there is a political or economic basis for a single public system which offers these services; nor that public ownership of the service facilities is mandatory.

Developments in electronic mail can shed a new light on the role of governments in ensuring the provision of telecommunication services. In particular, I will argue that specific government measures with respect to regulation of message handling services can positively influence the speed and direction of the innovation process (9).

Message handling services are fundamentally different from traditional telecommunication services. Telephone services in particular were provided directly for human beings, often leading to the inclusion of the user terminal as an integral part of the services being offered. Developments are now shifting the focus toward services being provided for computer systems instead of human beings, independent of the specific use that human beings are making of these computer systems. This will result in different concepts for the provision of public service and the role of government in this respect.

First the notion of equal access will change: it will be more complicated to determine under what circumstances equal access to public facilities should be allowed and when it should be denied. The role of standardization will gradually shift to determining compatibility rather than uniformity. Governments will have a significant role in determining what equal access should cover and how an 'equal playing field' for the provision of services will be established.

Second, public directories will become more diverse and the complexity of compiling and maintaining public directories will increase enormously. Governments will have to make provisions for ensuring the availability and registration of communicating parties and their communication capabilities in public directories. This raises important questions about privacy and secrecy.

Third, an important change will take place with respect to cost-allocation. The tariff structure as applied for telephone services, will be inadequate for computer communications, which typically occur in short 'bursts' with generally frequent but short calls. Tariffs that are based on the quantity of data which is transferred are more appropriate for most types of computer communications. Another change will result from the interconnection of different networks, each with their own tariff structure. This can lead to disturbing delicate tariff policies aimed at recovering long-term investments in transmission and switching facilities.

Governments will have a definite role to facilitate the above change and to ensure services for message transport. In this study I will argue for the creation of a generic value-added network regulated by government.

Standardization can become an explicit government tool of technology innovation policy. It seems to me that in conjunction with regulatory policy this can have a positive impact on the creation of new message handling systems as the basis for a wide range of tele-information services. It will be a socially desirable objective to provide access to information: message handling can form the kernel of an 'open information network' in such a way that a market mechanism can determine the free flow of information.

Scope and nature of the study

This study has been undertaken to perform an analysis of the characteristics of the process of innovation in electronic mail, with the aim to identify the main business and government policy issues. In particular, the following questions are being addressed:

1. what is the nature of electronic mail and what are the new developments directing the innovation process?
2. what changes are anticipated in usage patterns of mail systems? which factors stimulate or facilitate the process of change? and what are the bottlenecks?
3. what is the impact of standards? and which are the most critical issues of innovation policy? what are possible government actions for directing and promoting the innovation process?

The nature of the study is one of innovation policy, covering the issues of the generation of new technology as well as the market and non-market selection environment (10). However, the developments in electronic mail, in particular those of new message handling systems, are in a very early stage. Therefore much emphasis is given to the technical aspects of the innovation process as an attempt to provide a clear and precise view of the trajectory of technical change.

My first explorations into the field of electronic mail have shown that standardization plays a very specific role in the innovation process: a certain level of common understanding between the developers of new systems is mandatory due to the rigid demand of system interconnection. In this way standardization is not an 'a posteriori' result of innovation but an 'a priori' requirement (11). Standardization is a critical element in the transition from invention to market acceptance. Moreover, the need for interconnection extends to ensuring the availability of publicly accessable services. For this reason standardization and regulation had to be vital elements of the study.

The investigation covered literature search, exploratory study tours and a user questionnaire (12). Also a number of expert discussions took place (13). The investigation is explorative and conceptual rather than quantitative. For quantitative estimates reference is made to note (14); in view of the early stage of developments, quantitative estimates must remain highly speculative.

Much emphasis has been given to the developments in the USA and Japan for two reasons. First, at the time that the research plan was designed, the market developments in the USA seemed to have progressed far more than those in Western Europe; as concerns Japan, government innovation policy seemed to be both more planned and more far-reaching than in Western Europe. The second reason was that the study of two, possibly extreme and contradictory situations (USA vs. Japan), could present a new view on the opportunities and threats for Western Europe. During the course of this study, Western Europe has become more concerned about its competitiveness in telecommunications: standardization efforts have greatly intensified as a way to forge new cooperative structures. This study may particularly offer a complementary view on the ongoing and confusing developments in Western Europe.

Chapter layout

A brief overview of the nature of innovation research and, specifically, the methodological aspects of this study is given in the next paragraph.

The nature of electronic mail, the innovation policy aspects and the new developments affecting change are discussed in Chapters 1. and 2.
First the concept of fusion in telecommunications due to the merging of computers and communications is discussed. This merger necessitates that one clearly distinguishes between technology, system, network and service. Chapter 1. also discusses the relationship between innovation and policy: an approach to analysing the potential of innovations, i.e. substitution analysis, is taken as a basis to show the richer understanding offered by the theory of Nelson and Winter. This gives the theoretical framework for this study, in particular with respect to the impact of innovation policy on current issues in public telecommunications.

Chapter 2. gives an historical overview of the developments in electronic mail: while in essence a step-by-step process, new developments are putting a new challenge to the concept of 'mail'. This leads to ambiguity with respect to its definition. Three definitions are discussed in Chapter 2. In a limited sense, electronic mail is defined as CBMS and voice mail. A more comprehensive definition includes CBMS and voice mail as well as facsimile, communicating word processors, telex/TWX, message switching and electronic document distribution (15). The third definition is even broader and based on the functional aspects of message handling systems. I will opt for this broad definition of electronic mail, which includes both person-to-person as well as person-to-computer communications.

Note that electronic mail from a functional point of view is placed at the application layer of the OSI model. The various mail systems are grouped in four categories, as given in Chapter 2.

The function of a mail system is to provide message handling services: which services are included, the importance of the directory, and the type of public services for future message handling, is the second topic dealt with in this chapter. It provides an argument for a systems approach as developed by ISO and CCITT. However I will show that associations between systems can have effects for communications, in particular for message handling, that are generally not taken into account.

Chapters 1. and 2. are primarily discussing the technology and science base of the innovation process. The introduction of new mail systems is dealt with in Chapter 3. First the importance of the large organization is analyzed; to this end a questionnaire investigation has been carried out among the members of the International Communications Association (ICA) which is a major user organization of telecommunication managers. The needs of the large organization are specifically related to the development of office automation and office communication systems; bottlenecks which were found in the organizational and user acceptance, the financial justification and the availability of the appropriate equipment, software and services, are also dealt with.

The second part of Chapter 3. discusses the applications of electronic mail for communications between organizations, in particular for the small and medium size companies; in this respect electronic mail and message handling can form the kernel for value-added network services.

The issue of standardization is dealt with in Chapter 4. Because of the technical complexity of the standardization process, a technical overview of the involved standards is given. Next, the role of governments in promoting the standards in Western Europe, USA and Japan is studied. Standards, as will be shown, have a very important role in marking the transition from the innovation period to the selection environment.

Chapter 5. analyzes the main policy issues with respect to innovation in electronic mail. The revision in regulatory regimes for the provision of telecommunication services, has profound impacts on innovation processes in telecommunications in general; the developments to create an 'equal playing field' will influence the success of new message handling systems. In particular, message handling can denote a new borderline between those functions in telecommunications which contribute to public utility, and those which should be regulated by the market mechanism, i.e. by way of free competition with only a minimum of government involvement.

On the basis of the critical factors which mark the innovation process in electronic mail, in particular the possible effects of standards, four scenarios are proposed: a liberal-technology scenario, a contrived-technology scenario, a market-led and a government-led standards promotion scenario. Finally a possible message handling policy for the Netherlands is proposed.

Chapter 6. outlines the evolutionary path of telecommunication networks and

FIGURE I.1 CHAPTER LAYOUT

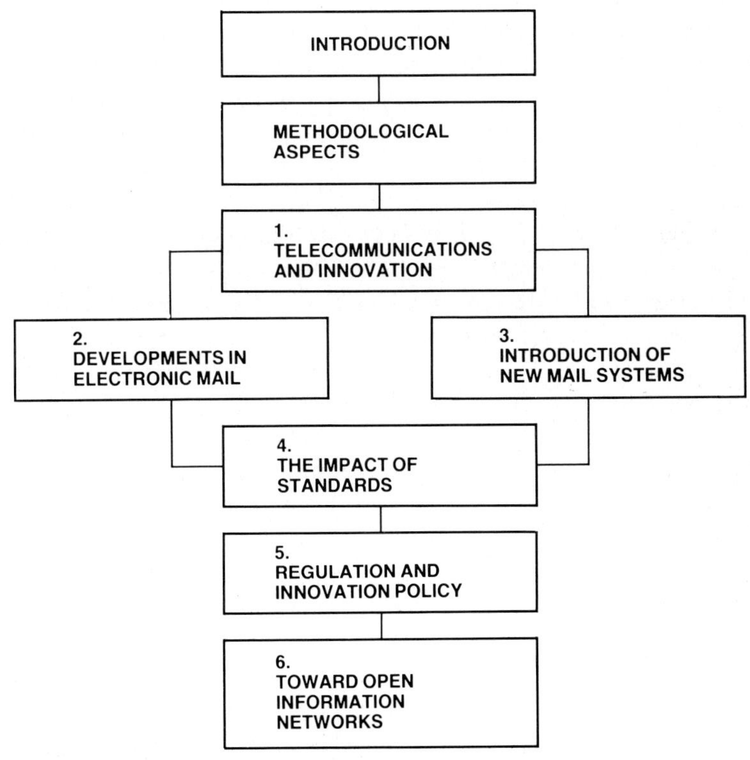

the role of message handling with respect to the creation of open information networks. Message handling is seen as a way of shielding the application processes from the specific characteristics of the lower-layer communication processes. As I have argued, this will be an important and basic innovation for the creation of many new tele-information services. Some of the current mail systems will be deeply affected by the trajectory set forth by message handling: however, telex, analog facsimile and newer systems such as those which enable telematic services, seem outside this development.

The current innovation process in electronic mail is characterized by the competition among different technological possibilities and the simultaneous emergence of a new – scientific, technological, political and market – regime to determine the selection environment for the new technologies. I will call this process of competition between technological alternatives 'technological Darwinism'. However, particularly in the case of technology, 'survival of the fittest' does not mean that our ideas about 'the fittest' cannot change. Selection environments do change with time and are heavily determined by social values, market factors and government policies. In this respect, students of innovation theory should pay more attention to the standardization factor. The study of standardization processes can give substantially different insights in the ways and procedures of adopting new technological ideas within our society and may give a different perspective on the possibilities of technological innovation policy.

The chapter layout of my thesis is shown in Figure I.1. In order to facilitate the technical understanding of message handling, an overview of the Open Systems Interconnection / Message Handling Systems Model as developed by ISO and CCITT is given in the appendix.

NOTES
INTRODUCTION

(1) Cf. Vallee (1984) p. 4, 10-16.
(2) Id. p. 8-10; as will be discussed in section 2.2, conferencing is not included in the definition of electronic mail as applied for this study.
(3) Licklider and Vezza (1978) present an overview of the possibilities of information networks, identifying electronic message transport as a kind of generic application for these networks. Stamps (1982) describes the origins of document communications and the specific importance for human progress. In 'The Network Revolution' Vallee (1982) analyzes how computer communications will tranform social interactions. Lee (1983, p. 49) mentions the possible importance of non-conventional forms of message transfer, such as between human and machine.
(4) Cf. Uhlig, Farber and Bair (1979) p. 31-45; Vallee (1984) p. 52-55; Vervest (1985) p. 68-70.
(5) Cf. Uhlig (1983); Vervest (1985) p. xvi-xvii.
(6) 'Information Processing Systems – Open Systems Interconnection – Basic Reference Model', International Organization for Standardization, IS 7498, ISO/TC97/SC16, Geneva, 1983.
(7) Recommendations Series X.400 on 'Message Handling Systems', approved during the October 1984 Plenary Assembly of the International Telegraph and Telephone Consultative Committee (CCITT), ITU, Geneva 1984.
(8) According to Shannon (in: Shannon and Weaver (1963), p. 31) the semantic aspects of communication are irrelevant to the engineering problems. I will argue, however, that message handling systems can be used for the management of associations between distributed information-processing systems: message handling can form the basis for tele-information services in such a way that the inter-operability of services can be maintained.
(9) Within this study the terms 'de-regulation' and 'regulation' cover three different aspects: first, the legal and government rules to influence the behavior of market actors. Secondly, the regulatory measures with respect to the provision of telecommunication services, in particular the demonopolization of telecommunication service provision. The third aspect of regulation concerns the role and possible dismantling of state-owned companies or public agencies. I will use the term regulation particularly in the first meaning; where necessary, I will indicate in which way the term has been used.
(10) Cf. section 1.1. A general treatment on government policy is given by Rothwell and Zegveld (1981, 1985). Goody Katz and Phillips in 'Government and Technical Progress' (Nelson, 1982) discuss the impact the US government had on the emergence of the computer. With respect to the new communication networks, Ganley and Ganley (1982, pp. 200-205) argue for specific government policy attention.
(11) Mueller and Tilton (1969) point out that a sequential process typically occurs in the development of a new industry around a radical innovation. After the innovation has taken place, imitation leads to closer attention to marketing. The subsequent stage of technological competition focuses on R&D-led improvements which make it increasingly difficult for new firms to enter the market. This also eliminates existing firms that cannot succeed in making important improvements on the basic innovation. Standardization takes place after the ideal product has been found: R&D concentrates on improving production and on prolonging the product life cycle, and technological competition shifts to price competition (in Rogers (1983) p. 141-143).
In the case of electronic mail innovation, however, standardization plays a pre-eminent role in the very beginning of the innovation itself, and pervades the whole process from invention and innovation to diffusion.
(12) The research strategy is explained in the following heading. Reference is also made to the initial research proposal (Vervest, 1983).
(13) The following research proceedings have been published:
Vervest, P.H.M., 'Electronic Mail and Message Handling', Frances Pinter (Publishers) Ltd,

London, 1985 – published in Japanese by Kogaku-Sha Publishing Company Ltd, Tokyo, 1986

Vervest, P.H.M., Wissema, J.G., 'Electronic Mail and Message Handling in the USA – Results of the May 1984 Study Tour', Erasmus University Rotterdam, October 1984

Vervest, P.H.M., Wissema, J.G., 'Electronic Mail and Message Handling in Japan – Results of the February, March 1985 Study Tour', Erasmus University Rotterdam, April 1985

Vervest, P.H.M., Wissema, J.G., Visser, M, Aller, J. van, 'The Introduction of Electronic Mail – Perspectives for Telecommunication Managers, Results of the April/ May 1985 Questionnaire for the International Communications Association (ICA), Dallas, Eburon, Delft, March 1986

(14) Quantitative estimates have been made in a number of studies, notably Mackintosh Consultants Company (1978, 1983), International Data Corporation (IDC, 1983, 1984), Frost & Sullivan (1983). Also of interest is the Eurodata Report on 'Data Communications in Western Europe in the 1980s' (Logica, 1980). The problems of early projections on new technologies lie in the lack of stability of such new technologies, rather arbitrary assumptions on the target market and the possible degree of penetration into this market. Moreover, samples are often limited and based on the opinions of users, who are often not knowledgeable.

(15) Cf. section 2.2; McQuillan (1984).

METHODOLOGICAL ASPECTS

Innovation research

The scientific investigation of technological change is an outstanding example of inter-disciplinary research. It requires that one seeks help from a variety of branches of science and that one combines the different research methods into a coherent and plausible strategy. Each individual research method should comply with the standards that have been set by the originating discipline, while the overall strategy should remain consistent with the research objectives.

As a management study, a number of additional criteria should be met, defined by Bomers (1983) (1) as follows:

1. the problem to be investigated should be based on an identified need in society and should have practical relevance;
2. anticipated results are operational and can be implemented, if so desired;
3. results are non-evident, i.e. they augment our knowledge in excess of common sense conclusions;
4. the investigation is carried out in time and can indeed contribute to managerial decisions at the right time.

Innovation research, however, is still a highly heterogeneous and dispersed scientific activity. Rogers (1983) (2) describes the variety of approaches to the problem. It leads to a saddening incompatibility of results: the low predictive value of innovation research is striking.

One of the major obstacles to innovation research is the lack of a coherent theory about innovations. First of all, the term innovation is not an unambiguous one. Innovation in the economic sense is accomplished only with the first commercial transaction, involving the new product, says Freeman (1982) (3), although the word is used to describe the whole process from conceptualization or invention to widespread use.

The macro-economic view on innovation defines technical change as the residual factor in explaining differential productivity growth and as an explanation for economic waves (4). Diffusion research focusses on the spread of technology in time, but does not account for the underlying reasons of the process itself.

Research into the adoption processes gives more information on the reasons and methods for assimilating new technologies, but the results are often limited to individual organizations. Marketing sees technological innovation as a way to generate new products or to stretch the product life cycle (5). The study of consumer and organizational buying behaviour gives some valuable models for assessing market needs and demand variables (6); these models, however, often lack a way to deal with the intrinsic complexities of technical progress. Another point of view on innovation stems from organizational theory and the role of managers in organizational innovation (7).

Technology assessment and innovation policy studies gain increasingly more interest as they try to relate micro-, meso-, and macro-factors to the complicated process of technical change. Moreover government policy seems an indispensable factor in generating new technology and in determining its 'fate' (8).

Objectives and research strategy

The objective of the study is to perform an analysis of the characteristics, applications and global introduction of electronic mail, with the aim to provide decision support for governmental and business institutions when considering the introduction of new mail technologies. The study has been carried out in the following modules (9):

- technical and market survey (10);
- investigation of theories on the introduction of technological innovations and the relation with electronic mail;
- investigation of standardization and regulatory issues;
- market survey of large user organizations.

In particular the influence and possible role of government policy has been studied.

A number of experts have been interviewed during two study tours in the USA and Japan (11). A structured mail questionnaire has been carried out among the members of the International Communications Association (ICA) (12). Membership of the ICA consists of representatives who are responsible for telecommunications services and facilities of companies, corporations and other organizations (13):

1. which operate multi-city offices and/or plants with total billings from communications common carriers approximating one million dollars annually;
2. which are extensive users of owned or leased point-to-point communications circuits, or services (other than toll) in lieu of same, between these multi-city locations;
3. which are not predominantly engaged in the production, sale or rental of communication services or equipment, and are not subsidiaries or affiliates of companies so engaged.

The study has been guided by a liaison group of representatives from Dutch government, PTT, industry, users and universities (14).

Evaluation of research methodology

Because the innovation is still at an early stage, the study emphasizes the understanding of the basic model for innovation, the underlying technology, the stimulating factors and the bottlenecks. This can form the basis for detailed assessments of the market potential, the social effects and the possible strategies of government, user organizations and producers.

A comprehensive survey and research of innovation in electronic mail is carried out in this study. It must be seen as an exploration of the opportunities and threats of message handling and as the analysis of a new technological trajectory.

As technology progresses, more quantitative studies are needed with respect to:

- policy research as to the effects and direction of government policy instruments with respect to procurement, regulations, subsidies to individual firms, scientific and technological infrastructure and policies toward the small and medium size companies;
- standardization policy and standards promotion and acceptance;
- the role and position of PTT both with respect to post and telecommunications;
- technology assessment and impact analysis of OSI/MHS developments;
- the progress and commercialization of public message handling services;
- the development of terminals and networks;
- case studies of the adoption of electronic mail and message handling at various levels of the market (the individual, the organizations, industry sector, and the government).

In particular, follow-up studies are recommended with respect to:

1. industry-specific use of electronic mail and message-handling as part of branch networks;

Electronic mail and message handling provides a new challenge for cooperation and competition both between and within industry sectors. Examples are trade and retail networks, transportation, banking, insurance, and agriculture. How can branch networks be constructed and what is the application of message handling systems as part of these networks? How will this influence the industry structure? What are the leading user applications and what is the role of standardization, regulation, and government policy as part of business strategy of individual market players?

2. case studies and field implementation of electronic mail and message handling systems for both intra- and inter-organizational communications;

Practical field implementations in critical branches of Dutch industry, such as agriculture, trade and transportation, as well as in educational and research areas, will support the building of expertise with respect to the current and future use of electronic mail and message handling.

Figure R.1 RESEARCH PLAN

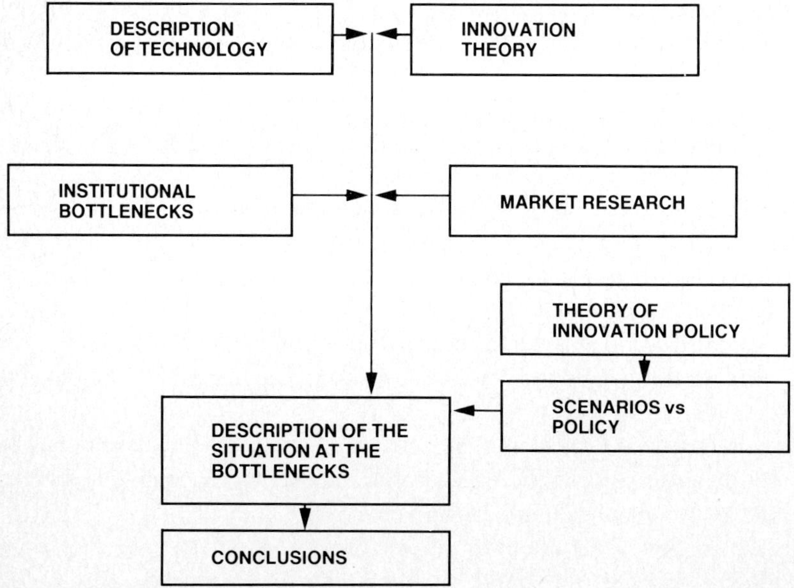

3. standardization as an international competitive tool for government and industry;

The current theoretical framework with respect to the relationships between standardization, government policy, and industrial innovation should be developed in more depth; a clearer understanding of the exact relationships can assist in applying standards – or the lack of standards – as a tool for international competition.

NOTES
METHODOLOGICAL ASPECTS

(1) Bomers 'Ontwikkelingen in de Bedrijfskunde' ('Developments in Management Science') (1983) p. 84-89.
(2) Rogers (1983) p. 38-86.
(3) Freeman (1982) p. 7.
(4) Cf. Van Duijn (1979).
(5) Levitt (1965).
(6) Cf. Zaltman and Wallendorf (1979).
(7) Cf. Drucker 'Business and Technology' in Drucker (1981) p. 37-61.
(8) Cf. section 1.2; Nelson and Winter (1977, 1982); Rothwell and Zegveld (1981, 1985).
(9) Document RGMT-T11, Erasmus University Rotterdam, January 1983.
(10) Cf. Vervest and Wissema (1984, 1985); Vervest (1985).
(11) Cf. Vervest and Wissema (1984, 1985).
(12) Cf. Vervest et al. (1986).
(13) International Communications Association by-laws, 12 January 1983.
(14) 'Research Group Management of Technology – Liaison Group Tele-Communication and Information', Document RGMT-T10, Erasmus University Rotterdam, January 1983.

CHAPTER 1.

TELECOMMUNICATIONS AND INNOVATION

1.1 INDUSTRY IN TRANSITION

1.1.1 The concept of fusion in telecommunications

The large-scale use of computers for communications obscures the conventional distinctions between the computer, telecommunications and media industries. Computers enable an economic way to store user-designated information inside the telecommunications network; in this way they facilitate the exchange and processing of information. A large number of new facilities for telecommunications become possible which have a profound impact on traditional services such as post and telephony (1).

Kitahara (1983) (2) explains the new directions in telecommunications and the enlarging range of applications due to the integration of computers. Figure 1.1 shows the broad spectrum of methods and carriers of communication which will be covered by future telecommunication systems and services.

The figure points two important directions:

1. future telecommunications will increasingly merge with mass media,
2. telecommunications will increasingly expand to information processing.

The merger of personal-type media and mass media will be made possible via a common communications infrastructure for transmission with adequate bandwidth to accommodate different types of media, or information formats, such as voice, text, facsimile, video, audio, etc. It must be remembered, however, that a full-scale integration of personal and mass media is not expected before the year 2000 because of technical problems in high bandwidth switching (3).

In particular, developments lead from interpersonal to machine-to-machine communications. It will result in a situation where the exchange of information is performed by a machine, a computer-based terminal, which can act 'intelligently' on behalf of its end-user, the human being. Whether the pattern of com-

FIGURE 1.1 ENLARGEMENT OF THE RANGE OF TELECOMMUNICATIONS

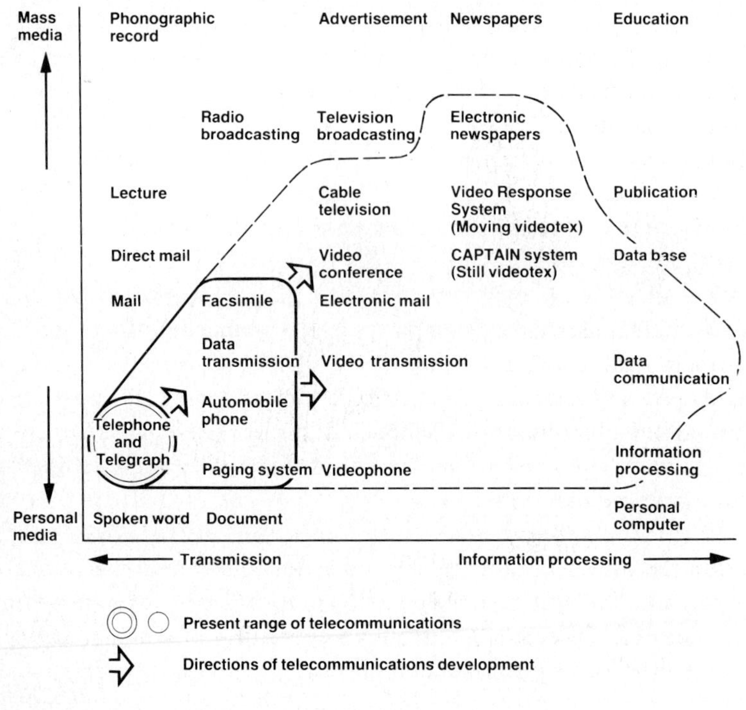

Source: Kitahara (1983)

munication is one-directional such as conventional radio and television (broadcast information delivery) or bi-directional (such as in traditional telephony), will in future no longer determine the way in which the communications infrastructure will be constructed, operated and managed.

The second important direction is from transmission to information processing. In future it will not only be a matter of transferring data from one location to the other, but far more than before, means are needed both to facilitate the transfer ('communications processing') and to process the information itself. Communications processing offers convenience to the users, such as speed, protocol and media conversions, without altering the content of the information being transferred. Information processing, however, changes the content of the information itself.

1.1.2 Technology, system, network and service

The industrial transformation taking place in telecommunications, computers and media, seems largely determined by the mutual usefulness of the technologies one to the other. The sharing of technology leads to new products and new methods of production: both product and process innovation will occur. However, it also creates uncertainty with respect to the degree of commonality of technology and to the definition of new products. In particular, technology will not have the same definition in each of the respective industries.

Freeman (1982) uses the expression 'technology' as a 'body of knowledge' related to the production, distribution and transportation of goods (4): technology has a growing scientific content and the specialization within science itself has led to major problems of communications (5). Let me emphasize that although technologists are primarily concerned with the application of knowledge for practical use, they increasingly need progress in science – and therefore must be engaged in science – in order to effect technical change. The fact that telecommunications and computer technologies shared much of the same bodies of scientific knowledge (in systems theory, mathematics, physics and electronics) may have been the major factor enabling the fusion.

Technical change starts with an invention, defined by Rothwell and Zegveld (1985) (6) as: 'the creation of an idea and its reduction to practice', such as a prototype, or practical trial, leading to a novel concept that in principle can be patented. Industrial innovation, however, concerns not only invention but 'includes the technical, design, manufacturing, management and commercial activities involved in the marketing of a new (or improved) process or equipment' (Freeman, 1974) (7).

Products are therefore the output of technology: and innovation is seen as the successful delivery of new products to the market, or the improvement of production methods. Note that a product can be either a material thing or a service.

A system is defined as 'the collectivity of entities that are related with each other' (8). Because there is a relation among the entities, the system can act as a 'whole', or have a specific function with respect to its environment. ISO defines the term system as 'a set of one or more computers, the associated software, peripherals, terminals, human operators, physical processes, information transfer means, etc., that form an autonomous whole capable of performing information processing and/or information transfer' (9).

The principal function of a telecommunication system is to transfer data from one location to another, or more precisely, from one system access point to another. Networking and transfer, therefore, are the main functions. For the purpose of this study, transfer is defined as the actual remittance of data, i.e. the transport as well as the carrying over.

Telecommunication systems are composed of transmission media – copper cable, optical fibre, radio links, satellite, etc.; multiplexers and de-multiplexers; switching exchanges which perform the routing (selection) and coupling (connection set-up, maintaining the connection and disconnection) functions; and network organization (numbering, switching and transmission plans as well as tariff plans) and management facilities, as well as the human personnel to operate the system.

Terminals are needed at the access points of the telecommunication system to convert user information to system information, and vice versa.

The output of a telecommunication system is a service to exchange data at distance. The elements of a telecommunication service are:

- a means to enable access to the system services and to ensure compliance with the access rules;
- a way to identify the parties connected at the access points;
- a way of reliable transport of data between different access points.

Critical user aspects of service provision are (10):

- reliability of data transfer;
- speed of data transfer;
- availability of service, as much as possible independent of time or place, and enabling priority setting of data transfer;
- connectivity, defined as transparency of data transfer from the point of view of the source and destination;
- flexibility of access possibilities;
- security and privacy of data transfer;
- cost performance.

Note that a telecommunication system performs data transfer as opposed to information transfer: the data carried along the transmission paths and exchanges, signifies information to the end-user but from a telecommunications system point of view they are meaningless. A principle distinction should be made between the technical design of a telecommunication system and the design of a telecommunication service. The system function is specifically the transfer of data between different access points. A telecommunication service is only provided to the user if the data transfer satisfies the conditions which enable the user to add value to his information state, i.e. the user can assign meaning to that data. A service is therefore highly dependent on the user applications.

Let us remember the principle distinction between 'data' and 'information'. IFIP defines these terms as follows (11):

- data: a representation of facts or ideas in a formalised manner capable of being communicated or manipulated by some process;
- information: in automatic data processing, the meaning that a human expresses by or extracts from data by means of the known conventions of representation used.

IEEE (12) defines the terms as follows:

- data: any representations such as characters or analog quantities to which meaning *might* be assigned;
- information: the meaning assigned to data by known conventions.

The important characteristic of data is that they are carriers of a potential, i.e. they *might* be assigned a meaning. Or: data are carriers of information unless they cannot be assigned a meaning. Data have a positive value assumption. Whether they are assigned this value by the user, is an entirely different matter.

This does certainly not imply that the user requirements are unimportant for the technical design of a telecommunication system. On the contrary, from the point of view of tele-information services, user requirements are specifically important: in these cases the source and destination are related to each other and can assign certain meaning to the content of a 'message'. I will return to this in Chapter 2.

With the above distinction between data and information, the term 'tele-information' service can be explained: tele-information services provide information transfer via a telecommunication system (or systems). This assumes an a-priori relationship between the sender and receiver of information, which sets the conventions for assigning meaning to data. Examples of tele-information services are radio and broadcast television, but the technical facilities (i.e. the tele-information system) should be distinguished from the service aspects. In a similar way telephony can be seen as a tele-information service.

However, the distinction between tele-communication and tele-information service is not always obvious; most current and new services have elements of both services. In particular in the case of electronic mail, there is a tele-information part (the meaning assigned to the content of the message) and a telecommunication part (the message transfer aspects). In Chapter 2. I will explain the way in which message transfer can be seen as a common boundary between tele-communication and tele-information; this can be a helpful method for clarifying the distinction.

The transition in telecommunications from interpersonal to machine-machine communications is one of major importance (13). The immediate user of telecommunication services becomes a computer system instead of the human being. Terminal equipment is no longer an integral part of a telecommunication service: a distinction is made between data circuit-terminating equipment (DCE), primarily for access to the telecommunication system, and data terminal equipment (DTE). The latter ensures access from and to the end-user (a human being or computer application process).

The separation of the terminal from the telecommunication service leads to different requirements as to the telecommunication systems: they are to provide 'interconnectivity' services, i.e. they must ensure that cooperation can be established among distributed information processing systems, which perform a common information processing task. Against this background, the following sections discuss the relation between technology, market and policy to enable a theoretical understanding of the process of innovation in telecommunications.

1.2 INNOVATION AND POLICY

1.2.1 The viewpoint of diffusion

Technology and innovation

Freeman (1982) (14) sees technology primarily as part of the economic process of production. Technological change can lead to new products (product innovation) or new production methods (process innovation). It is important to be aware of this concern with technology as a way of human progress: it can lead to the neglect of social innovation, i.e. the design and organization of new social values and structures. Social innovation is an equally important factor for human progress, and often an indispensable companion of technological innovation.

It was Schumpeter (1912) who correlated technological innovation and economic progress as an explanation of the long economic cycle (15). The initial model of Schumpeter said that the entrepreneur would be the main cause of innovative activity. His second model, Schumpeter 2 (1942), pointed to the large firms as the managers of innovation. Schmookler (1966), however, sets out a demand-led model. Walsh et al. try all these various models as well as a model of technology and demand-led science (after Hessen, 1931) (16). Their conclusion is that the relationship between science, technology and the marketplace is rarely unequivocally unidirectional, nor is it a simple one, and within particular branches of industry causality can switch from being mainly in one direction to being mainly in the other (17). In other words: there is no simple explanation for technological innovation such as technology push/market pull.

In particular when fundamental changes are involved, the concepts of technology and market are often obscured and require redefinition in the light of change. Of course, not all innovations are that profound. Schumpeter himself distinguished various types of innovations (18). Although only very few innovations can be seen as basic innovations (19), it will often not be possible to determine beforehand whether something will be a basic or trivial innovation. Therefore traditional perceptions of market, science and technology cannot serve as the filter of new ideas. We should appreciate that the diffusion of new technology demands social innovation as well.

Diffusion and adoption

The foregoing remarks imply that innovation should not only be approached from the production side, but also from the user point of view. Rogers (1961, 1971, 1983) (20) defines diffusion of technological innovation as 'the process by which an innovation is communicated through certain channels over time among the members of a social system'. He defines communication as 'a process in which participants create and share information with one another in order to reach a common understanding' (21). Adoption concerns the decision

FIGURE 1.2 STANDARD-NORMAL DISTRIBUTION OF ADOPTER CATEGORIES AND CUMULATIVE DISTRIBUTION CURVE

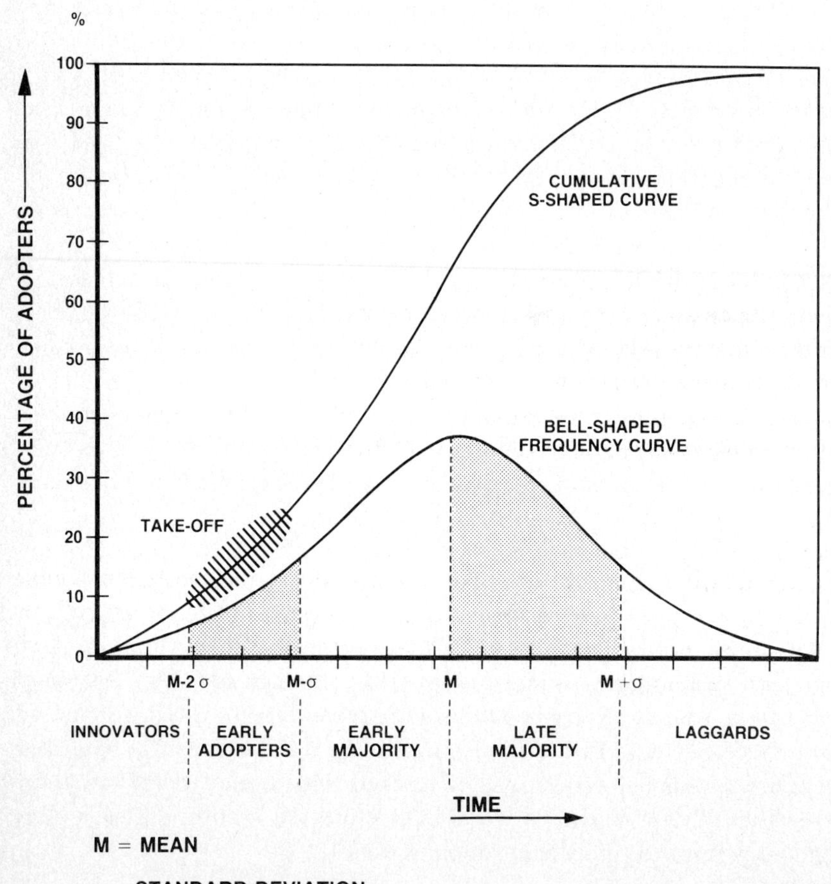

of an adopter unit, i.e. an individual or an organization, to make full use of the innovation as the best course of action (22). Thus it entails a commitment to the continued use of the innovation, or alternatively, its rejection.

Rogers and others found that the distribution of adopters over time forms a standard-normal (or Gaussian) distribution in most cases. Rogers uses this distribution as a method to classify ideal types of adopters on the basis of innovativeness (23) (see Figure 1.2). The mathematical integration of the standard-normal distribution gives the cumulative number of adopters with respect to time, called the diffusion curve (24).

Diffusion models are used in particular by scholars of marketing to forecast demand for new products.

The basic model is as follows (25):

$$\frac{\mathrm{d}N(t)}{\mathrm{d}t} = a\{\bar{N} - N(t)\} + bN(t)\{\bar{N} - N(t)\} \qquad [1]$$

where

$\mathrm{d}N(t)/\mathrm{d}t$ = rate of diffusion at time t
$N(t)$ = population of potential adopters at time t (or saturation level)
$N(t)$ = cumulative number of adopters at time t
a = coefficient of innovation
b = coefficient of imitation

The distinction between innovation and imitation originates from Schumpeter model 1 (1912) (26): in the early stage of diffusion the process is activated by 'innovators' or entrepreneurs who ignite the innovation process. Once the innovation has started to become known and accepted by the 'early adopters', the effects of imitation are becoming more apparent: this is expressed in the constant 'b'. Imitation is dependent on the number of actual adopters at time t.

The diffusion model has the problem that one has to assess market potential and the innovation and imitation parameters. This is particularly difficult for new products. Moreover, diffusion does not deal with the quantity of usage by different adopter categories.

Substitution

These problems can be overcome via the substitution model as proposed by Fisher and Pry (1971). Their assumption is that innovation is basically the result of the competitive replacement of one method of satisfying a need by another. Once substitution has progressed as far as a small percentage, it will proceed to completion (27). They define a take-over point in the substitution curve at point $t(0)$ equal to the time at which substitution is half complete. Take-over time is defined as the time needed for substitution to increase from 10% to 90%. Their formula is as follows:

$$f/(1-f) = 2^{a\{t-t(0)\}} \qquad [2]$$

where

f = fractional ratio of substitution at time t
a = the annual fractional growth in the early years
$t(0)$ = take-over point where $f = 1/2$

The Fisher-Pry model yields a symmetrical S-shaped curve or in loglinear form:

$$^{2}\log\{f/(1-f)\} = a\{t(0)-t\} \qquad [3]$$

In order to use the substitution model, one has to find pairs of competing products and comparable measures for consumption levels. The model cannot account for growth; nor does it deal with partial substitution or complex substitution of overlapping product capabilities.

Although more sophisticated models have been proposed (28), the fundamental problem stays: how can user research assist in understanding the early decisions as to the adoption or rejection of new technology? This is a crucial question for the innovative firm in order to monitor technological developments and in order to assess the size and development of the market. In fact users are as vital for the innovation as the body of technical knowledge and expertise. Innovation happens all along the process of diffusion when minor improvements are made; at the early stages of innovation diffusion, this process of reinvention and re-innovation will happen all the time and will be critical for the success of the innovation (29).

Adoption-decision research is also the crucial question for the government policy makers who have to assess the social, economic, political, environmental and other impacts of new technology as early as possible. We must appreciate, however, that innovations vary with respect to their degree of newness, both from the point of view of the producer of innovative products and from the point of view of each individual adopter (30). It means that market development is part and parcel of the whole process of technological innovation. Market development, as well as the development of our social structures to embody new technology, is needed for successful innovation and diffusion. It is a too narrow view to see technical change only as a matter of the competitive substitution of one technology for another.

1.2.2 Theory of Nelson and Winter

In a seminal paper Nelson and Winter (1977, 1982) lay down a basis of a general theory of innovation as a way to disentangle the interrelatedness of market, technical, and government factors. They relate both micro- and macro-economic factors to the innovation process and are among the first to exemplify in a theoretical model the impact of public policy on innovation processes (31). Nelson and Winter develop the concepts of 'natural trajectories' and 'selection environments'.

They propose a rigid analytic break between the development of new technologies (the 'generation of innovation'), for which they introduce the concept of natural trajectories; and second, changes in the use of existing technologies, or the selection of new technology (the 'fate of innovation') (32).

Natural trajectories

Which factors guide and motivate the development of new technologies is a key question in innovation theory. Schumpeter was the first to recognize the importance of the entrepreneurial firm (33), to develop new technologies because of high initial profits. Nelson and Winter, however, argue against the validity of a profit maximization hypothesis: R&D strategies, due to the intrinsic uncertainty of R&D projects, cannot be explained by profit maximization behavior of the researching firm. R&D strategies are the result of interacting heuristic search processes; this means that R&D activity has a goal, and a set of procedures for identifying, screening, and homing in on promising ways to get to that objective or close to it (34). They continue: 'However, it may be that there are certain powerful project heuristics that apply when a technology is advanced in a certain direction, and payoffs from advancing in that direction that exist under a wide range of demand conditions. We call these directions 'natural trajectories'. If natural trajectories exist, following these may be a good strategy' (35).

Thus the rate and direction of technological advance will be determined not only (as economists would argue) by demand conditions but also, as Rosenberg says, by 'technological imperatives': bottlenecks in connected processes, obvious weak spots in products, clear targets for improvement, etc. (36).

Technological advance, therefore, is seen as an autonomous process, that follows a natural trajectory. In his treatment of the Western European semiconductor industry, Dosi contends that, once a path of technical change has been established, technology gains a momentum of its own (37). The momentum defines in which way problem-solving activity moves. Continuous feedback from markets and production accelerates or slows down the technical progress along a given trajectory. This will eventually facilitate or hinder the emergence of alternative paths. Market factors as well as institutional factors function as the selective mechanisms within the field of technological possibilities.

Dosi compares the concept of technological trajectory with Kuhn's scientific paradigm (38): The concept of trajectories assumes that at some instance in time, a technological break occurs and 'old technologies' are substituted by new trajectories. Changes in scientific paradigms, says Dosi, precede the creation of new trajcctories; changes in scientific paradigms, however, cannot be scientifically understood, nor can they be planned (39). The same would be the case for technological trajectories (40).

Selection environments

Nelson and Winter define selection environment as follows: 'Given a flow of new innovations, the selection environment determines how relevant use of different technologies change over time. The selection environment influences the path of productivity growth generated by any given innovation, and it also feeds back the influence strongly of kinds of R&D that firms and industry will find profitable to undertake' (41).

A selection environment is composed of both market related and non-market related variables. The market as a selection mechanism is generally accepted; the market provides a clear distinction between producing firms on the one side, and consumers and regulators on the other side. Under assumption of consumer sovereignty, the 'laws of demand and supply' determine the relative use of technology. Regulators set the 'rules of the game', they determine what constitutes an 'equal playing field'.

Non-market selection variables, determined by regulatory and political factors, are less widely recognized. These factors determine how markets are structured, and which non-monetary and non-market criteria affect the choice process of new technologies. Non-market selection variables articulate the values of a socio-political system. Governments and public agencies have a task and social obligation to influence the choice of technology. They can effectively filter out harmful developments and accelerate the search for socially more desirable alternatives. Government regulations can have a powerful influence on both the rate and direction of technical change (42).

1.2.3 Regulation and technological innovation

Although Nelson and Winter see regulation as an integral part of their theory, they do not give a clear view on the way and direction in which government regulation influences the innovation process. Rothwell and Zegveld (1985) (43) note that regulation rarely is an important factor affecting the innovation process except perhaps for compliance regulations. Regulation, lack of regulation and deregulation can all influence business-led innovations (44), they claim, and it is often not possible to assess the direction of this impact, or to isolate the effect from a myriad other factors which influence the innovative behavior of a firm.

Ashford, Heaton and Curtiss Priest point to the great difference with respect to regulations of business as opposed to compliance regulations (45). The latter type clearly encourages technological change, as Ashford et al. found in the case of environmental, health and safety regulations. Figure 1.3 gives the effects of regulation on main business innovations as seen by Ashford et al. (46). They point to two goals for regulatory policy concerned with innovation (47):

1. within the current legal framework, regulation should be neutral with re-

spect to the direction of innovation for ordinary business purposes;
2. regulation should encourage innovation by compliance.

There is, however, a third dimension to regulatory policy, i.e. with respect to the diffusion of innovation. As I argued for social innovation and market development as an integral part of the innovation process, regulatory policy has direct relevance for the market acceptance of technical change. The change in social values and market structures which is often necessary for innovation diffusion, can very much be influenced by altering current regulatory regimes. Rothwell and Zegveld (1985) (48) explicitly mention the (positive) effects of deregulation on the American Telegraph & Telephone corporation (AT&T). They say that deregulation could stimulate AT&T to enter new areas; this may certainly have been the case, but the objective of deregulation was for AT&T to innovate equipment rather than to create the demand for telecommunication services and to entail new producers and more discriminating purchasers in the market process.

Ashford et al. mention standardization as an important policy instrument for compliance-related innovation (49). There are two basic legislative approaches to the design of standards: specification standards are technology-based standards and have a positive impact on compliance innovations as long as regulators can keep the standards up to state-of-the-art. The second approach is that

FIGURE 1.3 EFFECTS OF REGULATION ON MAIN BUSINESS INNOVATION

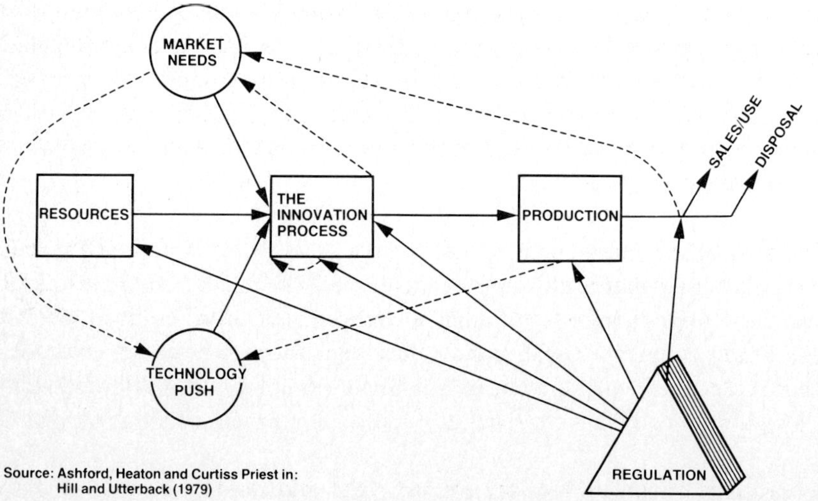

Source: Ashford, Heaton and Curtiss Priest in:
Hill and Utterback (1979)

of performance standards which define functional criteria. Performance standards can have a more direct influence with respect to the speed of innovations, but they are not always possible from a technical point of view, according to Ashford et al. In particular, performance standards can introduce uncertainty in the market place.

Governments can also use standardization as part of other innovation policy instruments, e.g. via government purchasing. A classification of government policy tools by Rothwell and Zegveld (1981, 1985) (50) is shown in Table 1.1. The objectives of a government standardization policy can be embodied in almost all of these tools: if so, however, it should fit in a deliberate standardization policy. As indicated in the foregoing discussion, legal and regulatory policy tools can have an important contribution to this standardization policy: regulatory policy should not only encourage compliance innovation, but also direct the selection environment and stimulate social innovation.

1.3 PUBLIC TELECOMMUNICATIONS AND TECHNOLOGICAL INNOVATION POLICY

Economic-political background

Throughout the history of telecommunications, government policy has had a deep impact on the ways and methods of provision of telecommunication services (51). There were both economic and political reasons for state intervention. In the early days of telephony, most observers acknowledged that the construction and operation of telephone networks was subject to diminishing returns to scale in the sense that the cost per subscriber increases with the number of subscribers, leading to reverse economies of scale. Vail (1907) (52) argued:

'The value of any exchange system is measured by the number of members of any community that are connected with it. If there are two systems, neither of them serving all, important users must be connected with both systems. Given the same management, the public must pay double rates for service, to meet double charges, on double capital, double operating expenses and double maintenance'.

Inter-system arrangements can be more efficient than suggested by Vail, but

TABLE 1.1 CLASSIFICATION OF GOVERNMENT POLICY TOOLS

Policy tool	Examples
Public enterprise	Innovation by publicly owned industries, setting up of new industries, pioneering use of new techniques by public corporations, participating in private enterprise
Scientific and technical	Research laboratories, support of research associations, learned societies, professional associations, research grants
Education	General education, universities, technical education, apprenticeship schemes, continuing and further education, retraining
Information	Information networks and centers, libraries, advisory and consultancy services, data bases, liaison services
Financial	Grants, loans, subsidies, financial sharing arrangements, provision of equipment, buildings or services, loan guarantees, export credits
Taxation	Company, personal, indirect and payroll taxations, tax allowances
Legal and regulatory	Patents, environments and health regulations, inspectorates, monopoly regulations
Political	Planning, regional policies, honours or awards for innovation, encouragement of mergers or joint consortia, public consultation
Procurement	Central or local government purchases and contracts, public corporations, R&D contracts, prototype purchases
Public services	Purchases, maintenance, supervision and innovation in health service, public building, construction, transport, telecommunications
Commercial	Trade agreements, tariffs, currency regulations
Overseas agents	Defence sales organisation

Source: Rothwell and Zegveld (1981, 1985)

the cost of interworking and conversion remain as a minimum penalty. The existence of reverse economies of scale, or marginal costs above average costs in case production crossed over a certain quantity level, provided strong arguments for monopolizing the provision of telecommunication services (53).

Not only economic but political arguments as well have played a major role in determining state intervention. Communications, including telecommunications, was seen as a constitutional right of the individual person, and formed the basis of the political argument to provide services to all with equal and non-discriminatory conditions (54). I will refer to this as the 'utility' argument.

The convention of the International Telecommunications Union (ITU) defines this right of the public to use telecommunication services as follows (55):

'Members recognize the right of the public to correspond by means of the international service of public correspondence. The services, the charges and the safeguards shall be the same for all users in each category of correspondence without any priority or preference'.

Telecommunications is also seen as a vital part for the functioning and progress of society and is very sensitive to national interests. The result has been that governments exercise direct control over telecommunication service provision. In some countries the management of telecommunication business has been given to a public enterprise. In others, private agencies operate the business under government license or other regulations, e.g. price.

A new framework for tele-information services

However, the impacts of modern computer technology on telecommunications give a different perspective on the monopolization of telecommunication services and facilities, and on the role of public enterprises and government regulation. In particular, the provision of new tele-information services are principally different from traditional telecommunications, necessitating a re-thinking of their social, regulatory and technical frameworks.

According to Bordewijk (56) a classification of new tele-information services should not be based on technical capabilities, but on:

- the traffic patterns of information transport;
- the format of presentation of information; and
- the intentions of communicating parties.

Bordewijk describes four patterns of information traffic (57):

1. conversation - two communicating parties exchange information between themselves according to a mutually agreed time schedule;
2. allocution - information is distributed from an information center to a specified group of recipients according to a time schedule defined by the center;
3. consultation - the retrieval of information from an information center at times and upon request of the recipient party;
4. registration - the collection of information from different parties by an information center according to a time schedule defined by the center.

A particular tele-information service, according to Bordewijk, is the result of a fixed combination of these four traffic patterns. The format of presentation, voice, music, text, images, moving pictures, etc., determines to a great extent the costs and quality of the service; while the intentions for the communications are specifically important for the operational and legal issues (58).

On this basis the availability of tele-information services concerns:

- first the installation, exploitation and maintenance of technical facilities for networks;
- the same for terminal equipment;
- the provision and exploitation of information services.

The exploitation and possible regulation of services relates both to the management of capacity (systems operation) and to the exploitation of the information itself (contents) (59).

Booz, Allen and Hamilton (60) make a similar distinction in their discussion of the four roles that companies will take in the creation of the future information society:

- infrastructure suppliers install, maintain and exploit the networks;
- hardware manufacturers supply the necessary equipment, in particular the user terminal equipment;
- system operators are responsible for the management of system capacity, in particular of the information centers;
- content providers provide the information, i.e. application software in its broadest sense.

The four roles are complementary to each other and necessary for the provision of services to the end-user, as shown in Figure 1.4. Some roles cannot be held together by the same organization, for instance the roles of infrastructure supplier and hardware manufacturer are inconsistent with that of system operator.

Structure of policy issues

The transition in telecommunications raises a great number of policy issues (61). The 'BIT-report' (62) enumerates a variety of government policy issues such as culture and education, employment, the creation of monopolies, standards setting and regulation, and the financing of the communications infrastructure.

FIGURE 1.4 PLAYERS IN THE CREATION OF NEW TELE-INFORMATION SERVICES

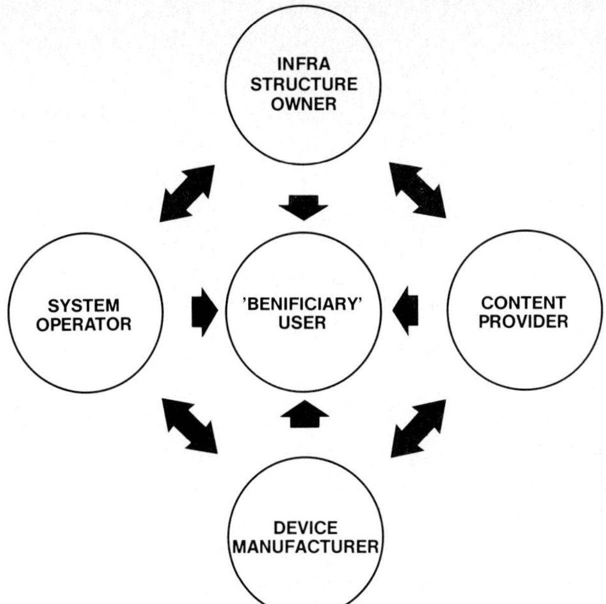

The US Congress Office of Technology Assessment (OTA) (1981) (63) structures the policy aspects in four groups:

- system level issues relating to the design, implementation, and operation of particular information systems. Example issues: government procurement, efficiency and economy of operation, security of information systems;
- information level issues relating to the handling of data (collection, storage, use, and dissemination). Example issues are privacy (recordkeeping), freedom of information, copyright and patents;
- secondary policy impacts exist independent of the particular information systems, but are changed in magnitude or character by use of technology. Examples: privacy (surveillance), freedom of speech, protection of the individual, social vulnerability;
- long-term social effects on society.

Taking inventory of the ongoing policy issues is not an easy task, let alone the task to set out appropriate goals for government policy. Government intervention is unavoidable, regardless of the emotional evaluation, in order to overcome the rigidities in current industrial structures and regulatory regimes. A new organization of the infrastructure for the provision of communication and information services is needed. It is in this framework that technological innovation policy must be formulated. Five lines of this policy can be defined as follows:

1. the design, development and organization of the technical infrastructure;
2. the definition and regulation of public functions as part of this infrastructure, in particular with respect to access, directories and reliable transfer;
3. the factual organization, provision and management of public facilities as part of the overall provision of telecommunication and tele-information services;
4. promoting the creation and use of innovative services from outside the government sector;
5. the monitoring and control of the side-effects, both short-term and long-term.

Before the policy issues can be discussed in more detail, an investigation of the history, of the nature and the technical aspects of electronic mail is necessary. In addition, the applications and user viewpoints are indispensable ingredients of the design of innovation policy.

NOTES CHAPTER 1
TELECOMMUNICATIONS AND INNOVATION

(1) Cf. Nora and Minc (1978) in 'The Computerization of Society' and Kitahara (1983) in 'Information Network system'; an interesting overview of developments is also given in the Proceedings of the International Conference on New Systems and Services in Telecommunications, held November 24-26, 1980 (Cantraine and Destine, 1981); in 'Mapping the Information Business' by McLaughlin and Birinyi (1980); an overview of the new media industries and the strategic implications is given in Compaine (1984) 'Understanding New Media'.
(2) Kitahara (1983) p. 9.
(3) The development of an 'Integrated Broadband Network' is part of RACE (cf. section 4.2). See also DTS-90, BECOM (1985) p. 26.
(4) Freeman (1982) p. 15-17.
(5) Id. p. 17.
(6) Rothwell and Zegveld (1985) p. 47.
(7) Id. p. 47.
(8) Cf. Angyal, A., The Logic of Systems, The Commonwealth Fund and Harvard University Press, 1941, in: Emery (1969), p. 17-30; see also Kramer and De Smit (1974) p. 22.
(9) ISO (1983), IS 7498, p. 4.
(10) Cf. Licklider and Vezza (1978, 1981).
(11) Cf. Gould (1971). See also Bordewijk and Arnbak (1983) p. 3.4-3.5.
(12) IEEE Standard Dictionary (edition 1984).
(13) Kitahara (1983) p. 8.
(14) Freeman (1982) p. 15-17.
(15) Id. p. 207-210; van Duijn (1979) p. 43-54.
(16) Cf. Freeman (1982) p. 211-214; Rothwell and Zegveld (1985) p. 61-66.
(17) Rothwell and Zegveld (1985) p. 65-66.
(18) Schumpeter made a distinction between five different types of innovations: the introduction of new products; the introduction of new production methods; the development of new markets; the utilization of new raw materials or semi-finished products; and the implementation of new organizational and market structures (Schumpeter, 1934, p. 66). See Van Duijn (1979) p. 44.
(19) Cf. Mensch (1975); van Duijn (1979) p. 44-45.
(20) Rogers (1983) p. 5.
(21) Id. p. 5-6.
(22) Id. p. 21.
(23) Id. p. 241-270.
(24) The formula of the Gaussian distribution is:

Id. p. 241-270. $f(x;\mu,\sigma) = (1/(\sigma\sqrt{2\pi}))e^{-(x-\mu)^2/2\sigma^2} \quad -\infty < x < \infty$ [6]

In the case of a standard-normal distribution: $\mu = 0$ and $\sigma = 1$. The cumulative distribution $f(x_0)$ is calculated as follows:

$$f(x_0) = \int_{-\infty}^{x_0} f(x)\mathrm{d}x = 1/2 + \int_{0}^{x_0} f(x)\mathrm{d}x \qquad [7]$$

which leads to an incomplete Gamma function (cf. Abramowitz, 1970). Graphically this is represented by the S-shaped curve as given in Figure 1.2.
(25) Wind (1982) p. 452-456. See for a general discussion Rogers (1983) p. 38-86.
(26) Van Duijn (1979) p. 43-54; see also the 'laws of imitation' by Gabriel Tarde (1903) in Rogers (1983) p. 40-41.

(27) Fisher and Pry (1971) p. 76-77.
(28) For instance, Dodson and Muller (1978) have proposed a model which includes changes in the number of potential adopters over time, i.e.: $\bar{N}(t) = f(S(t))$ where $S(t)$ is a vector of all relevant exogenous and endogenous variables affecting $N(t)$. Another model is suggested by Peterson and Mahajan (1978) who combine substitution and the basic diffusion model. See for a discussion Wind (1982) p. 452-456.
(29) Cf. Von Hippel (1977, 1978).
(30) Cf. Johnston and Jones (1957).
(31) Nelson and Winter in 'In Search of Useful Theory of Innovation' (1977) and 'An Evolutionary Theory of Economic Change' (1982).
(32) Nelson and Winter (1977) p. 48-49, p. 71.
(33) Freeman (1982) p. 211.
(34) Nelson and Winter (1977) p. 52-53.
(35) Id. p. 56.
(36) Rosenberg (1972); Rothwell and Zegveld (1985) p. 67.
(37) Dosi (1981) p. 7.; cf. Dosi (1984).
(38) Dosi (1981) p. 7.
(39) Id.; cf. Kuhn (1970).
(40) Dosi (1981) p. 8.
(41) Nelson and Winter (1977) p. 61.
(42) Id. p. 66-74; cf. Nelson (1982); Rothwell and Zegveld (1981, 1985)
(43) Rothwell and Zegveld (1985) p. 128; cf. p. 127-136.
(44) Id. p. 132.
(45) Ashford, N.A., Heaton, G.R., Curtiss Priest, W., Environmental, Health and Safety Regulation and Technological Innovation, in: Hill and Utterback (1979) p. 161-221.
(46) Id. p. 173
(47) Id. p. 190-191.
(48) Rothwell and Zegveld (1985) p. 132.
(49) Ashford et al. in: Hill and Utterback (1979) p. 191-196.
(50) Rothwell and Zegveld (1981) p. 57-66; Rothwell and Zegveld (1985) p. 83-88.
(51) Cf. Stamps (1982) p. 161-175; Beesley (1981); Evans (1983); Trebing (1979).
(52) Bornholz, R., Evans, D.S., The Early History of Competition in the Telephone Industry, p. 29, in: Evans (1983) p. 7-40.
(53) Cf. Evans, D.S., Heckman, J.J., Natural Monopoly, in: Evans (1979) p. 127-156. The economic theory of monopolies can also be found in Samuelson (1973) p. 516-572; Lipsey and Steiner (1972) p. 283-308.
(54) Cf. Stamps (1982) p. 161-175; see also Willig, R.D., The Theory of Network Access Pricing, in Trebing (1979) p. 109-152.
(55) Article 18 of the International Telecommunications Convention, International Telecommunications Union, Geneva.
(56) Bordewijk and Arnbak (1983) in their report on 'Foundations of a Tele-information Policy' for the Dutch Ministry of Science and Education, p. 1.3-6; Bordewijk and Van Kaam (1982).
(57) Bordewijk and Arnbak (1983) p. 1.6-1.12. See also the economic study on new services by CCITT GAS 5 (1984) p. 6. This study distinguishes four modes of relationships between communicators: conversation, broadcast (polling), conference and gathering (browsing).
(58) Bordewijk and Arnbak (1983) p. 1.12-1.14.
(59) Id. p. 1.15-16
(60) Booz, Allen and Hamilton (1980) in their contributions for the US Congress Office of Technology Assessment study on 'Computer-based National Information Systems'.
(61) Cf. Ganley and Ganley (1982); Compaine (1984); Bordewijk and Arnbak (1983); US Congress Office of Technology Assessment (OTA) (1981, 1982, 1982a).
(62) Bordewijk and Arnbak (1983) p. 3.13-3.17.
(63) OTA (1981) p. 57.

CHAPTER 2.

DEVELOPMENTS IN ELECTRONIC MAIL

2.1 FROM POST TO COMPUTER MESSAGE-HANDLING

From the early days to the 1960s

More than twenty-five centuries ago the Persian king Darius established a courier messaging service; via relays of staging posts the king's messengers could bridge a distance of 1600 miles from Sardes in the western part of the empire to the capital Persepolis within a week (1).

Less costly derivatives were deployed for civilian use; in ancient Rome horse relay services were commercially available (2). During the sixteenth century a regular postal service became established in England. It was later endorsed by state law, and the example was followed all over Europe and in North America. By 1800 postal services offered, by the standards of the time, a convenient way for communications over distance (3).

But man's quest for faster, cheaper and more efficient ways for tele-communications was paramount. The intensified trade between nations, the discovery of the new countries, the glimmering industrial revolution, new transportation systems, all contributed to the need of telecommunications.

Reuter's system of pigeons and Chappé's system of optical semaphores, revealed the potential of such fast telecommunications. Their systems employed the known possibilities of their time (pigeons, signalling posts); the major inventions, however, came from the technical pioneers, trying the useful application of a recent invention, electricity (4).

Samuel Morse engineered his telegraph during the 1830s, and with the funding of \$30.000 from the US Congress, he gave the first succesful demonstration of electrical telecommunications. From Washington to Baltimore it read 'what hath God wrought' on 24 May 1844 (5).

The telegraph became a success almost immediately after Morse's seminal demonstration; telegraph lines quickly spanned the American countryside, along railroads and connecting the major cities. Western Europe followed and in 1866 the first permanent transatlantic cable was laid (6). The first global telecommunications means was founded; it did not require the physical transport of a letter, it was faster than postal mail, and the economies of the new system were soon proven.

The telephone was patented by Bell in 1876; in a way, simultaneous speech communication was easier than the telegraph as it did not require the human encoding and decoding of the user message and enabled direct two-way speech communications (7).

In the mid-1930s an exchange was developed with special signalling between the exchange and the terminal. It enabled a fully automatic subscriber selection. The use of special exchanges led to the separation of telex from the telephone system (8).

Also facsimile was developed as a means for message communications but its use remained restricted to specialized applications like the transmission of weather charts and newspapers (9); post, telegraph, telex and telephone were the most commonly used means of telecommunication until the 1960s.

Computer communications

The first mass production and commercial delivery of computers started with the Univac I during the 1950s (10). In the decade thereafter, communications between computers developed as a definite need. First it was necessary to enable remote access to the central mainframe via a user terminal (man-to-machine, or terminal-to-mainframe communications). Initially manually operated modems were used via leased lines, i.e. fixed connections from one point to another.

Soon remote mainframes had to exchange data among themselves (machine-to-machine, or computer-to-computer communications). With the growth of computers and the need of communications between different computer systems and terminals, the public switched telephone network came into use for non-telephone service. Via modems and automatic calling and answering devices, the public telephone network could provide an automatic and switched service for machine-to-machine communications.

However, call set-up times could be time consuming in view of the relatively short connection times needed for most applications for computer communications; moreover, a more efficient access scheme was needed. More computers being distributed led to the higher need for faster communications and a more variegated pattern of communications. The concept of public data networks evolved during the late 1960s (11). The first public data networks used circuit-switching, but gradually a newer technology, packet-switching, became used (12). Circuit-switching deals with information as binary streams at a prescribed speed while packet-switching deals with information as short messages at any convenient speed (13). Note that in this context a 'message' is used from the communications point of view. As I will explain in the next sections, messages for my study are defined from the applications point of view.

Messaging

Another development that began in the 1960s was the use of computers for electronic message switching, in particular to add new functions to conventional systems such as telegraph and telex: a complete user message (normally text) was stored in memory and forwarded to the appropriate destination (14). This allowed direct message input by the originator, automatic message multiplication and automatic delivery. The procedure was used in messaging networks of PTT's and international organizations, such as ICAO, WMO, NATO, SITA, AIRINC and SWIFT (15).

Message switching was primarily a way of increasing the efficiency of message transport from a telecommunications point of view: message forwarding became fully automatic and independent of the availability of the addressee at the time of forwarding.

Computer-based message system

A new viewpoint in the 1970s, however, was to store user messages in an 'electronic mailbox' on a computer system and not to deliver the message directly to the terminal of the addressee. Simple terminals were connected to a central (mainframe) computer and message preparation was done on-line. Messages could be sent to anybody who was registered on the central computer system. As computers were linked in a network, messages could also be exchanged across the various central computers, but the message itself would remain on the user file of the central computer, until the addressee could collect the message via his computer terminal. This is what the first experimental systems, developed in the early 1970s, were designed to do.

Arpanet, the Advanced Research Projects Agency computer network of the US Ministry of Defense, was one of the first packet-switching networks. It linked university and defense computers over the USA and it was the first to experiment during 1970-1975 with the exchange of computer-resident 'messages' between human beings, called Computer Based Message System (CBMS). Arpanet also stimulated the development of computer-mediated conferencing (16).

The first CBMS was designed for the exchange of short text messages. It was conceivable, however, that on similar principles a system could be built for voice mail (17). Moreover, why would a computer message not combine many different data formats and let the application processes determine in which way data could be interpreted? This is also referred to as 'compound document structures' (18).

The most immediate stumbling block, however, became the 'global' function of a computer-mediated communications system: a critical number of users is necessary to provide a communications value. It was necessary to connect the various independent CBMS. It was not only a matter of technical interconnection but also of the telecommunications service aspects.

With the spread of computers in the 1970s, the need for communications between computers increased dramatically. In private environments local networks were developed; manufacturers designed proprietary protocols which enabled their equipment to interconnect but precluded competitors' systems. Examples include the protocols developed for data terminal connections to mainframe; communicating word processors (WP); and communicating personal computers (PC). Major incompatibilities were showing themselves as critical points for future growth.

In the early 1960s the International Organization for Standardization (ISO) organised its Technical Committee 97 on Information Processing Systems. In 1978, TC 97 established Subcommittee (SC) 16 on Open Systems Interconnection to develop a reference model that would provide an architecture for the future development of standards for worldwide distributed information systems (19).

The efforts of PTT's

Post, Telegraph and Telephone administrations (PTT) became concerned about the profound impacts that computers would have on their business; in particular the lack of standardization in the computers industry would hamper the use of their telecommunications systems and could severely jeopardize their investments in present and new facilities. There was an equally important issue at stake, however: who would ensure the availability of the appropriate networking and transfer capabilities, numbering plans and directories, for making computer communications as easy as possible? The wild growth in the computer industry formed a real threat for providing a global service for system interconnection.

The International Telegraph and Telephone Consultative Comittee (CCITT) particularly commissioned its Study Groups (SG) I, VII, VIII and XVIII to define new standards and services for computer communications.

SG VII on data communications networks adopted OSI in Series X.200 and at the same time conceived a Message Handling Systems (MHS) model to enhance OSI, laid down in Series X.400 Recommendations (20) in 1984. This MHS model defines, from an applications point of view, a method for computer systems to exchange messages among themselves, so as to make the message content indifferent for the communications processes. Note that SG VII had laid down recommendations for packet-switching (X.25) and circuit-switching (X.21) in 1976, 1980 (21).

SG VIII (on terminal equipment for telematic services) promoted a set of new services, referred to as the telematic services or telematics (22). They did so in close cooperation with SG I on telegraph, telex and telematic service operation. These new services covered in the initial phase (1980) (23):

- broadcast and interactive videotex for information distribution;
- teletex as a document communication service;
- digital facsimile and mixed-mode teletex/facsimile communications.

The Recommendations define service aspects, terminal specifications as well as the networks which can be used.

SG XVIII has been working on digital networks: they have laid down the Series I Recommendations for Integrated Services Digital Networks (ISDN) (1984)

(24). Originally ISDN was defined as 'a network which provides end-to-end digital connections, to support a wide range of telecommunications services to which users have access by a limited set of standards, multi-purpose customer interfaces' (25). ISDN is ear-marked as the future infrastructure for telephony and other telecommunication and information services, with the aim to satisfy the demands of private and public computer networks.

New opportunities

Since the inception of the telegraph during the previous century, electronic mail has become a far from clear service in telecommunications. Computers have an impact on conventional mail systems, post, telegraph, telex, in two different ways: first, computers as part of the telecommunication system enable new ways to store and process user messages. New systems emerge, such as CBMS, voice mail, communicating word processors and personal computers, MHS and telematic systems.

Second, because user terminals themselves have become computer systems, the complexity of the mail system is increasing enormously. Terminals which are capable of using compound documents with many different bit formats, i.e. data records, text, voice, images, or even audio and video, make it difficult to assess which services are needed, and which of these services should be provided on a common basis.

Computers change our perception of telecommunication service: the user terminal will act on behalf of the human user and arrange his information transfer needs, calling on different telecommunication services and information processing systems. From a telecommunications points of view, this necessitates the integration of telecommunication services. At the same time the variety of terminals is increased. These developments lead the way to the construction of an integrated services network such as the ISDN.

To conclude, the main issues in (non-voice) telecommunications today seem to be:

1. the implementation of global – ISDN type – networks that enable the access to information by many different communication parties and for many different purposes;
2. the conception of 'compound' document structures that can accommodate

many different bit formats, such as structured data, text, voice, and images;

3. the design and dissemination of multi-functional, human-friendly and integrated terminals to support a variety of functions, including automated message handling;
4. the construction of distributed data bases that can be accessed from the network(s) and constitute a single resource that yields information in the right format for the application processes.

As has been shown, the developments in telecommunications and computers moved step-by-step till the 1970s but have been wildly accelerating since then. Some of the most difficult points are the transition from the present situation to the future and the role of public service in this process of change.

2.2 DEFINITION OF ELECTRONIC MAIL

2.2.1 A basic electronic mail system

There is no agreement about a definition of the term 'electronic mail' in present literature (26). In a limited sense, electronic mail is defined as CBMS and voice mail. Uhlig et al. (1979) (27) speak of a 'message data bank', referring to the Arpanet experiments. The computer-based message system (CBMS) takes a central place in the innovation process, but the concept of electronic mail is much broader than that.

In an early survey, the Mackintosh Consultants Company (1978) (28) defined electronic mail as:

> 'the transfer via electronic transmission paths of addressed messages, which are effectively person-to-person and which may be paper-based at either or both ends'.

Transmission paths, says Mackintosh, are not a key issue from a user's point of view, but they may offer added features that enhance their suitability for electronic mail. Packet-switched networks are of major significance as a backbone network that would enable the interconnection of incompatible computer systems and the provision of intelligence inside the network. In this way terminal-to-computer mailing becomes possible and electronic mail would be extended beyond interpersonal messaging.

Also McQuillan (1984) (29) applies a comprehensive definition. He defines electronic mail as 'a system for electronically transmitting information from sender to receiver in the form of a message'. This definition includes facsimile, communicating word processors, telex/TWX, message switching, CBMS, voice mail, and electronic document distribution (for physical delivery of documents which are transmitted in electronic form along some part of the path from sender to receiver).

The fact that most electronic mail messages are effectively person-to-person, should not obscure the future direction. CBMS and voice mail systems assign an 'electronic mailbox' to each individual user. Flexibility is gained both with respect to the communications aspects and to the information manipulation aspects, e.g. for office automation. The concept of an electronic mailbox opens the way to applications that will extend far beyond those of interpersonal communication.

Two developments exemplify the potential impact. First, the development toward multi-media communications. Multi-media message systems allow the transfer of 'compound documents', i.e. units of information which are composed of a variety of data types, or bit-stream formats, such as text, facsimile, bit-map images, vector graphics, compressed speech, PCM sound, still picture (colour) and full video.

Another important development is toward 'active messages', or 'messages as messengers': messages that contain procedures which are activated on receipt at destination (30). Such procedures can interact with the human user, data bases, computing resources, and other resources at destination. This interaction may lead to new messages which return to the sender or are transferred to a new destination. A simple example is computer-generated messages, but the concept also extends to the management of distributed data bases.

A definition of electronic mail should be precise with respect to the functional aspects, indicative of the practical applications and as much as possible, independent of the present state of technology. In this way electronic mail is defined as (31):

> *'the electronic, one-directional transfer of information in the form of a message, via an intermediate (tele-)communication system, from an identified sending party to one or more identified receiving parties'.*

This definition is broader than those of Mackintosh and McQuillan, and includes anything from a telegraph message to electronic funds transfer. In fact, it also includes computer-to-computer communications. However, a very specific type of traffic pattern has been defined: message transfer in one direction between two or more equal parties, which are at least known to the sender.

At first sight electronic mail, defined in this way, is a special case of 'conversation': however, electronic mail can be a one-time message without any further reply. According to the definition of Bordewijk, conversation implies the 'exchange' of information, which is certainly not a requirement for electronic mail. It is not the same as correspondence if the latter term is used to include a sequence (or chain) of messages.

Moreover, an agreement as to the time schedule of information exchange, as required by Bordewijk, is not necessary. Since both sender and receiver have been identified, the message can be a totally self-contained unit; the telecommunication system ensures a time-independent message transfer without bi-party, or multi-party agreement for that specific session.

In line with the above definition, electronic mail can also be applied to Bordewijk's other traffic patterns. Allocution-type of electronic mail is defined as the multiple-addressing to a specified group; consultation is an active message in one direction and registration in the other direction.

Bordewijk does not define whether the status of 'information center', which is fundamental to allocution, consultation and registration, can be changed depending on the type of session. If each communication party can assume the status of information center, the flexibility of communication patterns would be increased as well as the possibilities for information systems to adapt to each other.

The definition of electronic mail is strictly limited in the following respect: information should be packaged in self-contained units, i.e. messages, from the point of view of the application layer. Electronic mail does not include information exchange where the message is not a self-contained unit for data transfer, i.e. where the identity of the addressee is not an integral part of the message. Each time that information is submitted to the communication system for transfer from one point to another, the identity of the receiving party must be indicated.

Note that packet-switching also captures user data in self-contained units, i.e. packets, but this has no relevance from an application layer point of view.

Communication via self-contained messages must be the intention of the communicating parties and not because of a technical limitation (such as for some cases of half-duplex voice communications). The repeated addressing for electronic mail is absent in two-way, simultaneous communications, such as telephony.

The identification of sender and receiver distinguishes electronic mail from many other forms of broadcast-type communications, which convey messages in one direction, but to a non-specified or loosely defined audience.

Figure 2.1 shows a basic electronic mail system. A system user in the broadest sense is composed of:

FIGURE 2.1 A BASIC ELECTRONIC MAILING SYSTEM

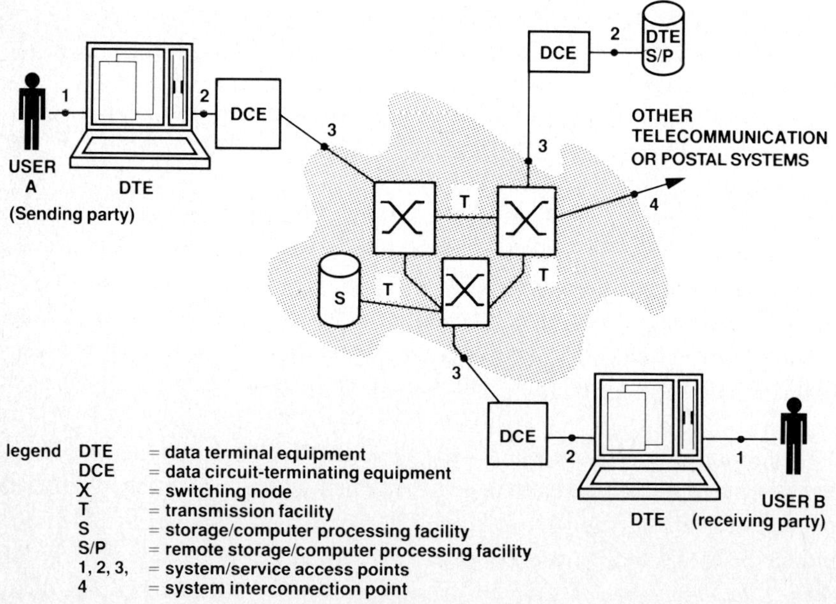

- the end-user (a human being or application process of an information processing system)
- the data terminal equipment (DTE), which could be a computer, a communication processor terminal or a terminal;
- data circuit-terminating equipment (DCE) which provides the interface between the DTE and the physical transmission circuit, or network.

A data-base computer system can be an end-user from the viewpoint of the telecommunication system, even though it provides tele-information services to a multiplicity of users.

There are four important interface points in this basic mail system:

- between the telecommunication system and DCE;
- between DCE and DTE;
- between DTE and human user and between DTE and computer system;
- between two (or more) telecommunication systems (internetting) or to/from a physical delivery system.

Each of these interface points can be seen as the system access point. Regulatory regimes will differ along the boundary which they take.

The intermediate communications system serves as the transfer mechanism for the message; it will be dealt with in more detail in section 2.3. First the various types of mail systems are discussed.

2.2.2 Mail systems

Over the past years a number of systems have developed for the provision of message transfer services. They are different with respect to technology, services and applications. Below a classification of mail systems in four groups is given. The criteria for clustering have been as follows:

1. is message transfer by the mail system fully electronic?
2. is the mail system standardized by one or more recognized international standardization bodies?
3. is it a CCITT Telematic system?

1. Postal and hybrid mail

The first group of mail systems are conventional postal or courier services, and hybrid forms of postal and electronic mail. The latter are generally termed Generation 1 and 2 electronic mail systems (32). Postal delivery is based on physical collection, processing, transport and distribution. Conventional postal systems use letters and parcels as the carriers of information; the message handling process is all hardcopy and transport goes by physical means such as handcarrier, truck, rail, and plane.

Generation 1 electronic mail messages are submitted and delivered on hardcopy, but electronic transmission is used by the service provider. Telegram and facsimile post are examples of Generation 1 electronic mail.

A system of both electronic message submission and electronic communication, with hardcopy delivery, is referred to as Generation 2 electronic mail (33). Other hybrid forms are hardcopy submission of messages, but electronic delivery.

2. Conventional electronic mail

The physical component is no longer present in so-called Generation 3 systems which are fully electronic.

In the first classification of Generation 3 mail are the conventional electronic mail systems, such as telex, TWX and analog facsimile (34). Telex and TWX are end-to-end electronic mail systems (i.e. without intermediate message storage from sender to receiver); they are usually based on a public service for forwarding text messages; specialized terminals, protocols and exchanges are used in accordance with national and international standards. Telex employs International Telegraph Alphabet No. 2 (ITA 2, see S.1); TWX uses the ASCII character set (IA5, see V.3).

Analog facsimile is an end-to-end electronic mail system for picture transmission, using analog techniques for scanning, transmission and reproduction of image documents. CCITT has developed a number of Recommendations for analog facsimile, called Group 1 (approved by CCITT in 1968) and Group 2 (approved in 1976) and which have often been based on available equipment (see CCITT Recomendations T.0, T.2, T.3).

Store-and-forward message switching is classified as conventional because it was initially an improvement of conventional mail systems such as telex (store-and-forward telex) rather than a new user system. Messages are relayed via a number of central switches, equipped with message storage facilities; user-originated messages are stored for a certain period of time, sometimes very short, and re-transmitted to the appropriate destination. Store-and-forward was first used for automatic telegram service and CCITT has defined the service in F.350. It is also applied for store-and-forward facsimile, while the same principle is part of new CCITT Recommendations on Message Handling Systems (Series X.400).

Conventional electronic mail systems have a relatively long history (35) and have often been standardized and regulated by national administrations. CCITT has been a stimulating factor affecting international standards and, indirectly, for national standards (36).

3. Telematic systems

When computers started to affect conventional telecommunications, CCITT promoted – on the basis of national, mostly Western European initiatives (37) – the creation of new services. This resulted in a set of new service definitions referred to as 'telematics' or telematic services. They are defined as services, but the Recommendations define system requirements as well as 'service' facilities.

Teletex, conceived by initiative of the German PTT (38), is end-to-end electronic mail for the exchange of textual information in a similar way to communicating word processors, but using medium-speed communications and a comprehensive character set. The definition by CCITT is as follows:

'Teletex is an international service, offered by administrations or Recognized Private Operating Agencies (RPOA's), enabling subscribers to exchange correspondence on an automatic, memory-to-memory basis via telecommunication networks' (F.200).

Teletex offers textcommunication between word processors and personal computers, which comply with the Recommendations. Conversion between Teletex and telex is also foreseen. The Teletex Recommendations have been laid down by CCITT in an extensive set of Recommendations in 1980 and were substantially improved and enhanced in 1984 (F.200, F.201, T.51, T.60, T.61, T.62, T.63, T.70, T.71, T.72, T.73, T.90, T.91, X.430) (39).

Digital facsimile is another telematic system which allows end-to-end electronic mail of pictorial information, using primarily digital techniques. CCITT approved Group 3 in 1980 (see T.4, T.30); this class of machines uses digital data compression and analog transmission of one A4 document over the ordinary telephone network in less than a minute. Group 4 has been defined in 1984 (T.5, T.6, T.62) and uses digital transmission in addition to digital scanning techniques. Dependent on the digital network, transmission speed may be as low as 5 seconds for one A4 (40).

During its General Assembly of 1984, CCITT also approved a set of Recommendations on mixed-mode Teletex/digital facsimile. The mixed-mode capability provides the means of document communications where the document content has been encoded using different techniques (i.e. in all forms of facsimile and Teletex character coding); moreover the document structure is fully identified, enabling the recipient to reprocess the message contents. The mixed-mode is defined in T.5 (Group 4, class 3; class 2 for reception only), T.62, T.72. T.73. Equipment exists in protype stage (41).

Interactive videotex (F.300, T.100, T.101) is the third group of telematics: in essence it is an information distribution system for data, text, and graphics via a central computer and simple terminals and retrieval procedures, as used for instance, in British Telecom's Prestel service. These systems can include a message exchange facility, both with store-and-forward and with store-and-retrieve operations. Note that there are at least five different standards (Prestel, Télétel/Antiope, CEPT, NAPLPS, CAPTAIN) (42), selected by national administrations.

4. Non-standardized new electronic mail (43)

Along with the standardization work of CCITT on telematics, manufacturers of computer and office automation equipment have designed proprietary electronic mail systems. Word processors and personal computers were adapted for communications via public or private (global, or local area) networks; in this way office personnel could mail data and textual information, although they were restricted by the incompatibilities of manufacturers' equipment.

TABLE 2.1. MAIL SYSTEMS

1. Postal and hybrid mail

   *postal and courier, Generation 1 Electronic Mail System
   *Generation 2 Electronic Mail System

2. Conventional electronic mail

   *telex, TWX
   *analog facsimile
   *store-and-forward message switching

3. Telematic systems

   *Teletex
   *digital facsimile
   *mixed-mode Teletex/digital facsimile
   *interactive videotex

4. Non-standardized new electronic mail

   *communicating word processor, personal computer
   *computer-based message system (CBMS)
   *voice mail

As discussed before, the computer industry designed computer message systems (CBMS) which were based on store-and-retrieve operations. Similar to CBMS are voice mail systems: while CBMS stores data and text messages, voice mail systems store spoken messages. They require no specialized terminal except a push button telephone set (44).

2.3 MESSAGE HANDLING SYSTEMS

2.3.1 CCITT message-handling functional model

A mail system typically provides a service for the transfer of mail items, which are defined as messages if they contain information. The developments in mail systems show a movement toward fully electronic, computerized systems with computer-based terminal equipment connected to them. In a way the function of the computerized mail system remains message transfer, but the facilities to handle the message, i.e. to transfer, store, and process the message, are increasingly more sophisticated. In particular, a new conceptual framework is needed to define the functions and basic architecture involved in electronic mail systems. First we need a clear understanding of the relationships between message on the one hand, and data and information on the other.

Three levels of communication problems

Figure 2.2 is a schematic diagram of a communication system (45). The transmitter and receiver are the same as the DCE, and the information source and destination are comparable with the DTE. The channel is the medium used to transmit the signals from transmitter to receiver; for the purpose of this discussion, one may view the channel as the intermediate (tele-)communication system (see Figure 2.1). It is indifferent whether the channel is switched or not, as long as there is a permanent or virtual circuit between transmitter and receiver.

The problem of communication – following the scheme of Figure 2.2 – is how the information source can affect the information state at the destination. Ac-

FIGURE 2.2 SCHEMATIC DIAGRAM OF A COMMUNICATION SYSTEM

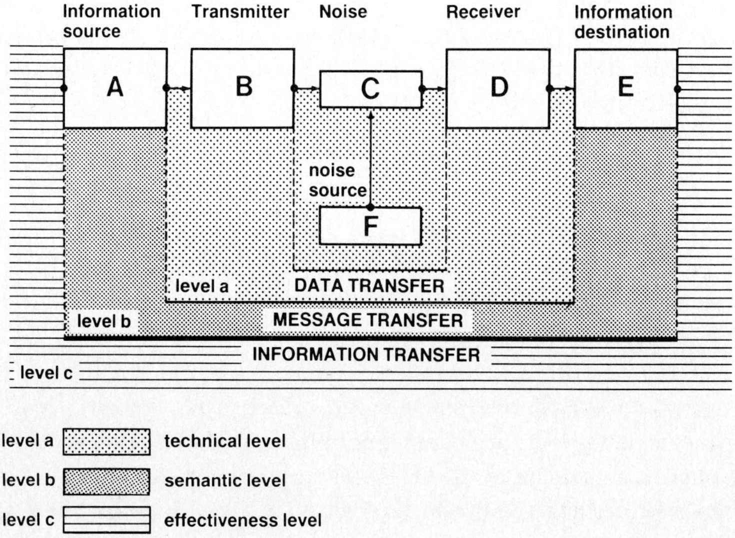

cording to Weaver (1963) (46), this problem can be analysed on three levels:

- at the technical level: how accurately can the symbols of communication be transmitted?
- at the semantic level: how precisely do the transmitted symbols convey the desired meaning?
- at the effectiveness level: how effectively does the received meaning affect conduct in the desired way?

A 'message' can be viewed either from a communication point of view (the technical level) or from an application point of view (the semantic and effectiveness levels). This leads to different definitions.

According to Shannon (1948) (47), 'the fundamental problem of communications is that of reproducing at one point either exactly or approximately a message selected at another point. Frequently the messages have meaning; that is they refer to or are correlated according to some system with certain physical or conceptual entities. These semantic aspects of communication are irrelevant to the engineering problem'.

Relative to the view of Shannon, telecommunications is a system for reliable message transfer. A message is defined as a sequence of symbols that have been selected from a pre-defined set (for instance a character set). Shannon defines information as a measure of one's freedom of choice when one selects a message. In its simplest form, the amount of information of a message is measured as a Markoff process of repeated choices from a set of options. This set of options should be an exhaustive enumeration of the available possibilities, while each option excludes the other. The probability of selecting a certain sequence (i.e. a set of choices in time order) represents a certain amount of information, or a message. From an engineering point of view, the design of the communication system must be such that it can handle each message that the source can produce (48).

A concise definition of a 'message' is one by Wiener (1948, 1961) (49): 'the message is a discrete or continuous sequence of measurable events distributed in time'. Wiener relates message to automata: the coupling of automated systems to the external world is not only a matter of energy exchange, but also of incoming messages and of the actions of outgoing messages (50). As part of a control system, messages must be stored so that they can be released in a timed manner (51). In other words: a message is not an isolated unit, but a means to an end that is determined by its lock in time.

Ackoff and Emery (1972) (52) define message as 'a set of one or more signs intended by its producer to produce a response either in another or in himself'. According to Ackoff and Emery, communication only takes place when a message produced by a sender produces a change in one or more of the parameters of the receiver's state. Both sender and receiver must have choice as well as purpose (53): a message must have a desired or non-desired effect, or it is no message.

Because of the use of formalized information processing systems as communication entities, an orientation on 'message' as 'meaningful data' is necessary. Increasingly the higher levels of the communication problem form the bottlenecks for the overall design of a communication system. When human beings are the immediate user of the communication system, the semantic and efficiency problems are solved via natural language and the memorizing of past communications. The natural language provides the means to assign meaning to data (defined as in section 1.1); and via the use of memory, past relations can be recalled and associations to shared knowledge can be made (i.e. the referencing to a declarative knowledge base). Because the interpretation of the data is performed by human beings, it is sufficient to have a 'technical' knowledge of the characteristics of the signals in order to be able to design the communication system. For instance, the analog telephone system has been designed for transmission of voice signals on the basis of 3.4 kHz bandwidth as an acceptable quality level for the reproduction of human speech: the availability of a technical infrastructure was adequate, the users took care of the common understanding of the data transferred from one point to another via the network.

The fact that computers are the direct user of the communication system, is not an immediate problem for the technical infrastructure that transfers signals from one point to another. The main bottlenecks are the incompatibilities at the higher levels, i.e. the interpretation of the received messages. In the case of computer communications, it is insufficient to transfer a message as a 'sequence of probable options from a defined set': agreements on the semantics are necessary so that the message may act as a control mechanism (Wiener), or as response producer (Ackoff and Emery). The issue is not as simple as redefining the set of options from which a message can be composed: like human communication, flexibility is needed with respect to the meaning assigned to symbols. It must be possible to adapt during the communication session, and moreover it must be possible to maintain a selective memory with respect to communications for subsequent use (54).

A general architecture: Open Systems Interconnection

The above realization that formalized information systems require detailed agreements on semantics and effectiveness, led to the development of an architectural design for 'Open Systems Interconnection' (55). The three-level problem of communication has been split into seven layers in an hierarchical order:

- layers 1-3 are network oriented layers with the aim to provide data transfer service to the higher layers, in such a way that the syntax of the transmitted symbols are independent of the underlying physical media;
- layers 4-6 are service oriented layers with the aim to provide communication service to the application layer, in such a way that the semantics of the transmitted symbols are independent of the syntax;
- layer 7 embodies the application of systems interconnection, i.e. the effectiveness of communications, or, according to Ackoff and Emery (56), the pragmatics of communication that considers the relationship between the 'sign' and the response.

One of the main difficulties of the architecture is to segregate the various layers and to group the common functions. In particular layer 4, the grouping of network-independent transport functions, and layer 7, the grouping of communication service-independent applications, constitute complicated boundary definitions.

CCITT Message Handling System

CCITT has defined message-handling as a function on the application layer. It forms one of the first specifications of a user system that is part of the application layer in accordance with the OSI model (57). A Message Handling System (MHS) is defined by CCITT as the collectivity of user processing equipment, referred to as User Agent (UA), and Message Transfer Agents (MTA) (58). A related number of MTA's constitute a Message Transfer System (MTS), which provides the following types of services (59):

1. interacting with originating UA's via the submission dialogue;
2. relaying messages to adjacent MTA's based upon recipient designations and the networking plan;
3. interacting with the recipient UA's via the delivery dialogue.

The MTS is the interconnection of distributed systems on the level of message transfer, called the Message Transfer Layer (MTL). The MTL is the conceptual boundary between the application layer and the lower-level communication layers. Its position is on the lowest part of the application layer. Note that layers are a conceptual grouping together of similar functions of distributed systems.

In this layered model other application functions are positioned on top of the MTL. As of October 1984 CCITT has defined the Interpersonal Messaging service (IPM) – or User Agent Layer (UAL) – for the relaying of messages for human end-users. The MTS functionality, however, extends beyond that of interpersonal messaging. It should be remembered that the IPM services are limited in respect to group communications possibilities.

A detail examination of the variety of message handling facilities and the Open Sytems Interconnection / Message Handling Systems model is given in the appendix. Let me emphasize that in view of current and future developments, message handling should not be seen in the restricted sense of store-and-forward electronic mail services: it forms the critical boundary between user data transfer and information transfer from the point of view of application and effectiveness. This is schematically indicated in Figure 2.2. While earlier mail systems, in particular the conventional postal system, delivered a service for message transfer with no relevance to the application, the newer systems will provide message handling facilities, that will have a bearing on the application data.

X.400 introduces a functional model of the MHS that should be applicable to a variety of physical and organizational configurations. The next sections discuss which services should be provided in a public message-handling environment in order that a global transfer of messages between different configurations is possible. In the first place, these are directory services which will become more important in proportion to the growth and variety of 'open' systems. Secondly, services are necessary for the factual transfer of messages, in particular access, interworking, conversion, message storage and message processing.

2.3.2 Directory services

If formalized information systems are the users of the message handling system, the directory is not only a means to find the access number of another communication entity, but also the information base to find the commonality of communication capabilities.

First, the directory service enables one to identify the other party. The variety in message handling systems and the different conventions for naming and addressing, will make the compiling and maintenance of a public directory a formidable task.

The updating of the public directory will be a continuous effort of processing the mutations of various directory systems. This may lead to a distributed directory management system in such a way that every private MTA has an associated Directory Service Agent (DSA), to which all relevant information from the other directory systems must be copied, under the management of the overall public directory.

Second, the directory services will include information on the type of messages (at presentation layer and/or application layer) and the method to obtain access to private or specific public systems (60).

Two more types of services relate to the directory. First, the directory can be seen as a means to control access and to provide specific facilities for security. Second, it may provide domain management services and conformance testing services.

Access authorization and security services relate to (61):

- key management for access authorization, including verification of sender and receiver identity, terminal identity and location, resource and cost allocation;
- secure transfer and storage of messages (message authentication, transmission error detection/correction, data encryption, fail-safe message storage, verification and maintainance of message identity, such as conversion protection);
- maintaining system integrity (secrecy of messages, program control, protection against fraud, mutilation or loss of information, etc.).

Domain management services refer to management facilities of a closed user group within a public domain. The user group is the authority for naming and access management, deciding on message processing facilities, cost allocation and the quality of service.

Finally, the more complicated the applications, the more urgent are services for conformance testing.

2.3.3 Public message-handling services

Acknowledging that users may be formalized information systems, the facilities for message transfer extend beyond those of straightforward data transfer. Facilities are necessary that ensure that the messages can be interpreted by the receiver systems. In addition the public domain should be able to deal with a variety of both 'intelligent' and 'non-intelligent' user systems.

Access, interworking and conversion

Public domain facilities for access, interworking and conversion include:

- uniform access to public networks; 'transparent' interworking among these networks, including the use of PSTN as access network to CSPDN and PSPDN; interworking between CSPDN and PSPDN; interworking with foreign public networks;
- access to, and interworking with traditional services, i.e. post, telex/TWX, and analog facsimile. This requires specific conversion facilities, i.e. for telematic services and non-standardized new electronic mail services, see Figure 2.3;
  The interworking with Generation 2 EMS, i.e. the delivery of electronic messages independent of their origination, is needed for most of the mail technologies and requires distributed printing and enveloping facilities, in a similar way to post office decentralization (62).
  As far as interworking with telex/TWX is concerned, this is mandatory in the Teletex Recommendations (63) while some major operators of public CBMS systems automatically deliver telex/TWX messages to and from the subscriber's mailbox (64).
- specific interworking and conversion between public networks and communicating word processor/personal computer, and CBMS. The latter will usually support 'Teletype', using ASCII character coding (IA5), and speeds at 50-300/1200 bps, full duplex modes (65).

Message transfer and gateway services

A public service is needed for message transfer between private and public domains, as well as for connecting two or more private domains via the public domain. The Reliable Transfer Service (RTS), defined in X.411, enables the

FIGURE 2.3 INTERWORKING AND CONVERSION OF MAIL SYSTEMS

from \ to	1 postal and courier, Generation 1 EMS	2 Generation 2 EMS	3 telex/TWX	4 analog facsimile	5 S&F message switching	6 Teletex	7 digital facsimile	8 mixed mode Teletex/facsimile	9 interactive videotex	10 communicating WP/PC 1)	11 CBMS 1)	12 voice mail
1. postal and courier, Generation 1 EMS	•	c	c	c	c	x	c	c	c	c	c	x
2. Generation 2 EMS	i	•	c	c	c	x	c	c	c	c	c	c
3. telex/TWX	–	c	•	c	•	c	c	c	c	c	c	c
4. analog facsimile	–	c	x	i	x	x	c	c	x	x	x	x
5. S&F message switching	–	c	•i	c	•i	c	c	c	c	c	c	c
6. Teletex	–	c	c	c	c	•i	c	ci	c	c	c	c
7. digital facsimile	–	c	x	c	x	x	•i	c	x	x	x	x
8. mixed mode Teletex/facsimile	–	c	xc	xc	xc	ci	ci	ci	c	x	x	xc
9. interactive videotex	–	c	c	c	c	c	c	c	•i	c	c	c
10. communicating WP/PC 1)	–	c	c	c	c	c	c	x	x	c	c	c
11. CBMS 1)	–	c	c	c	c	c	c	xc	c	c	c	c
12. voice mail	x	x	x	x	x	x	x	x	x	x	x	•i

legend: • = no interworking and/or conversion necessary
x = interworking and/or conversion not possible/practical
i = interworking necessary, but not conversion
c = conversion necessary
– = not applicable

1) character coding most commonly used is ASCII (IA5) at 50-300/1200 bps full duplex

routing of messages on store-and-forward basis between various management domains (MD's) (66). It has been defined in such a way that other services can easily make use of it without major constraints on the semantics of the bit-strings. All types of UA's can access or be accessed via the MTS.

Three types of message transfer services in the public domain are (67):

- RTS based on interconnected, public MTA's, and which can use the various public networks in a 'transparent' way for the connected private domain UA's; access to this service should be possible for private UA's as well as private MTA's;
- gateway services for private MTA's in such a way that 'transparent' end-to-end transport is possible between two or more private MTA's crossing the public domain (68);
- gateway services between two or more public MTA's of different Management Domains, i.e. the national and international relaying of messages.

TABLE 2.2 PUBLIC USER AGENT FACILITIES (INTERPERSONAL MESSAGING)

1. Message send		
	– addressing	user identification
		copy (cc., bcc., copy to file)
		directories
		multiple addressing
		distribution lists
		bulletin boards
	– delivery	acknowledge receipt
		obsoletion/withdraw
		reply requested
		auto-/forced delivery
		message waiting indicator
		delivery priority
		deferred
		private
		periodic
2. Message compose		
	– basic editor	character input and insert
		delete character, word, line
		line feed/continuous typing
	– optional editor	full screen
		search/replace
		spelling
		connected software package
		off-line word processor/ personal computer
	– forms handling	form set-up and definition
		forms transfer
		forms processing
3. Message reading		
	– scanning	user identification
		scan lines on name/ address/ date/ subject
		message read
	– disposition	auto reply form
		forward plus comment
		delete/ delete back-up
		file
4. Filing and retrieval		
	– file input	messages/ text
		file labelling
	– retrieval	cross file search
		retrieve on sender name
		retrieve on address field
		retrieve on copy field
		retrieve on subject, combination of various subjects
		retrieve on date, between dates, before/after dates
		retrieve on message number
	– access to data bases	

Source: Vervest (1985)

Basic electronic mail (UA)

A basic interpersonal messaging service is needed in the public domain, either for individuals to use or for closed user groups that wish to operate a UA service via public facilities. Note that such a service is similar to a CBMS service. A package of facilities has been given in Table 2.2 (69).

In addition a public voice mail system coupled to a data base can importantly enhance the ability to use the public CBMS, e.g. via speech output of text messages, voice annotation to messages and voice response systems (70).

Specialized services

Basic message-handling services are communication-oriented and facilitate message transport; specialized message-handling services are application-oriented, aiming to enable message processing. Our discussion of value-added services has shown that resource-sharing is the essential purpose of message-handling based networks. This may lead to very specific services, which are not always offered non-discriminatorily to the public, but for which a public system should provide the necessary support functions. These services cover (71):

- access to public and private data bases;
- forms processing support, i.e. for purchasing, banking, shipping or other types of transactions;
- decision support services for specific branches, i.e. for logistics, trade, energy management, cash management;
- interconnection of different office automation systems through the public domain.

2.4 OSI/MHS AS TECHNOLOGICAL TRAJECTORY

2.4.1 Communications and meaning

The question now arises whether OSI/MHS will act as a new technological trajectory, i.e. as an autonomous route for technical change. This question is difficult to answer in view of the early stage of development, but some comments can be made.

First, as explained in the Introduction and the foregoing sections of this chapter, the concept of the 'electronic mailbox' is definitely different from previous designs of electronic mail systems. It raised uncertainty as to the definition of 'electronic mail' itself, as well as to the arrangement of telecommunication systems to provide electronic mail services.

The development of the first experimental electronic mailbox system (as part of Arpanet) was more the result of an idea put into practice than one of careful scientific analysis and planning of R&D efforts (72). However, after the idea was proven, it could only result in success if a number of other conditions were met. In particular, a paradigm had to be developed for the connection of computer systems with each other via tele-communication networks in such a way that 'meaningful communication' between these systems was possible. It is for this reason that the OSI Basic Reference Model was a pre-requisite for progress. It laid down a common basis for the design of 'open' computerized information systems. Within this context 'openness' refers to the mutual recognition of the applicable standards; it does not imply any particular system implementation, technology, or means of interconnection (73).

Following the same methodology, CCITT developed the MHS functional model. The two models together, of which the MHS model is a specific elaboration of the OSI model, constitute the terms of reference for the future development of mail systems. While the specification work on OSI/MHS is still ongoing, the first systems have been built which are supposed to comply with the model requirements (74). It seems that OSI/MHS is leading the way of technical advance in messaging systems (see also section 4.3).

The basic ideas of OSI/MHS as a new path for technical change may be summarized as follows:

1. a user of a telecommunication system, i.e. a communication entity, is seen as a formalized system capable of information processing and/or information transfer; the fact that a human being is the end-user of this system is irrelevant to the construction of the technical means for system interconnection;
2. the interests of each communication entity are represented via a User Agent (UA) which is the formalized domain for the management of user messages;
3. the distribution of messages is performed via a Message Transfer System (MTS), which acts as a boundary between application processes and the

lower-layer (technical) facilities and services for telecommunications;

4. a message can be anything which has relevance to the application processes; from the application point of view, the integrity of the message should be maintained, but this does not prohibit message processing for the purpose of message transfer.

The above 'rules' should ensure that distributed information systems can cooperate with the common (distributed) task to provide 'meaning' to the human end-user, i.e. the timely delivery of appropriate information.
However, what does 'information' mean within this context? It should be recognized that at the highest layer of communications, information has a different definition than the one applied by Shannon. From an application point of view, information deals with the effectiveness of the message, i.e. its useability to determine the course of action of the receiver.

Shannon defines information as (75):

$$H = -\mathop{\mathrm{SUM}}_{i=1}^{n} p(i) * {}^{2}\log p(i) \qquad [4]$$

where

H = degree of information (of a discrete source)
$p(i)$ = probability for selecting message i
n = total number of available messages

H is an expression for the degree of freedom of an information source when selecting a message from a defined set n. The definition of the set of available messages, however, is the focus of interest of behavioral scientists, such as Ackoff (1958) (76) and Watzlawick (1967) (77). Communication is determined by a meta-relation between communication parties, that determines the significance of symbols which are communicated between the two parties, according to Watzlawick (78).

Ackoff (1958) (79) quantifies information as a measure of the information state of the receiving party. Information is measured as the receiver's freedom of choice to determine the 'course of action'. A message contains information to the extent that it can change the state of the recipient's course of action. The available number of courses of action, and the likelihood of choosing a certain course, determines the degree of information (80):

$$A = n/2 * \sum_{i=1}^{n} \mid p(i) - 1/n \mid \qquad [5]$$

where

A = degree of freedom of choice
$p(i)$ = probability of state i
n = number of states

As has been analyzed by Galjaard (1979) (81), the information concepts of Ackoff and Shannon are fundamentally different. Shannon's H is a measure for the information content of a message: a high value of H means that there is a low degree of freedom, or choice, of the recipient. Thus A would have a low value (82). The relation is not this easy, however. A is a measure for the information state of the receiver: it relates to the meaning that is assigned to a message by the receiver, rather than to the intents of the sender.

With the advent of computers Ackoff's concept is increasingly important. Open systems interconnection will require that machines can communicate more intelligently, i.e. by building a-priori associations with each other and by exchanging the knowledge states of each machine (83). The more applications are distributed over separate systems, the more difficult it will be to manage the system within an OSI environment without explicit management of associations between application-entities. It is this aspect of system interconnection which has not been dealt with by the current specifications of OSI/MHS (84).

Figure 2.4 gives the OSI environment for distributed user applications. One application process transfers information to another via application entities, which use other services through their common access point. OSI distinguishes between Common Application Service Elements (CASE) and Specific Application Service Elements (SASE). The first provide the capabilities required by application processes for information transfer independent of the nature of the application (e.g. setting up an association between application processes, terminating an association). Specific Application Service Elements provide information transfer capabilities (e.g. file transfer, data base access, job transfer) or capabilities to satisfy the needs of a particular application process (e.g. banking, shipping, logistics). The User Element (UE) represents the capabilities needed to interface the remainder of the application process to the application layer service elements (85).

In order to have the two application processes of system A and system B inter-

FIGURE 2.4 INTERCONNECTION OF DISTRIBUTED APPLICATION PROCESSES IN OSI ENVIRONMENT

OSI environment. One application process transfers information to another via application entities, which obtain other services through their access point.

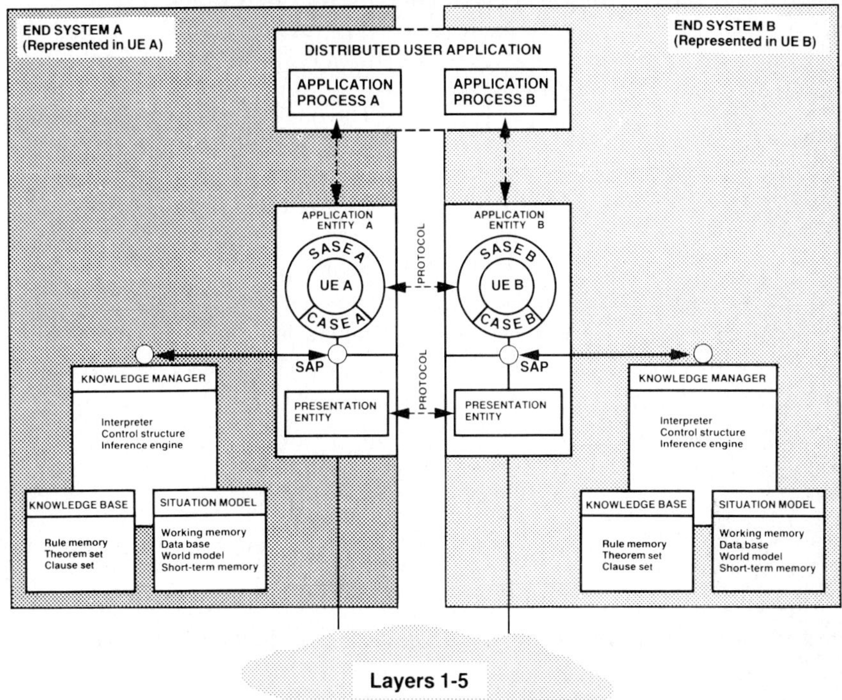

legend **UE** = **user element**
SASE = **specific application service elements**
CASE = **common application service elements**
SAP = **service access protocol**

act, i.e. to act and react to each other's behavior, an association must be established. This is what some scholars of OSI refer to as the application context (86). The effectiveness of highly interactive systems will largely be determined by the speed and nature of building and maintaining the associations. The use of a memory is needed in this process so that associations can be stored.

The management of system memories is necessary for the management of system interconnection at the application level. For the same reasons this can affect interconnection at the lower levels of the OSI model. Memory is not necessarily a function at application level (87). OSI memory must be seen as a kind of expert system (88) capable of building, maintaining and applying information in a communications context.

Meaningful communications requires that the information states of communications partners are exchanged. For the same reason as OSI has been conceived, we need a model to signify information states; in this way 'open' systems can adapt to one another before, during, or after the communications session.

Adaptivity is essential for meaningful communications as is connectivity. It determines in which way network communications can result in effective access to information. Computer networks can share data among different systems; data can be transferred, stored and processed as a single network resource. But the essence for the network user is the implementation of data for the application: this is what produces information. For this reason we need a model to represent knowledge in information networks in a way which is independent of the application.

2.4.2 Developments in system technology

The foregoing section looked at the scientific basis of OSI/MHS; another viewpoint is the immediate effects on technological developments itself. Table 2.3. shows an outline of the key technologies involved. It should be kept in mind that OSI/MHS is specified in terms of system facilities; it is not a particular technology, but part of an overall system.

The importance of OSI/MHS as a system technology is particularly relevant for the arrangement of the telecommunication networks. The message-handling functional model requires that different networks are interconnected in order to offer a Reliable Transfer Service independent of the underlying telecommunication means.

Figure 2.5 shows, as an important example, the configuration of the facsimile communication network (FCN) in Japan (89). FCN utilizes both analog and digital paths which have been rearranged from the available PSTN and PDN to provide dedicated facilities for facsimile transmission.

In future, complicated network arrangements are necessary to interconnect the

Table 2.3 KEY TECHNOLOGIES

1. Public communication networks
   - message handling facilities integrated in central office equipment
   - distributed message communications; X.400 networking
   - gateways for private systems
   - international gateways
   - X.400 adaptive network routing mechanisms
   - global directory systems
   - access systems to distributed (public) data bases
   - access systems to (public) transactional systems
   - public key systems; privacy and integrity systems

2. Private communication networks
   - message handling facilities integrated in PBX
   - message handling servers for LAN's
   - global message handling systems for WAN's; X.400 networking
   - message handling integration in EDP systems
   - office document handling processors
   - message processors for manufacturing, logistics, etc.
   - company directory systems
   - private gateways

3. Inter-organizational networks
   - message handling system for inter-organizational transactions
   - forms processors
   - private-to-private, private-to-public gateways
   - access systems to private data bases
   - X.400 adaptive routing systems
   - inter-company directory systems

4. Message management systems
   - MTA/message switching systems
   - access, interworking and conversion systems
   - maintenance and operational control systems
   - UA/CBMS
   - IPM, Pc processing systems (see section A.2.3)
   - directory systems
   - control & certification equipment

5. Workstations
   - compound document processors
   - integrated office terminals
   - portable terminals
   - home terminals
   - modular message handling devices
   - dedicated user interface modules for message handling

Source: Expert discussions

different mail systems as part of an all-encompassing message-handling system. The different networks are used as the means of transport for different forms of mail while the overall compatibility is maintained in separate message handling facilities.

FIGURE 2.5 CONFIGURATION OF THE FACSIMILE COMMUNICATION NETWORK (FCN) IN JAPAN

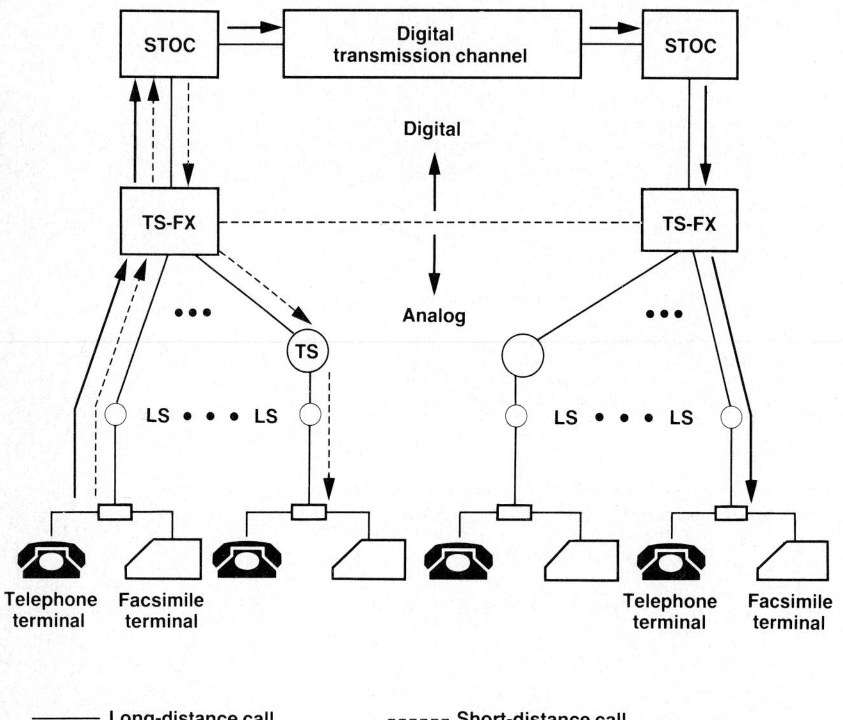

Source: Nippon Telegraph & Telephone Public Corporation (NTT), 1985

NOTES CHAPTER 2
DEVELOPMENTS IN ELECTRONIC MAIL

(1) Roebuck in 'The World of Ancient Times' (1967) p. 167.
(2) Daumas in 'Technology and Invention' (1969, Vol.1) p. 242; Stamps (1982) p. 15, p. 41.
(3) Stamps (1982) p. 15-18.
(4) Daumas (1969) p. 376-390; Stamps (1982) p. 40-47.
(5) Stamps (1982) p. 47; Vervest (1985) p. 41-47; cf. Freebody (1958).
(6) Stamps (1982) p. 44-46
(7) An extensive review of the history of telephony can be found in Chapuis, '100 Years of Telephone Switching 1878-1978', (1982).
(8) Stamps (1982) p. 47-51; Friedrich (1934).
(9) See Costigan (1978) for a review on facsimile history and trends. Facsimile has been designed by Alexander Bain who received a British patent in 1843 (Costigan, 1978, p. 2). Cf. Vervest (1985) p. 48-54.
(10) Goody Katz and Phillips in: Nelson (1982) p. 172-178; Stern (1981).
See for a general discussion on computer networks: Davies, Barber et al. (1979), Meijer and Peeters (1982), NCC (1982) and Tanenbaum (1981).
(11) Davies, Barber et al. (1979) p. 21-26; Sjöström (1982).
(12) Davies, Barber et al. (1979) p. 38-76; Davies (1968).
(13) Davies, Barber et al. (1979) p. 12, p. 38-74.
(14) Vervest (1985) p. 19, 21-25; see also Van Kampen (1969).
(15) Vervest (1985) p. 116-124; see also Van Duuren (1981). ICAO is the International Civil Aviation Organization; WMO is World Meteorological Organization, NATO the North Atlantic Treaty Organization, SITA is the International Aeronautical Telecommunication Organization (Société International de Télécommunications Aéronautiques); SWIFT is the Society for Worldwide Interbank Financial Telecommunications.
(16) Davies, Barber et al. (1979) p. 73; Uhlig, Farber and Bair (1979) p. 23-45; Vallee (1984) p. 52-68.
(17) Cf. Vervest (1985) p. 89-91.
(18) A compound document accommodates the widest possible variety of data types -or bit formats- for data representation, such as text, facsimile, bit-map images, vector graphics, compressed speech, PCM sound, etc.
(19) ISO (1983); for a review see Folts (1983).
(20) CCITT Plenary Assembly, October 1984; cf. Cunningham, rapporteur Study Group VIII during the Eighth Study Period (1983, 1984)
(21) Cf. Recommendation X.25, CCITT, 1976, amended 1980.
(22) The word 'telematics' or 'télématique' has been coined by Simon Nora and Alain Minc in their significant report on the 'L'informatisation de la Société', delivered to the French president in 1978 (Nora and Minc, 1978,1980). Since then it has been accepted as a general term for the whole range of new services made possible by the interconnection of computers and telecommunications. Within CCITT, however, it has a specific meaning for new non-voice telecommunication services.
(23) Cf. Series F. Recommendation on 'Telegraph and 'Telematic Services' Operations and Tariffs', in particular F.160, F.170 and F.180 on facsimile; F.200 on 'Teletex Service', F.201 on 'Interworking between the Teletex Service and the Telex Service'; and F.300 on 'Videotex Service' (Fascicle II.4 of the Yellow Book, CCITT, 1980). Digital facsimile and mixed-mode Teletex and facsimile are described in T.4, T.5 and T.72 (CCITT, 1984).
(24) Cf. Series I. Recommendations (CCITT, 1984); an overview of ISDN developments is given in Vervest (1985) p. 107-112. The use of ISDN for text and data communication has been analyzed by Bocker and Gerke in Uhlig (1981) p. 53-65.

(25) Irmer (1981).
(26) Important but mostly incompatible definitions can also be found in Schicker (1981), Sirbu (1981), Nothhaft (1982), Connell and Galbraith (1983), Datapro (1983), Siegman (1983), Vallee (1984) and Wilson (1984)
(27) Uhlig, Farber and Bair (1979) p. 23.
(28) Mackintosh Consultants Company (1978), Volume 1, p. 1, p. 11, p. 27-41.
(29) McQuillan (1984), conference lectures on electronic mail, p. I.1, p. 2.1-43, 4.15-17.
(30) Vittal, J., Active Message Processing: Messages as Messengers, in: Uhlig (1981) p. 175-195. Cf. McQuillan (1984) p. 4.14-4.23.
(31) Vervest (1985) p. 15-16.
(32) The distinction between three generations of electronic mail has been introduced at the National Research Council in 1976 (NRC, 1976) and has been widely used in the impact study of electronic mail for US Postal Service by the US Congress Office of Technology Assessment (OTA, 1982)
(33) OTA (1982) p. 28; cf. Vervest (1985) p. 12, p. 33-41.
(34) TWX is an acronym for teletypewriter service, cf. Vervest (1985) p. 2, p. 45-48, p. 101; cf. Stamps (1982) p. 47-51.
(35) More details on the history of telex and facsimile can be found in Vervest (1985).
(36) Although CCITT is formally restricted to international harmonization of telecommunications, its work serves as the guideline for national standards.
(37) Videotex found its origins in British Telecommunications; text communications for office use, or Teletex was promoted by the German PTT; the French PTT have been leading with respect to nation-wide plans for tele-information.
(38) The first conceptions have been attributed to the 'Kommission für den technischen Kommunikationssystems' (1976) and subsequently it became an official Study Question in CCITT Seventh Study Period 1977-1980; cf. Schenke, Rüggeberg, Otto (1982) p. 9-14.
(39) Cf. Vervest (1985) p. 54-68.
(40) Cf. Vervest (1985) p. 48-54.
(41) Cf. Maurice (1984).
(42) An overview of current status and trends is given in the proceedings of the Videotex '84 International (Online, 1984).
(43) The term non-standardized does not mean that there are no applicable standards for the types of electronic mail systems described in this section. Standardization for these types of systems is the result of autonomous technological and market developments, and not of prior definition by PTT's and CCITT as with the telematic services.
(44) Cf. Vervest (1985) p. 89-92; see also Diebold (1984) in 'Voice Communications in the Office'; Lee and Lochovsky (1983) on voice response systems.
(45) Cf. for this diagram Shannon and Weaver (1963) p. 6-8; p. 33-35.
(46) Id. p. 4; p. 24-28.
(47) Id. p. 31.
(48) Id. p. 14.
(49) Wiener (1948, 1961) p. 8.
(50) Id. p. 42.
(51) Id. p. 197.
(52) Ackoff and Emery (1972) p. 176; cf. id. p. 179-192.
(53) Id. p. 144-153; p. 133-134.
(54) Brok, W.F., in an interim report BECOM-DTS90, PTT, The Hague, May 1985, describes the distinction as follows:
'Suppose as application (of the OSI-model) two persons who are discussing the useability of the OSI-model. Which is the protocol governing the discussion? The answer is as follows: Both need to understand each other's language and both need a common knowledge of the OSI-model. This knowledge does not only demand a procedural knowledge, i.e. knowledge about the ways and manners to perform tasks, but more importantly, it requires a declaratory knowl-

edge base; this is not a collection of unrelated facts that one should retrieve in a laborious manner via electronic directories, but facts which have been stored within a context, within specific patterns of associative relationships. This is what enables us to retrieve information from a data base, even if the question is ambiguous. This is due to the fact that our (human) brain only accepts new knowledge elements if it can activate associated knowledge units to establish new associations or to enforce existing ones'.

(55) ISO (1983) IS 7498.

(56) Ackoff and Emery (1972) p. 162-163.

(57) Cunningham (1983) p. 1334.

(58) X.400, p. 4-5; see also Cunningham (1983) p. 1425-1427 and Myer (1983) p. 413-415.

(59) X.400 p. 6; X.401 p. 51; X.411 p. 4-6. Note that page numbers refer to the 'Final Report on the Work of Study Group VIII During the Study Period 1981-1984' , AP VIII-66-E (X.400, X.401, X.408, X.409, X.410) and AP VIII-67-E (X.411, X.420, X.430), June 1984.

(60) Cf. Steedman, D., CCITT Study Group VII, Draft Recommendations X.ds0 - X.ds6, Directory Systems, May 1985.

(61) Davies and Price (1984).

(62) Cf. MCI Mail in Vervest (1985) p. 39-44.

(63) F.200, F.201.

(64) This has become the overall strategy of one of the major US carriers, Western Union. Cf. Data Communications (August 1984) p. 79-84.

(65) Cf. Logica (1980) 'Successful Word Processing'.

(66) Cf. X.400, X.411.

(67) Cf. X.400.

(68) This means that the 'architecture' of the information is maintained across the private boundaries.

(69) Cf. Vervest (1985) p. 75-77.

(70) Cf. Lee and Lochovsky (1984); Vervest (1985) p. 89-91; Diebold (1984).

(71) Cf. section 3.3 on value-added network services; further reference is made to Yankee (1983) and Butler Cox (1984);

(72) According to Rosenberg (1982, p. 143, 159), scientific activities are more the result of technological advances than their determinant. The latter belief, science as the determinant for technological progress, is the one which is generally held among economists. Cf. Rothwell and Zegveld (1985) p. 59.

(73) ISO (1983) IS 7498 p. 2.

(74) The issue of compliance is discussed in section 4.3; implementations are – among other things – promoted by the X.400 Demonstrator Group organizaed by the US National Bureau of Standards.

(75) Shannon in Shannon and Weaver (1963) p. 45-53.

(76) Cf. Ackoff (1958), Ackoff (1960) , Ackoff and Emery (1972).

(77) Watzlavick (1967, 1983).

(78) Id. p. 34-37.

(79) Ackoff (1958); Ackoff (1960) in Emery (1969) 'Systems Thinking' p. 338-340; Ackoff and Emery (1972) p. 144-153.

(80) Id.; cf. Ackoff and Emery (1972) p. 35-47, p. 169-172, p. 179-195.

(81) Galjaard (1979) p. 71-73.

(82) Id.; basically Shannon assumes that both sender and receiver have the same set of possible messages; if a specific message is received, this relates uniquely to this common set, so it gives a specific amount of information to the recipient about the sender choices. Ackoff's measure A, however, relates to the choices available to the recipient before reception of the message: thus if the receiver receives a message with a high value of H, this means that before reception A had a low value.

(83) In this way 'open systems interconnection' would become a matter of changing the information states of related machines and not so much the transfer of information.

(84) This necessitated special provisions in OSI for connectionless data transmission, cf. ISO Draft International Standard DDDD, 'Information Processing Systems – Open Systems Interconnection – Addendum to the basic reference model covering connectionless data transmission', Geneva, October 1983. Cf. DIS 8473, 8348. See also the discussions by Chapin (1983) p. 1366-1367; Foley (1985) p. 184.
(85) Cf. Bartoli (1983).
(86) Id.
(87) Memory could be organized at the different layers of the OSI model, which is desirable in view of high response times, e.g. a transport memory at the Common Service Access Point between layers 3 and 4.
(88) For a detailed discussion on expert systems, see Waterman (1985); Hayes-Roth (1984); Feigenbaum et al. (1981).
(89) Cf. Vervest and Wissema (1985).

CHAPTER 3.

INTRODUCTION OF NEW MAIL SYSTEMS

3.1 FROM INVENTION TO PRACTICAL USE

Network-independent user services

The new developments in electronic mail have a strong technological bias, as was explained in Chapter 2. One of the remarkable points is that, because of the process of computerization and digitization of information handling, the telecommunication networks become independent of the type of information which they carry. A great number of new services become possible via the same technical telecommunication network. For instance, after the introduction of the telex service facilities by means of the telephone network, a dedicated telex network became necessary (i.e. specific switching facilities were needed: transmission facilities are mostly shared among different telecommunication services) (1). In future, however, new services will be offered without the resulting impact on the concurrent services of that network, nor will the optimization of service operation lead to dedication of the network to that service.

The multiplicity of services via a common network requires new arrangements with respect to the definition and inter-operability of services. Particularly important for this study are the tele-information services: these services use telecommunications for the transfer of data, but, as argued in Chapter 1, they include conventions with respect to the meaning assigned to that data, i.e. with respect to the information content of data. A certain degree of inter-operation via a common network of the tele-information services will be desirable. This should be done in such a way that the services with common conventions as to the interpretation of data are compatible and can work together.

Because of this cooperation of tele-information services, electronic mail has been defined as a specific pattern of data transfer in the form of a message. Common facilities such as those mentioned in paragraphs 2.3.2 and 2.3.3, enable information, packaged in a 'message', to be transferred independent of the telecommunication means being used.

Assessment of the role of the user

These new developments in telecommunications – specifically with respect to electronic mail and message handling – make it particularly difficult to assess the role of the human user in the innovation process. In past developments of new telecommunication services, the human being in general played an immediate role for the development of that new service: he determined the immediate applications and the ease of using the service. On that basis the technical infrastructure was developed. For instance, the telephone service was the result of a proven concept of voice communications over a distance; as technology progressed, more sophisticated transmission and switching facilities were developed which offered a higher degree of service (e.g. user dialling, automatic call set-up, higher speech quality) but the voice communication by the human user remained the guiding post for the technical development of the telephone system (2).

This role of the user is changing. The information needs and information-handling behavior of the human being will remain a critical factor for the determination of communication demand, but the technical infrastructure for communications will have to support a multiplicity of information-handling functions that go far beyond those of the human being. The latter will interface to the telecommunication system with a terminal that is far more intelligent than the ordinary telephone handset. For instance, the use of a communicating personal computer for the handling of information will make the physical location of the data irrelevant to the user application, i.e. data may reside on the personal computer or on the network, or both; the operating system should shield on-line or off-line activities from the application processes. This leads to different requirements as to the design of the telecommunication system, in particular with respect to the added-value of electronic message transfer. The user will increasingly become dependent upon these facilities to add value to the message.

The foregoing developments complicate the introduction of new mail systems. A 'total systems design' is needed in which a variety of user needs for the handling of information (often not well-defined) should be accommodated. Let me briefly summarize these points as follows:

1. *re-arrangement of networks* – the technical organization of a new mail system (i.e. the intermediate telecommunication system, or systems, and the user systems) should support a multiplicity of information-handling func-

tions. On the one hand the availability of networks and user terminals will facilitate the introduction of new mail systems; on the other hand the variety in networks and terminals will lead to problems in system management in order to guarantee 'reliable message transfer';

2. *integration of information-handling functions* – the applications of message transfer are to a far greater extent than before, integrated with other information-handling functions, such as processing and storage;

3. *user added-value* – from the point of view of the human end-user, the ability to add value to the electronic message, such as for improved group communications or faster access to data bases, will be more important than message transfer itself. Individuals will be dependent on the availability of such facilities.

Intra- and inter-organizational applications

The interrelatedness of network re-arrangement, the integration of information-handling functions, and user added-value, require that certain conditions are met before large-scale adoption of new mail technologies and systems can take place. In essence there are two development paths: first, the new mail systems can be introduced for intra-organizational applications. In this case the large organization will take the lead. Second, new mail systems can be introduced for inter-organizational applications; in this case, service providers may take the lead.

There are some strong arguments in favor of the large organization as the leading force for the adoption and continued development of new mail systems:

- the large organization has a substantial need of communications; for instance, Mackintosh (1978) (3) showed that 5% of the leading business establishments in the major countries of Western Europe account for 61% of total mail volume;
- large organizations have obvious economic benefits for better and more efficient communications;
- they can afford technical knowledge for tracing new developments and have the necessary resources for experiments;
- since internal communications are more important, innovation is less dependent on the choices of other organizations; large organizations tend to

disseminate their communications systems and procedures to the smaller organizations and individuals that depend on them;
- once innovations start to become adopted, they can spread more easily through the organization due to centralization of decision power.

The ability to monitor technical developments is particularly important. Gatekeeping is the communication behavior of individuals who withhold or reshape information that they control as it flows into their system (4). There is a strong role for the technology gatekeepers in the innovation process of electronic mail. They are the experts who are monitoring the environment of technological change; at the time which they believe is appropriate, they will pass new information on to their organization.

Large organizations will first use electronic mail as part of their office automation programs (5). Office automation gradually extends its scope from the department level toward intra-site communications via local area networks. At the same time there is a development toward inter-site and corporate systems that integrate different organizational processes (purchasing, manufacturing, logistics, marketing and administration in particular) via a company wide area network (see Figure 3.1).

FIGURE 3.1 OFFICE AUTOMATION AND VALUE-ADDED NETWORK SERVICES

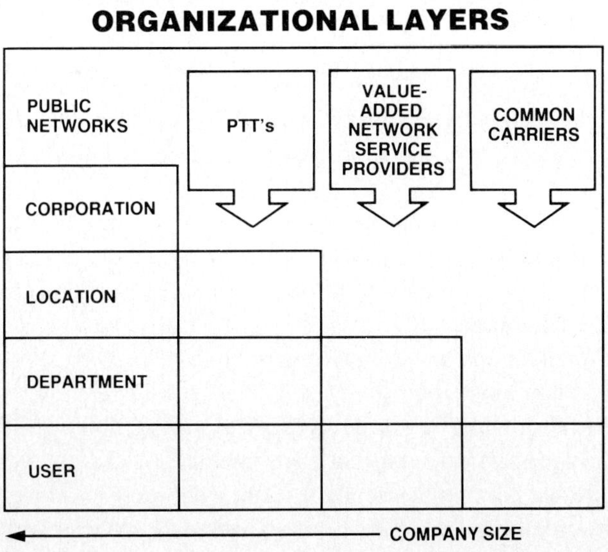

The development of corporate, and often international, wide area networks (WAN) by the large organization adds a new dimension for electronic mail. The WAN becomes a company resource for access by non-members of the organization, i.e. for the organization to communicate with its environment such as suppliers and customers. The large organization can then provide services such as information on products, organizational procedures or more general information; it can also share resources with its environment, like electronic mailbox, data bases or data processing/computer power. Even more important, transactions between the organization and the environment can be handled electronically and procedures could be imposed upon less powerful suppliers and customers. In fact the corporate network can be used as a strategic means to increase the competitive strength of the large organization.

Some trends are counterbalancing this possible dominance by the large organization.

1. Telecommunication service providers (PTT's and carriers) are extending their communication-oriented services into information processing.
2. Computer timesharing bureaux are entering networking businesses.
3. Cooperative leagues and associations of small and medium size companies are seeking a new opportunity to enforce the cooperative structure among their members via a similar concept as WAN (6).

This leads to the conceptualization of Value Added Network services (VAN), defined as (Butler and Cox, 1984) (7):

> 'A value added network service is a service based on a telecommunications network by which messages are processed or stored so that some value is added to the message as it is transferred from the message sender to the message receiver. In addition to the network operator, value added network services involve two other categories of participant: the service provider, and the service users (or subscribers)'.

Thus, the kernel of VAN services are electronic mail and message handling facilities; this usually narrows down to (8):

- connection of incompatible computer terminals of different manufacturers or of different models, by converting protocols, speeds, codes, formats and media;
- access to and from a variety of networks and the interlinking of different

nets ('internetting');

- concentration of traffic and optimal path selection; error detection/correction, improving reliability and security;
- message routing, storage and processing;
- access to data bases and computer application programs, including remote job entry and remote execution of jobs over distributed computer systems.

From an organizational/legal point of view, the difference between a wide area network and value-added network is the following: in the case of a wide area network the network provider, service provider and service user are all parts of the same organization. In a value-added network at least the service provider and the service user must be different juridical or organizational entities. It is obvious that a large organization can, depending on regulatory issues and organizational policies, easily extend its wide area network to incorporate value-added network services for third parties.

It will be clear that both intra- and inter-organizational applications will play an important role in the future of electronic mail.The leading role of the large organization will be discussed in the following section, presenting the results of the questionnaire survey among the members of the International Communications Association. Following that is an overview of inter-organizational applications of new mail systems.

3.2 INTERNATIONAL COMMUNICATIONS ASSOCIATION

3.2.1 Change in usage patterns

Survey method

The International Communications Association (ICA) is a non-profit making professional league of mainly North American telecommunication managers (9). A mail questionnaire was issued to the 557 member organizations, of which 116 (or 21%) completed the forms. The questions related to:

- introduction plans of new mail technologies (10);
- relative use and change in usage patterns of mail technologies;
- criteria for the introduction of new mail technologies;

FIGURE 3.2 INTRODUCTION OF NEW MAIL TECHNOLOGIES (ICA SAMPLE)

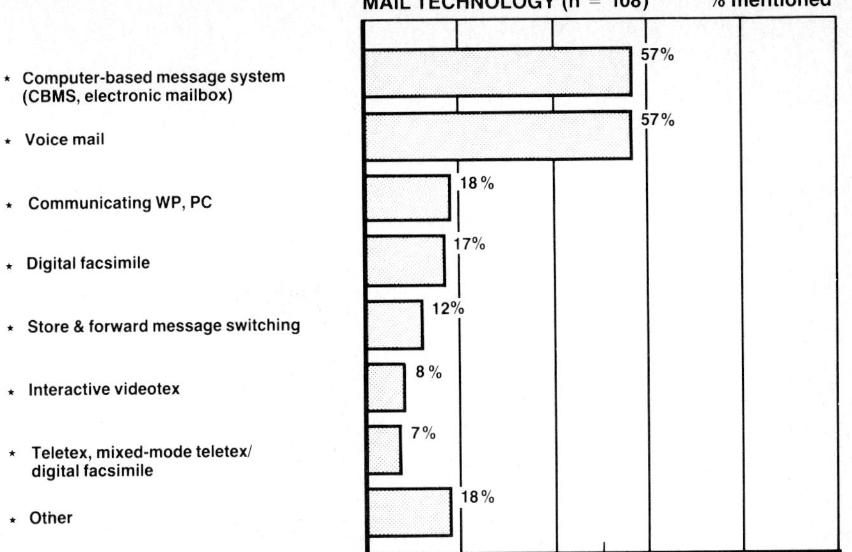

Source: ICA Questionnaire Survey April/May 1985

- bottlenecks for the introduction in the organization;
- the impact of standards and regulation.

The ICA sample is not representative of the potential adopter categories of new mail systems, but respondents should be viewed as experts in their field. The ICA was selected for the experience of American firms with respect to new mail systems such as CBMS and voice mail.

Most respondents (66%) reported a telecommunication manager function (11).

Introduction plans

Most respondents plan to introduce one or more new mail systems in the coming five years as shown in Figure 3.2. At the same time the use of new mail systems should increase significantly over the forecast period 1985 through 1995 (see Figure 3.3). CBMS and voice mail are the most important new technologies to be introduced; communicating word processors and personal computers seem to be already in use in most cases and are expected to grow significantly in usage over the forecast period.

FIGURE 3.3a CHANGE IN RELATIVE USE OF MAIL TECHNOLOGY 1985-1995 (ICA SAMPLE)

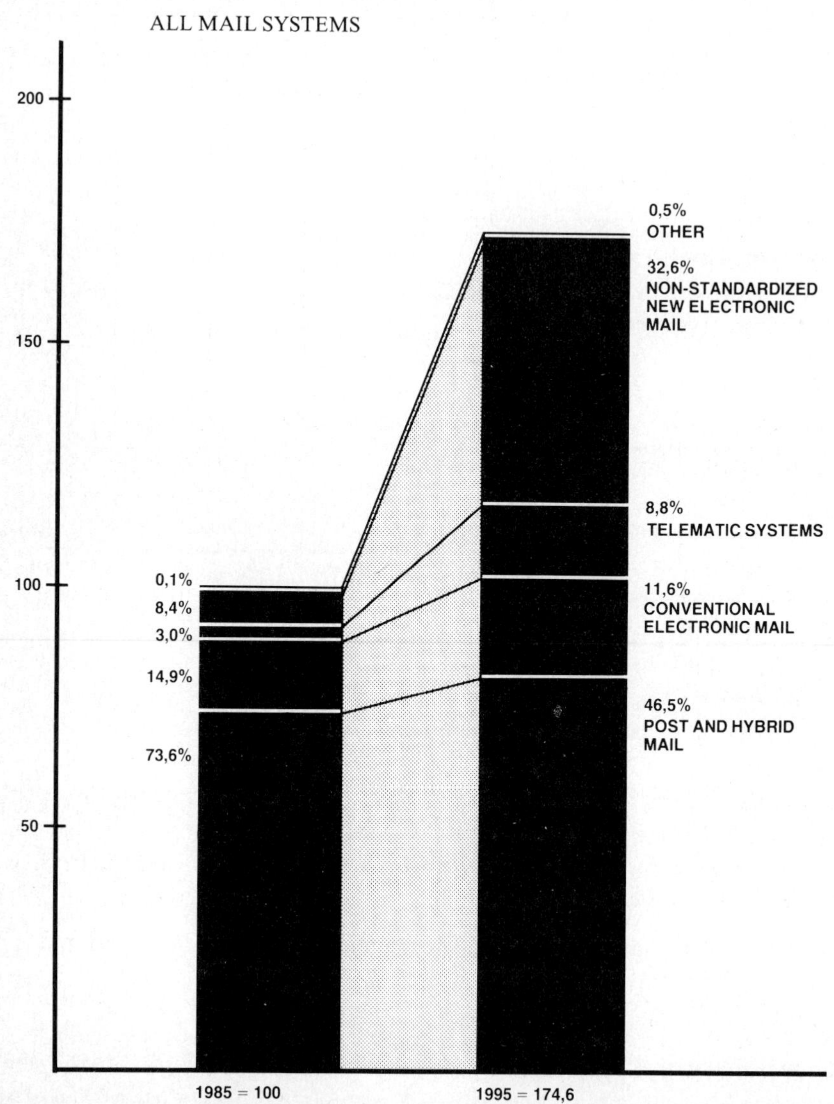

Source: ICA Questionnaire Survey April/May 1985

About 70% of the reported technologies to be introduced falls within the category of 'non-standardized new electronic mail'. In general telematic systems seem to be less important.

Substitution 1985-1995

Figure 3.3 shows the expected change in relative use of mail technologies for base years 1985 and 1995 as a percentage of mail volume. The average increase over this period will be 74.6% or 5.7% per year on assumption of annual linear growth.

As an indicator for the use of a specific technology or system implementation, the number of mail items or messages has been taken, because it seems a more reliable indicator than the number of users or systems installed (12).

The following trends are shown:

1. an overall growth in the use of new mail technologies which are defined as new electronic mail (telematic systems and non-standardized new electronic mail) as well as Generation 2 EMS. There will be a sharp increase from 13.9% in 1985 to 45.9% in 1995, which means a 19.2% annual growth on linear basis;
2. a rapid increase in the use of non-standardized new electronic mail from 8.4% in 1985 to 32.6% in 1995; voice mail will have the highest growth rate (29.8%) while CBMS will be the most important factor overall (15.6% of mail volume in 1995). Communications between word processor and personal computer will be another important area of growth;
3. telematic systems are expected to grow at a rate of 17.8% while non- standardized new electronic mail will grow at 21.1%. Due to the time involved in the standardization process, standardized new mail technologies obviously will take off later. This delay does not seem to be compensated by a higher growth rate. Digital facsimile is best established for continued growth; Teletex, mixed-mode Teletex/digital facsimile and interactive videotex are still in a beginning phase and are not expected to have more than 3.1% of the total mail volume in 1995.
4. the use of conventional electronic mail will decrease except for store-and-forward message switching. The growth of this latter technology (annual linear growth rate of 9.6%) is comparable to the newer mail technologies; it supports the view that telecommunication managers anticipate some major innovations in S&F message switching. For instance, the technology could be integrated with CBMS in order to provide a 'reliable message transfer service' as defined by the MHS model. Telex, TWX and analog facsimile will decrease in absolute figures during the study period.
5. there will be a moderate increase of approximately 1% per year in the use

FIGURE 3.3b CHANGE IN RELATIVE USE OF MAIL TECHNOLOGY 1985-1995 (ICA SAMPLE)

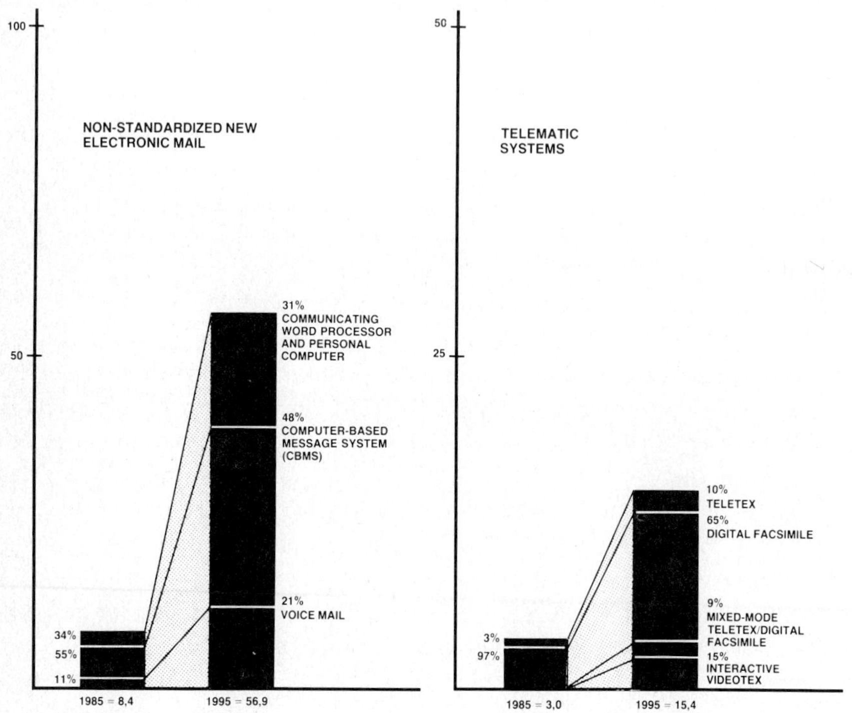

Source: ICA Questionnaire Survey April/May 1985

of post oriented services. However, the proportional share of total mail volume is likely to decrease from 73.6% in 1985 to 46.5% in 1995. Traditional postal services will remain about the same in absolute numbers (this does not imply that the content of physical mail will be unchanged; application patterns may change dramatically). Hybrid forms of postal and electronic mail (Generation 2 EMS including electronic input/physical output) will increase sharply at 12.2% on linear annual basis, but seems related to the stable pattern of use of post. Note that most investigations assume a 2% overall annual growth for physical and hybrid forms of mail (13).

The responses have considerable standard deviation from the mean (14): prob-

FIGURE 3.3c CHANGE IN RELATIVE USE OF MAIL TECHNOLOGY 1985-1995 (ICA SAMPLE)

CONVENTIONAL MAIL SYSTEMS AND HYBRID MAIL

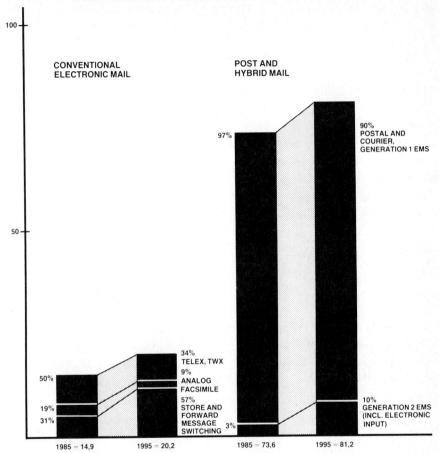

Source: ICA Questionnaire Survey April/May 1985

ably in most cases there is little reliable data on the current communication flows, nor is there much quantitative assessment about future needs. Another important factor seems to be the expected changes in the use of alternative technologies for post in order to cope with the anticipated growth of mail volumes.

The main conclusion from the figures may be that new technologies are to a great extent introduced for new applications and new methods of message handling, rather than as direct substitution of conventional technology.

In particular the high growth percentage of non-standardized electronic mail, i.e. 21.1%, is interesting. We may assume that the applications of these new technologies are related to company internal message handling. In that case standardization can be handled within the company itself.

The use of non-standardized new electronic mail in 1995 is directly proportional to the expected growth in mail volume, whereas the reverse is true for telematic systems (15).

Projection of take-over time

A theoretical projection of the take-over time as defined by the Fisher-Pry model can be made by taking the years 1985 and 1995 as base years (16). The fractional rates of substitution for 1985 and 1995 are 13.9 and 45.9 respectively. Thus take-over point $t(0)$ (see section 1.2.1) can be calculated as 1996 and the take-over time is 26 years. The substitution curve on semilog scale has a linear form as shown in Figure 3.4.

Fisher-Pry do not take into account the effects of absolute growth. Figure 3.4 shows the possible effect of growth: the upper boundary of the substitution curve is not a horizontal asymptote but rather a curved upper line. This results in a delay of substitution; $t(0)$ would become 2002 and take-over time is 41 years (17).

Figure 3.4 also gives the substitution curves for (18):

- Generation 2 EMS (incl. electronic input) for postal and courier mail and Generation 1 EMS;
- new electronic mail for conventional electronic mail.

The actual substitution can only be computed when more accurate data are gathered that encompass more potential adopter categories (19). However, it should be remembered that substitution assumes competition between different methods of satisfying a specific need under more or less stable conditions of demand. The theory has difficulty in accommodating a change of need and demand factors. This change is currently being experienced in most organizations with relation to communication and information management.

FIGURE 3.4 PROJECTED SUBSTITUTION OF MAIL TECHNOLOGY (ON BASIS OF DATA FROM ICA SAMPLE)

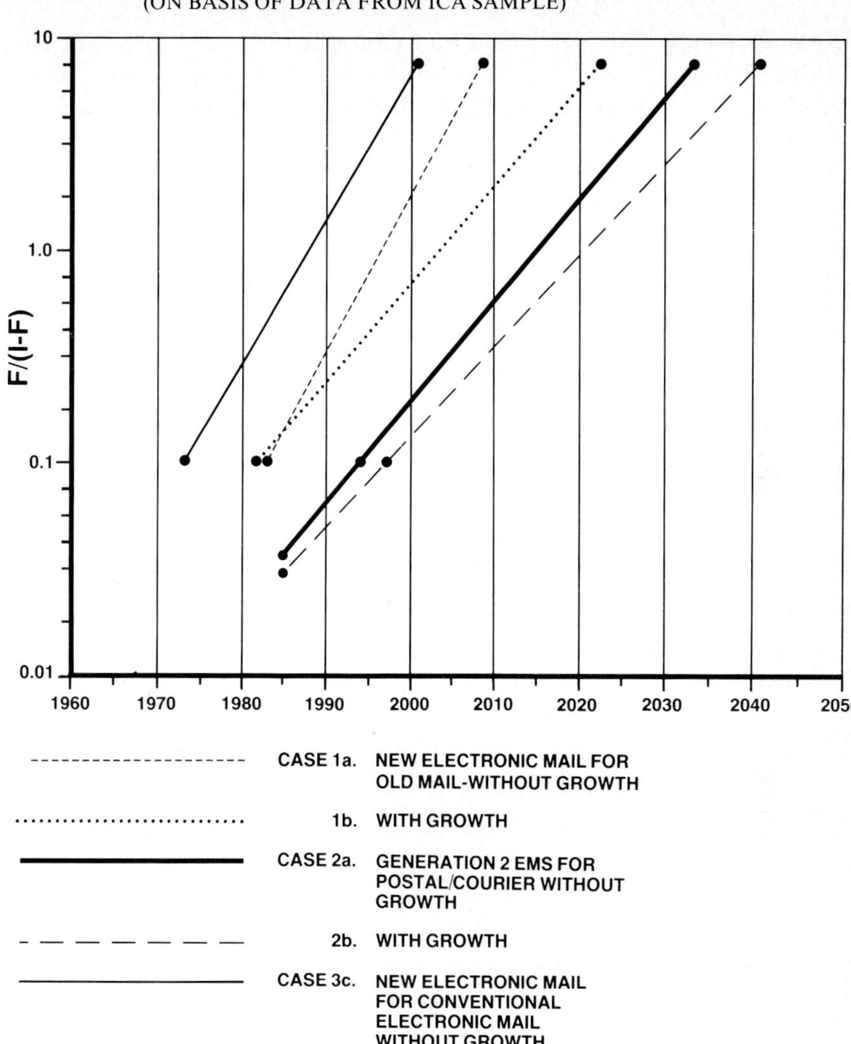

cf. notes (17), (18)

Moreover, substitution theory does not account for the motives of early adopters and the conditions for change in user behaviour. The experience with new means of communication is still very limited. Many organizations have difficulty in assessing the utility of new means of communication and establishing their information management policies.

The impact of innovativeness

Following the classification of innovator groups by Rogers, respondents have been subdivided on the basis of the relative use of new mail technologies in 1985 and 1995(20). Rogers takes the date of first use as the reference point of adoption, but in our case the quantity of use seems a more reliable measure for innovativeness (21).

Figure 3.5 shows the distribution of use of new mail technologies for 1985 and 1995 among the various innovator classes. The use of new mail technologies in 1985 and the expected use in 1995 are positively correlated in a significant way (Pearson's measure for rank correlation $R = +.55$) (22). An interesting pattern emerges:

- the use of new mail technologies in 1985 is positively related to the use of non-standardized electronic mail in 1995 ($R = +.54$); at the same time it is highly negatively related to the use of postal/ hybrid mail in 1995 ($R = -.49$);
- the anticipated increase in mail volume is positively related to the use of new electronic mail in 1995 ($R = +.19$); it is negatively related to the use of postal/ hybrid mail in 1985 ($R = -.46$) while there is a positive correlation with the use of conventional electronic mail ($R = +.24$), telematic systems ($R = +.20$), and non-standardized new electronic mail ($R = +.45$) in 1985;
- innovators use significantly less postal/hybrid mail technologies in 1995 than the others; they also use significantly more non-standardized electronic mail technology.
- of particular interest are the anticipated changes in usage patterns of the early majority: they hold a midway position between innovators/early adopters on the one hand, and the late majority/laggards on the other hand with respect to the use of postal/hybrid mail and non-standardized new electronic mail; at the same time they apply more conventional electronic mail in 1985 and telematic or standardized electronic mail in 1995.

Obviously the early majority holds an important position in the large-scale adoption of a new technology. The actual breakthrough of a new product will occur from the moment onwards that the 'early majority' accepts the innovation. The finding with respect to the use of mail technology by the early majority suggests that standardization is important in a particular stage of market development, namely in the transition from introduction to growth (23).

FIGURE 3.5. INNOVATIVENESS AND USE OF MAIL TECHNOLOGY 1985-1995 (ICA SAMPLE)

(PERCENTAGE OF USE BY RESPONDENT CATEGORIES)

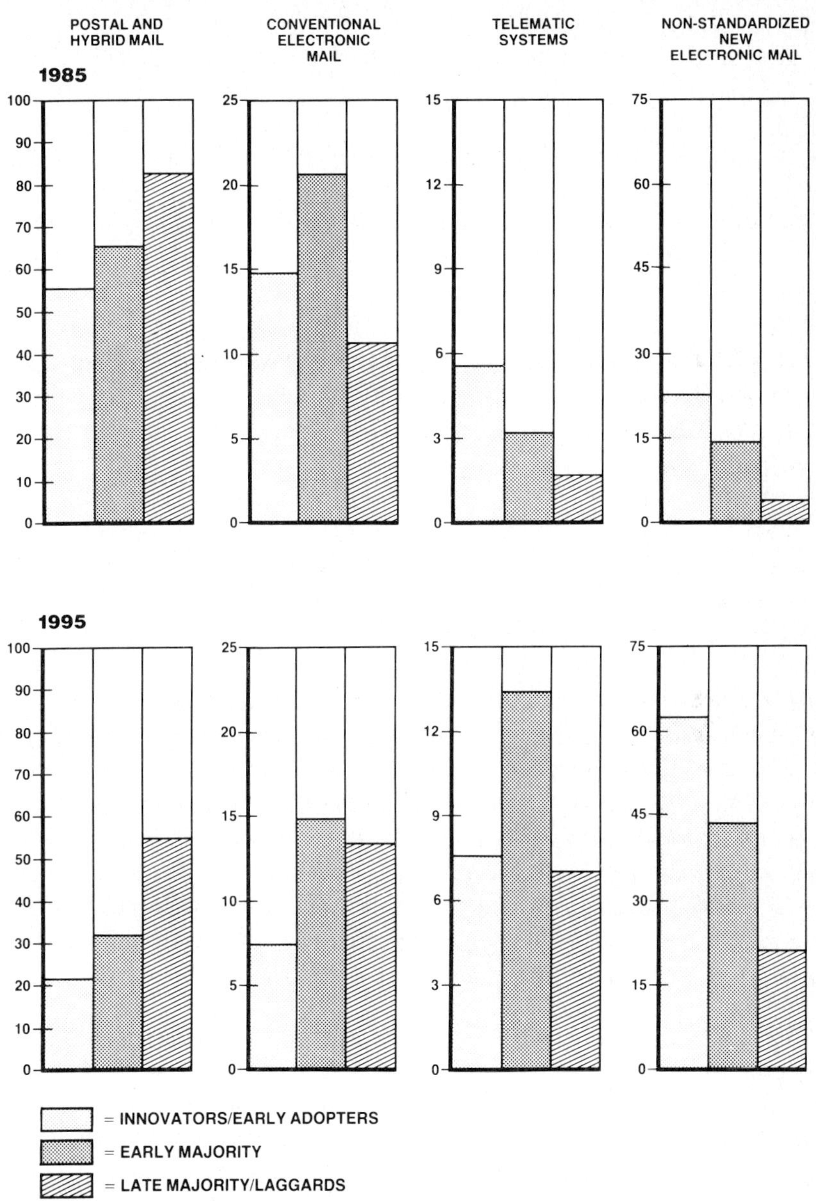

From the point of view of the product life cycle, the postal system is at the peak of its use and will gradually decline; the same applies to telex, TWX and analog facsimile, although these will suffer more competition from new electronic mail systems, and will therefore experience an earlier decline.

The growth of telematic systems, i.e. standardized new electronic mail, is strongest for the early majority; within the same time frame the innovators and early majority are adopting CBMS and voice mail, as well as extending their use of communicating word processors and personal computers. The larger growth in mail volume which is anticipated by innovators and the early majority, may partly account for their relatively earlier adoption of new technology.

Innovativeness, industry and centralization

Respondents have been classified in the following groups of industry sectors:

- primary industry/government/utilities 30%
- manufacturing 40%
- trade/finance/services 30%

Expectations with respect to the growth in mail volume differ among the different industry sectors; the usage patterns are also different. Companies in the trade/finance/services class expect lower increase in mail volume than do the others; they also anticipate the lowest usage of conventional electronic mail by 1995.

Primary industry/government/utilities will be the main users of postal and hybrid mail by 1995 and will use non-standardized new electronic mail systems the least. Statistically significant differences could not be established.

Centralization, defined as the number of sites, has a weak but positive correlation with the increase in mail volume. However, it seems that the degree of centralization has little influence on innovativeness.

3.2.2 Innovation criteria and bottlenecks

Reasons and criteria for the introduction of new mail technology

Figure 3.6 gives the user ratings of various criteria for adopting a new mail

FIGURE 3.6 CRITERIA FOR ADOPTING NEW MAIL TECHNOLOGY (ICA SAMPLE)

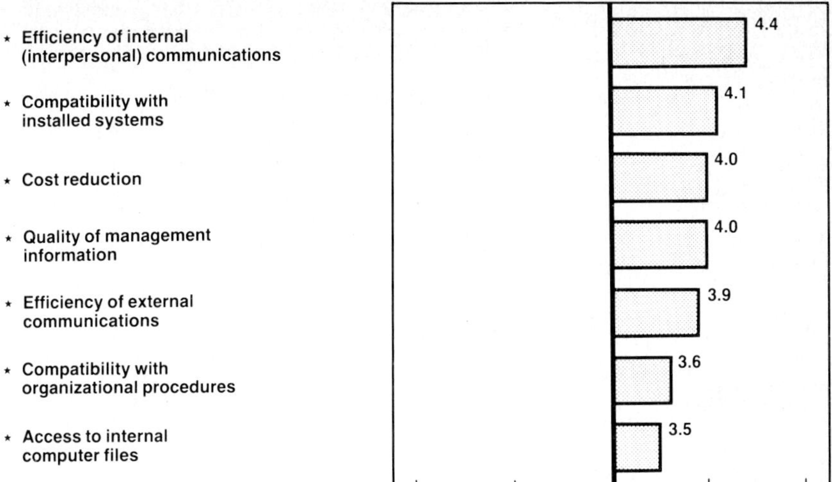

technology. Adoption is specifically motivated by efficiency of internal and interpersonal communications. The compatibility with installed systems is also important. The access to internal computer files and the compatibility with organizational procedures are rated the least important.

The reasons for introducing new mail technology, and the bottlenecks that users anticipate, have been probed via an open question; the results are given in Figure 3.7. A better communications system at lower cost seems to be the most important reason for innovation, whereas the organizational resistance to change is the most limiting factor. This was not significantly different for various industry sectors; nor did we find a significant relation between innovativeness and geographic centralization.

Most of the reasons for introducing a new mail technology, as given in this figure, are either need or cost driven. Need factors include orientation towards effectiveness and reliability of communication, the speed and the improvement of information flow and information access. Cost considerations are specifically expressed in the desire to reduce costs and to improve overall operations

FIGURE 3.7 REASONS AND BOTTLENECKS FOR INTRODUCING NEW MAIL TECHNOLOGY (ICA SAMPLE)

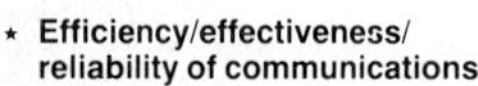

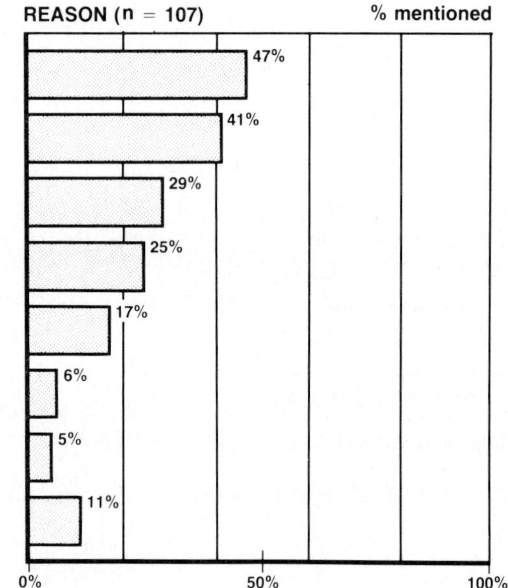

* Cost reduction
* Productivity/overall operational improvement
* Speed
* Improvement of information flow/information access
* New possibilities
* Competitive advantage
* Other

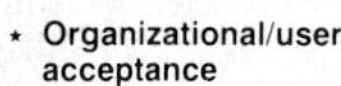

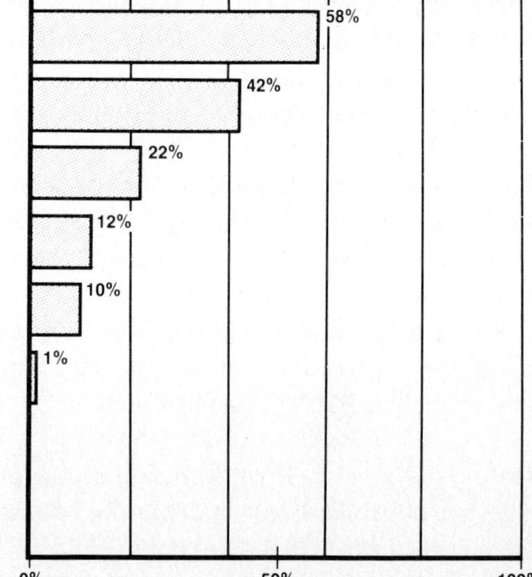

* Lack of standards/compatibility
* Financial/cost justification
* Choice and availability of equipment/software/services
* Regulation
* Other

Source: ICA Questionnaire Survey April/May 1985

and productivity. In view of the central role of communication and information in organizational processes, most of the factors mentioned are closely interrelated.

External factors get considerably less attention: competitive advantage, increased organizational responsiveness and the provision of new services are rarely mentioned.

An orientation towards needs requires an assessment of the organizational communication and information flows. Vallee (1984) (24) suggests a procedure for making communication audits: first the means of communication are inventorized, e.g. which means are used, how often per time unit, against which costs? The second step is to discriminate communication flows between various groups. Once this has been done, the possible application of new means for the target group can be assessed by comparing application requirements against technical possibilities.

The role of office automation

The need for electronic mail is often identified with office automation. The most important aspect of an 'automated office', say Uhlig, Farber and Bair (1979) (25), is that interactive computer tools are put into the hands of individual knowledge workers in the areas in which they are physically working. The stand-alone computer environment for dedicated and primarily simple tasks is gradually extended towards knowledge tasks. This leads to the need of communication means by which knowledge workers may access information on a global scale and perform information processing as a common resource of the organization. McQuillan (1984) (26) distinguishes four trends in the use of electronic mail for office automation and communication. These are:

- trend 1 – the evolution of a systems architecture to integrate all available organizational resources;
- trend 2 – total electronic connectivity so that independent devices are interrelated on a worldwide scale;
- trend 3 – evolution of a human interface to reduce the training and educational barriers for users; highly sophisticated knowledge representations must bridge the gap between the 'common sense' users and the rigid, arbitrary rules and conventions of current computer systems;
- trend 4 – office integration that fully integrates electronic mail with information

processing and file management both within and between offices; this will require multi-media communications (the exchange of compound-documents) and the automation of office procedures via 'active messages'.

Whether electronic mail can indeed satisfy specific user needs, depends on the critical evaluation of application requirements and the utility factors of the technology in question. Each industry sector will have different application requirements; thus the utility of a specific technology will yield different results. Many application studies quote the following industry sectors as important target users of electronic mail and message handling (27):

- banking/ finance/ insurance
- manufacturing
- government
- distribution trades
- transportation.

Specific bottlenecks

A number of bottlenecks which are foreseen with the introduction of new mail technology have been listed in Figure 3.7. The main bottlenecks are in the area of organizational adaptations, user acceptance and standardization. Standardization is in the first instance a technical, or supplier-side problem; this will be dealt with in the following section as well as Chapter 4.

1. Organizational and user acceptance

The acceptance of new mail technology, at the level of the organization as well as of the individual user, is given as the most important bottleneck. Organizational acceptance may be difficult as application requirements are different across organizations and between departments. New systems may be incompatible with already installed systems and/or organizational procedures; or the degree of change which is required may become too high. For instance, the extensive use of CBMS is said to flatten the organizational structure (28).

Individual users may have a negative attitude towards the use of new technologies; new systems necessitate the re-training of users and result in divestiture of existing skills. User procedures are difficult and rigid, the applications are not integrated and reliability of message delivery and receipt are unproven (29).

The introduction of new technology requires the understanding of user attitudes towards change. A phased implementation and extensive education seem to be prequisite for successful introduction (30).

2. Financial bottlenecks

Users who may want to implement a new mail technology, face a great number of choices that will affect the cost structure of their new system. In particular the cost elements of using mail technology are associated with (31):

- system use for message composition, sending, receiving and filing and administration
- transmission
- user terminal equipment
- initial expenses such as designing implementation programs, training users and project support

New users may want to minimize the initial expenses and may prefer low fixed costs and high variable costs. As their usage increases, they may want to increase fixed costs in order to lower the overall costs per message. However, 'intangible' tariff structures make such a policy very difficult.

A strong orientation towards costs often leads to a reluctant attitude for adopting new mail technologies. As was indicated by IDC in the case of CBMS and voice mail (1984) (32), cost justification is difficult, but generally not a deterrent for expanding the use once the organization has had initially positive experience. In the ICA survey financial bottlenecks were mostly indicated by the late majority/laggards who were not using new mail technologies at the time.

3. Availability of equipment/software/services

Another important bottleneck is the choice and availability of equipment, software and services. Critical for the use of new mail technology is the timely availability of a number of key technologies (33).

There are important bottlenecks in the generation of these key technologies. In a survey of developments in the USA (1984) (34) the major problem areas were found in workstation technologies, network message computers, voice mail and data communication technology in general.

Workstation technologies are of specific concern as their penetration will ultimately determine the accessibility of electronic mail facilities for the individual user. The major shortcomings are in the following areas (35):

- a modular design is needed which can handle compound document structures;
- the user interface must be improved significantly, for instance by having improved knowledge representation and less rigid user procedures;
- communication facilities must be integrated in the operating system of the workstation and allow easier access to and from the network (often referred to as the intelligent micro-mainframe link).

Figure 3.8 shows a sketch of an integrated though modular communications terminal, designed for office use. Network message computers are another important bottleneck. Most networks are not capable of transferring compound document structures in an economic and efficient way or do not provide facili-

FIGURE 3.8 INTEGRATED BUSINESS COMMUNICATIONS TERMINAL

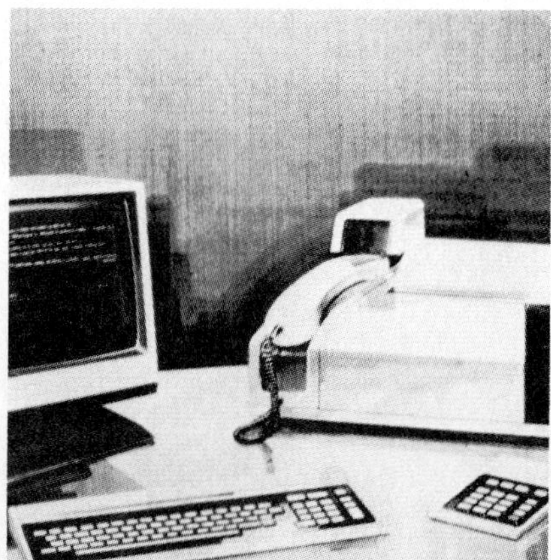

Courtesy: Philips' Telecommunicatie Industrie BV

ties for storage and conversion. Moreover users have subscriptions to a limited number of networks. This necessitates that different networks are interconnected and that each of them can be used for different purposes. Networks have to be re-arranged to meet user requirements, leading to network management problems.

It should be emphasized that the innovation of workstations and of network message computers are interrelated: there will only be an economic basis for multi-functional network arrangements if adequate numbers of communicating workstations are installed. Conversely the workstation will only be installed on the basis of the availabilty of network services. The two innovations will therefore be interlocked.

3.2.3 Viewpoint on standardization and regulation

One of the main objectives of the ICA questionnaire survey has been to investigate the relation between opinions on standardization and regulation on the one side, and innovativeness on the other side. To this end a number of standardization and regulatory issues have been defined (as given in Figure 3.9, 3.10a and 3.10b). The examination of the standards themselves and the process of making standards is dealt with in Chapter 4.; the discussion of regulatory aspects from a government policy point of view is part of Chapter 5.

Standardization issues

The effects of standardization on the introduction of new mail technology are far from straightforward. Roughly there are two conflicting views. The first viewpoint holds that the possible reach of a new communication system should be as extensive as it can be. Standards are therefore an a-priori requirement for the acceptance of a new communication system. The second viewpoint sees standards as an unnecessary delay of market development; the leading manufacturer will establish the standard as the result of the factual acceptance of his product, and not as an a-priori agreement on the applicable standard.

Standards in the area of electronic mail and message handling can be classified with respect to the following issues:

data communications for access, interworking and conversion of different communication networks and services;

- directory and submission/delivery facilities defining the methods and procedures for the naming and addressing of communication parties; it also concerns the human interface to the system;
- message transfer for the transport of messages over telecommunication networks;
- message structures that enable interchange of message formats among application processes;
- system administration and management including, among other things, the interconnection of different management domains, i.e. private and public systems.

Figure 3.9 gives the opinions of the ICA respondents as concerns electronic mail and message handling standards. The interconnection capabilities between private and public systems are considered the most important. These are followed by the message transfer capabilities and addressing and directory capabilities. A clear pattern does not emerge, but it seems that interconnection is particularly important since it increases the reach of company-internal mail

FIGURE 3.9 OPINIONS ON STANDARDIZATION (ICA SAMPLE)

Proposition: 'The widespread use of new mail technology requires complete standardization in respect of' –

* human interface capabilities
* message structures
* addressing and directory capabilities
* data transmission capabilities
* message transfer capabilities
* interconnection capabilities, i.e. between private and public systems

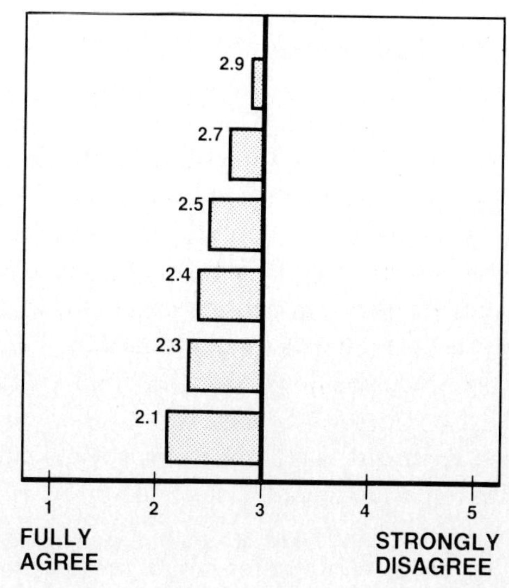

Source: ICA Questionnaire Survey April/May 1985

systems. Decentralized organizations are significantly more interested in standards for message transfer (36).

Some of the most pressing issues for standards from a Western European perspective have been identified in a survey on behalf of British Telecommunications (1984) (37). The findings of that study support the ICA results with respect to the need of standards.

Innovativeness and standardization

The impact of attitudes toward standards is different for the various innovator classes. Innovators/early adopters consider standards issues as more important than the other classes; this may be explained by the use of non-standardized equipment. This awareness, however, does not lead to a choice of standardized equipment in their future plans. It seems that the innovator/early adopter class can draw on experience or other resources to resolve the incompatibility issues.

The early majority views standardization as less important, but they plan the introduction of standard rather than non-standard equipment. Learning effects may have led to more foresight on behalf of the early majority. The late majority/laggards score in-between the innovators/early adopters and the early majority with respect to standards: this may be explained by the aversion to risks associated with the adoption of non-standard equipment in view of the absence of know-how within the organization.

Regulatory issues

Figure 3.10a and 10b give the opinions of the ICA respondents with respect to a number of regulatory aspects. The strict regulation of institutional/organizational aspects of communications (the position of traditional service providers, third-party traffic over private facilities, tariffs) is resisted. However, it should be taken into account that most respondents will have given their position from a North American perspective. Deregulation of telecommunications in the USA and the divestiture of AT&T will give a more liberal attitude. The differences with respect to regulatory aspects in Western Europe and Japan are discussed in Chapter 5.

FIGURE 3.10a OPINIONS ON REGULATION (ICA SAMPLE)

Proposition: 'The widespread use of new mail technology requires strict regulation in respect of' –

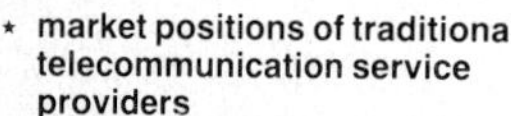

- market positions of traditional telecommunication service providers
- possibilities for third-party traffic over private telecommunication facilities
- tariffs for public services
- transborder data flow
- interconnection of private and public systems
- legal status of electronically transmitted documents, e.g. protection of copyrights
- liability for information transfer, fraud and mutilation of information
- security of computer systems
- privacy

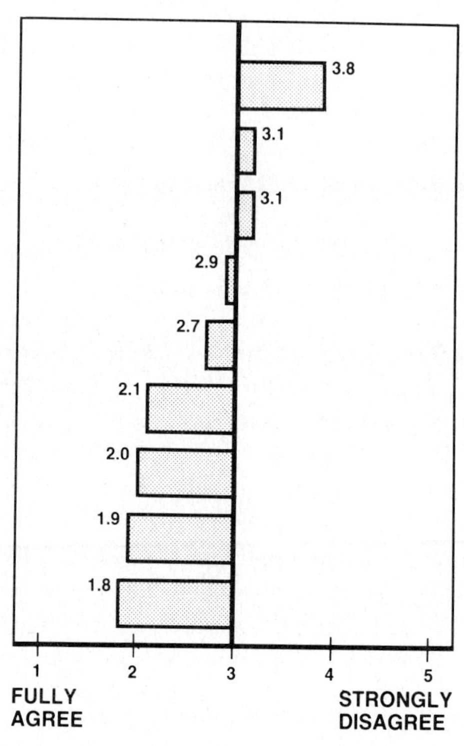

Source: ICA Questionnaire Survey April/May 1985

FIGURE 3.10b ROLE OF PUBLIC AGENCIES (ICA SAMPLE)

Proposition:

- 'Public agencies should have a monopoly to provide (postal and electronic) public mail services'
- 'Public agencies should provide public mail services in equal competition with private companies'

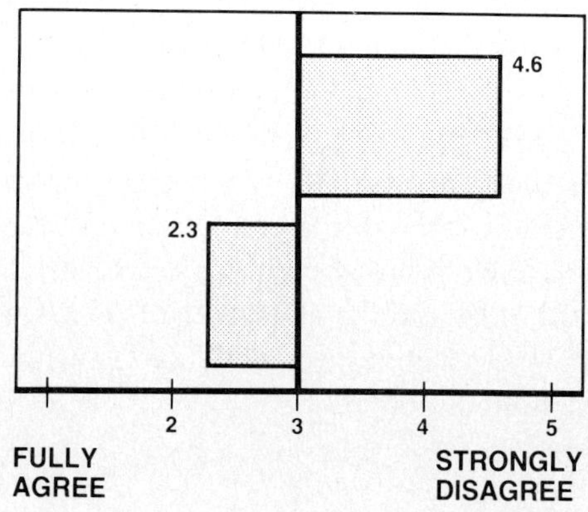

Source: ICA Questionnaire Survey April/May 1985

Important aspects of regulation are found in privacy as well as the security of computer systems.

It may be that, because of the early stage of the use of computer-based message exchange, there is a low perception of the possible impact of regulatory issues. Users are probably more inclined to support regulation once practical use has increased and they have experienced bottlenecks due to the lack or inadequacy of regulation. The degree of regulation can be viewed as that necessary for reducing user uncertainty with respect to the practical use and actual application of new systems.

Role of public agencies

Respondents share the position that public agencies should not have a monopoly to provide public mail services, but should compete on equal terms with private companies (see Figure 3.10b). The possible impact of this is discussed in Chapter 5.

Innovativeness, standardization and regulation (38)

In the early stage of the development of a new technology, the standardization process is still incomplete. It leads to uncertainty on behalf of the user with respect to the future value of investments and to risks of incompatibility when extending the present system and incorporating new applications.

The user has – in principle – three alternatives:

- invest in new technology with all risks associated with that choice;
- invest in proven technology that is more or less stable and standardized;
- postpone the investment decision.

Which course of action will be taken, will depend to a great extent on the available resources in the telecommunications and automation departments of the organization. Particularly important resources are: financial funds, in-house expertise, overall know-how in the computer and communications disciplines, (including data processing and office automation) and, perhaps most important, experience in implementing systems. The organizational attitude and the ability to experiment with a complicated new system seem prerequisites for innovative behavior.

Organizational know-how may be the factor explaining the seemingly contradictory behavior of the innovator/early adopter class. More than the other classes, they uttered a positive opinion on standardization and found the lack of standards a critical bottleneck. At the same time they anticipate significantly more use of non-standardized new electronic mail by 1995. This can be explained by the ability to deal with the problems of incompatibility and lack of standards, by internal know-how and expertise. As innovators/early adopters they are well aware of the painful consequences of incompatibilities. This leads to a strong positive attitude toward standardization.

The early majority, on the contrary, seem to avoid the problems of new technology by the introduction of standard equipment. The late majority/laggards follow a strategy of risk avoidance by postponing investment decisions. However, the postponement of investment leads to another risk: technological obsolescence of the organizations and the impossibility to catch up due to the lack of technical expertise.

The relation between innovativeness and opinions on regulatory issues could not be unravelled in the same way. Standardization seems to affect the introduction of new technology in a rather direct way. Regulation on the other hand is probably perceived as a general circumstance. It should be noted that there is a significant correlation between opinions on standardization and regulation (39). It seems therefore that regulation has an indirect impact on innovativeness.

Moreover, we suspect that new mail systems will first be used for internal communications. Regulation will become more important as and when the large organizations use the system for external communications.

3.3 INTER-ORGANIZATIONAL APPLICATIONS

3.3.1 The small and medium size company

The use of new mail systems for communication between different organizations will develop as result of the in-house use by large organizations. On the other hand small and medium size companies will have a more pressing need for external communications. The personal computer (PC), in combination with the word processor for secretarial tasks, has become a vehicle for office automation in the small and medium size company. Office automation can be especially productive when the organization has large internal resources combined with a low span of control, as seen in many large organizations. The small company, however, will usually have a high span of control but limited internal resources. As a result, the access to external resources is far more pressing for the small firm than it is for the large organization. The availability of communication facilities for its equipment, and services for accessing external information, have become critical in many cases where small and medium size companies apply personal computers (40).

Computer timesharing bureaux and telecommunication service providers will find new opportunities as increasing numbers of personal computers are installed. The timesharing bureau evolved during the 1960s at a time in which computer power was expensive and centralized in huge mainframes. Minicomputer developments during the 1970s deeply affected their business of selling space and time on the mainframe. The personal computer will provide a new challenge for offering complementary services (the 'intelligent' PC-mainframe link) (41), i.e.:

- increase the capability of the personal computer in terms of remote processing power and remote data manipulation
- link two or more machines via networking
- gain access to data bases and remote software
- take advantage of the service bureaux knowledge of specific market segments as well as support, training and consulting
- purchase and maintenance of personal computers.

With regard to the telecommunication service provider, the personal computer in the small and medium size company signifies grossly distributed computer power across their networks. The network services will shift from those directed towards use by human beings to intermediary services that support computer-mediated (personal computer) communications. Thus telecommunication services must in future include facilities for sharing resources among distributed systems connected to the networks.

Communicating personal computers and value-added network services can provide a new means for organizing small and independent firms to maintain, or improve their competitiveness against the large corporation. This is an area where cooperative leagues and associations of the small and medium size com-

FIGURE 3.11 PERSONAL COMPUTER COMMUNICATIONS AND VALUE-ADDED NETWORK SERVICES

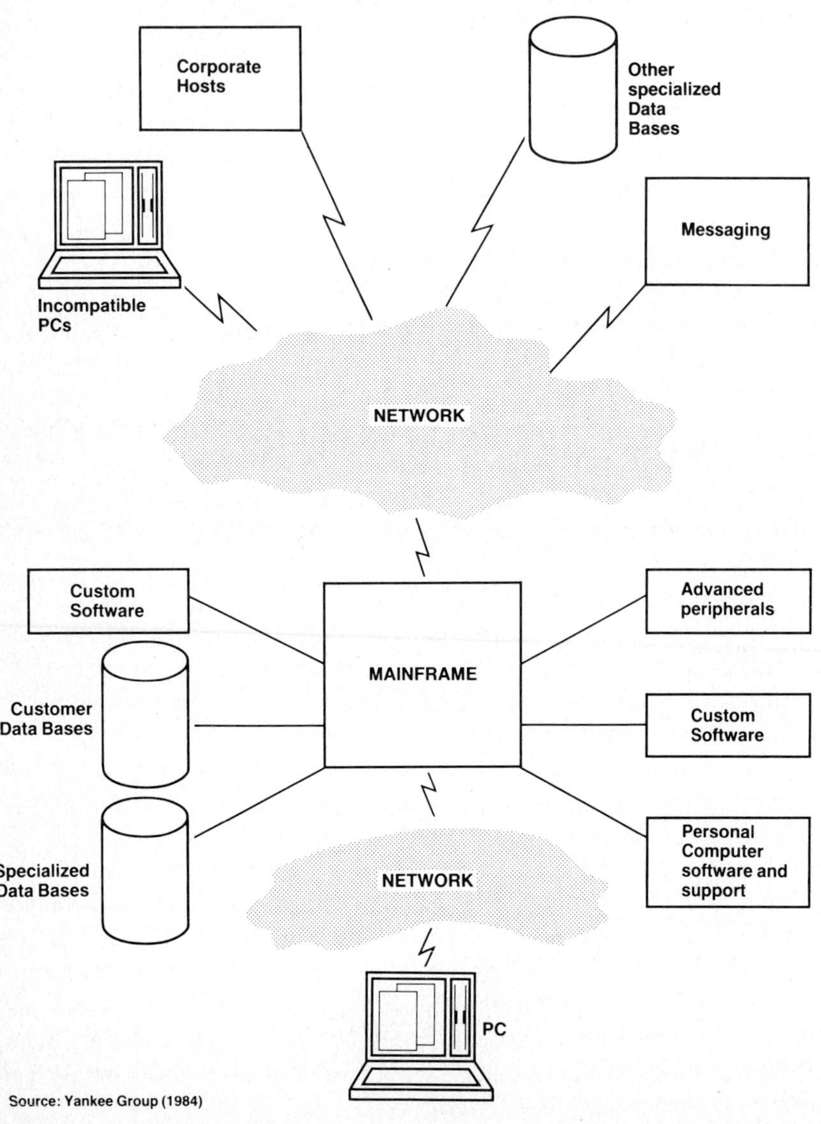

Source: Yankee Group (1984)

panies can be active to secure the availability of specialized resources and information.

3.3.2 Types of value-added services

Within the context of OSI, the functions of the value-added network are located on layers 4 through 7. Three types of value-added network services are classified as follows: facility-sharing, information-sharing and transactional. Note that most value-added network operators will offer a combination of these possibilities and are aimed at specific sectors of industry (42).

Facility-sharing

A facility-sharing value-added network service makes available network facilities, such as computer power, networking capabilities and message storage. The basic motivations for facility-sharing are the possible economies of scale and the availability of services at the moment the user needs them without heavy initial investments.

Facility-sharing is a basic application of computer networking where the computer can be seen as a 'place to park bits in' (43). Most of the value-added network operators will offer facility-sharing. American firms including ADP, AT&T, Compuserve, EDS, GEISCO, GTE-Telenet, ITT-Dialcom, The Source, Tymshare and most European PTTs as well as the NTT are offering VAN resource-sharing services of one kind or another (44).

Information-sharing

The information-sharing, value-added network service offers access to information residing in the network and which is either proprietary or gained via access to third parties. Butler and Cox (1984) (45) distinguish between information-monopoly services, where an organization has secured a monopoly, or near monopoly, on valuable information and can sell that information via a value-added network service; and information-utility services, where organizations in the same business sector use a value-added network service to pool and exchange business information.

An important function of the information-sharing value-added network service is the access to remote data bases where the service operator is a distributor or an information provider.

Information-sharing value-added network services can play a crucial role in decision support systems. Alter (1980) and Keen (1978) (46) describe a decision support system as a computer aided tool for facilitating decision processes (rather than making clerical transactions more efficient) specifically at the managerial level. This is different from traditional electronic data processing, which gives standard reports for decision makers: decision support is an active tool for both decision making and implementation.

Transactional

The transactional value-added network services facilitate interorganizational processes such as purchasing, physical goods distribution and financial transactions. They provide the necessary processing of information for effecting transactions between organizations in addition to the exchange of information. The information content of many transactions has increased to such an extent that enormous cost reductions are expected from electronic handling of these transactions (47). Major opportunities are seen in the transportation and distribution industries; grocery and retail; insurance and banking; hospital supply and government purchases.

The necessary data for electronic transactions are gathered from the involved organizations and converted into a standardized electronic form. This requires detailed cooperation among normally competing firms to define the data interchange formats, identifiers for the transactions (e.g. uniform article codes, transportation codes, bank transaction identifiers) as well as the updating procedures of the information and the clearing of the transaction itself.

Figure 3.12 lists the possible types of organizations that would be involved in a trade support system. Some of the major problems for the design and implementation of transactional value-added network services are:

- the nature, quantity and costs of the information flows among the involved parties;
- the invested equipment and the internal procedures and standards of each participant;
- the necessary level of standardization and service aspects such as availability, reliability and security;
- the participants' possible gains and losses using a VAN service and the willingness and legal possibilities for cooperating.

FIGURE 3.12 PARTICIPANTS OF A TRADE SUPPORT SYSTEM

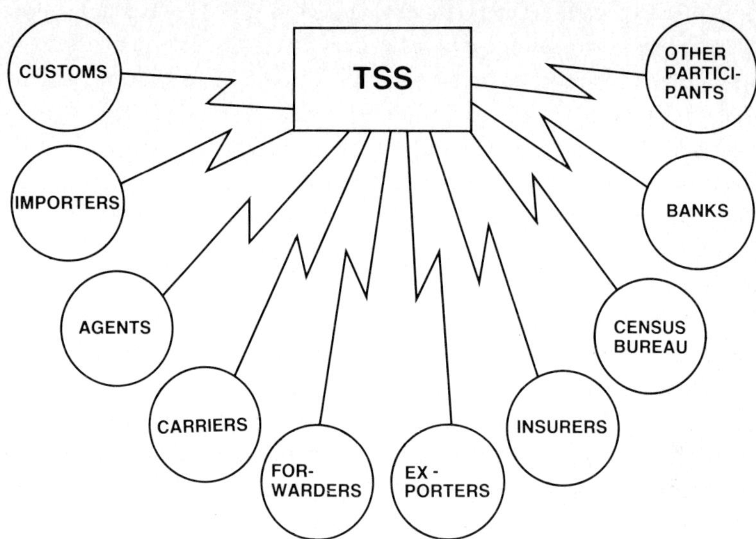

Some conclusions

It is probable that the introduction of new mail systems will take place both as the result of the application within company internal communication systems, and part of value-added network services, which are shared among different user organizations. I have pointed out the need for a 'total systems design' in which electronic mail should form part of a communication and information plan. The three main issues (re-arrangement of networks, integration of information-handling functions, and user added-value) may be better controlled in large organizations, but it is highly dependent on the available technical expertise. This expertise should include both the knowledge of the technical alternatives as well as the knowledge to implement new technology as part of organizational systems. The ICA study suggests that, even in the case of a large organization, technical expertise may account for variations in innovative behavior. This expertise, in computers and communications, including data processing and office automation, is also present in telecommunication service providers (PTT's and carriers) and timesharing service bureaux. Therefore they are clearly fitted to operate value-added network services. From this perspective the small and medium size companies are likely candidates to introduce new electronic mail systems at an early stage.

According to the ICA study, significant changes in the usage patterns of mail systems can be expected in the forthcoming period. CBMS, voice mail, communicating personal computers and word processors, and hybrid postal/electronic mail, will be important new systems by 1995. Some of the newer systems will actually be substitutes for existing systems, such as telex, TWX and analog facsimile. New systems can partially reduce the inefficiencies, costs, or inflexibility of conventional systems; more important, they will also add new means to deal with the increased need for communication and information exchange. The projected take-over times are long and highly uncertain in view of the growth in communication needs and the new applications.

One of the most important aspects is the 'engineering' of user added-value. Organizational and user acceptance are generally seen as the bottlenecks for innovation. The motivation to change current behavior will depend on the added-value which the user perceives in relation to the risks. Technical expertise, standardization, and readily available equipment, software and services, are important facilitators. In this respect value-added network services can play a vital role to lower the entry barrier: they offer a test bed with low fixed costs, proven equipment, and technical expertise capable of solving incompatibility and other problems.

The continuous guidance of the user in order to change his communication and information-handling behavior seems one of the most critical factors in the acceptance of new technology. This leads us to the conclusion that user innovation – i.e. the user as the actual creator of the innovation – is as important as the creation of new technical possibilities. The two are obviously related to each other, but technology has generally dominated the innovation process. In the case of communication and information, however, the success of new technologies is determined, by and large, by user-added value. It may be for this reason that standardization has a specific role: it forms the interface between technical innovation and user innovation by guiding new technologies into the market and providing the basis for user innovation.

NOTES CHAPTER 3
INTRODUCTION OF NEW MAIL SYSTEMS

(1) Cf. Friedrich (1934); Renton (1954); Freebody (1958); Vervest (1985) p. 100-101.

(2) A historical overview of the development in telephony is given in Chapuis (1982). The conventional telephone network that is most commonly in use, has a number of disadvantages for non-voice communications, such as (Kitahara (1983); Vervest and Wissema (1985) p. 13): the need of costly modems, limitations in transmission speed to generally 4.8 kbps, relatively long call-establishment times, and a tariff structure which is inadequate for new tele-information services.

(3) Connell and Galbraith (1982) p. 30-31.

(4) Cf. Rogers (1983) p. 350-355; Webster and Wind (1972) p. 79-80.

(5) Cf. IDC (1984); Yankee Group (1982); Vervest and Wissema (1984).

(6) Cf. value-added network concepts as discussed by Butler Cox Foundation (1984); Link (1983); Technology Analysis Group (1984), Yankee Group (1983, 1984).

(7) Butler Cox Foundation (1984) p. 1; cf. Beesley (1981) p. 3.

(8) Cf. Vervest and Wissema (1985) p. 33-34.

(9) Reference is made to the Appendix and Vervest et al. 'The Introduction of Electronic Mail – Perspectives for Telecommunication Managers', March 1986.

(10) In the questionnaire the term technology has been used; mail technology is defined as a specific way to perform a mailing function, and is therefore used as a synonym for 'mail system', as discussed in section 2.2.

(11) Other functions are: automation/ EDP manager (15%); general manager information resources (7%); electronic mail/ telecommunication specialist (5%); and administrative manager (4%). Cf. Vervest et al. (1986).

(12) See for a discussion of the possible indicators Vervest (1985) p. 83-85.

(13) Cf. OTA (1982); Blokland and Janssen (1984). The possible effects of change in the application patterns of existing systems, because of the introduction of new systems, is generally not taken into account, cf. OTA (1982).

(14) Cf. Vervest et al. (1986).

(15) Pearson's rank correlation $R = +.23$ for the correlation between growth and use of non-standardized mail in 1995; $R = -.17$ for the correlation between growth and the use of Telematics in 1995 (measured at the 5% significance level). Cf. Vervest et al. (1986).

(16) Cf. Fisher and Pry (1971); see also section 1.2.1.

(17) The Fisher-Pry model without growth is as follows:

$$(y) = {}^{2}\log\{f/(1-f)\} \qquad [8]$$

See also formulas [2] and [3] of section 1.2.1.

Adjusting the general model for growth factor *(gr)* gives:

$$(z) = {}^{2}\log \left| \frac{\{f/(1-f)\}}{g^{t}} \right| \qquad [9]$$

which can be transformed to:

$$(z) = (y) - t^{*2}\log(g) \qquad [10]$$

(y) = logarithmic fractional substitution curve
(z) = logarithmic fractional substitution curve with growth
(g) = compound annual increase on basis 1985-1995
(gr) = growth factor on basis 1985 $(gr) = t^{*2}\log g$

The substitution points $t(1985)$, $t(1995)$, $t(0)$, $t(f=0.1)$, and $t(f=0.9)$ are calculated as follows (see for the input figures, Vervest et al., 1985):

Case 1 – new mail for old mail technology
$g = 1.057$ $gr = 0.081*dt$

	without growth			with growth		
	year	$f/(1-f)$	(y)	year	(gr)	(z)
$t(1985)$	1985	0.161	-2.631	1985	0.	-2.631
$t(1995)$	1995	0.848	-0.237	1995	0.810	-1.041
$a)$	–	–	0.239	–	–	0.159
$t(0)$	1996	1.	0.	2002		
$t(f=0.1)$	1983	0.111	-3.170	1982		-3.170
$t(f=0.9)$	2009	9.	3.170	2023		3.170

(18) As indicated in note 17:

Case 2 – generation 2 EMS for postal/courier mail
$g = 1.01$ $gr = 0.014*dt$

	without growth			with growth		
	year	$f/(1-f)$	(y)	year	(gr)	(z)
$t(1985)$	1985	0.035	-4.837	1985	0.	-4.837
$t(1995)$	1985	0.108	-3.219	1995	0.141	-3.360
a	–	–	0.162	–	–	0.148
$t(0)$	2015	1.	0.	2018		
$t(f=0.1)$	1994	0.111	-3.170	1997		-3.170
$t(f=0.9)$	2033	9.	3.170	2041		3.170

Case 3 – new electronic mail for conventional electronic mail
$g = 1.134$ $gr = 0.181*dt$

	without growth			with growth		
	year	$f/(1-f)$	(y)	year	(gr)	(z)
$t(1985)$	1985	0.763	-0.389	1985	0.	-0.389
$t(1995)$	1995	3.566	1.834	1995	1.814	0.020
a	–	–	0.222	–	–	0.040
$t(0)$	1987	1.	0.	1995		
$t(f=0.1)$	1973	0.111	-3.170	?		-3.170
$t(f=0.9)$	2001	9.	3.170	?		3.170

? The calculated take-over time is irrelevant in view of the low level of substitution

(19) Cf. OTA (1982).

(20) For each respondent z-scores of the use of new mail technologies have been calculated for 1985 and 1995. Note that new mail technologies include:

- generation 2 EMS;
- Telematic systems (Teletex, digital facsimile, mixed-mode Teletex/digital facsimile, and interactive videotex);
- non-standardized new electronic mail (communicating word processor and personal computer, computer-based message system (CBMS), and voice mail).

For the purpose of our analysis, respondents have been classified as follows:

1. innovators/early adopters	$z(i) > 1$
2. early majority	$1 < z(i) < 0$
3. late majority/ laggards	$z(i) > 0$

where $z(i)$ = z-score respondent i of the relative use of new mail technology.
Cf. Vervest et al. (1986), trying a combination of z-scores as the mean of z-scores of 1985 and 1995.

(21) Cf. Rogers (1983) p. 241-254.

(22) All Pearson's rankcorrelations in this study have been tested at the 5% significance level.

(23) Thus there seems to be an important relationship between standardization, diffusion, and the product life cycle. See for the concept of the product life cycle Kotler (1980); Rothwell and Zegveld (1985); Wissema (1986).

(24) Vallee (1984) p. 38-50.

(25) Uhlig, Farber and Bair (1979) p. 13-22.

(26) McQuillan (1984) p. 4.7-4.21.

(27) Cf. IDC (1984); Pactel in its survey on telecommunications in Western Europe on behalf of Eurodata (Expert Panel discussions, 27-28 November 1984) gives similar results.

(28) Vallee (1984) p. 21-30.

(29) Cf. Vervest et al. (1986).

(30) Cf. McQuillan (1984); Vervest and Wissema (1984, 1985).

(31) Cf. Vervest (1985) p. 77-81; EMMS (1984).

(32) Cf. IDC (1984).

(33) Cf. section 2.4.

(34) Cf. Vervest and Wissema (1984).

(35) Id.

(36) Vervest et al. (1986).

(37) The Applied Telematics Group (1984, p. 65-67) identified in a survey on behalf of British Telecommunications, a pressing lack of standards in the following areas:

- means by which messages are reliably transferred from one message domain to another;
- means by which diverse terminal devices and privately operated computer systems can gain full access to the service;
- an agreed format for the information accompanying a message which can be used as directives to the recipient system control procedures;
- an agreed format for representing the contents of a message;
- common forms of user address across interconnected message (CBMS) services;
- universal directory assistance service providing a means to retrieve the address with a name (or another identifier);
- means by which to authenticate both the originator and recipient of a message, in order to maintain the security and privacy of the communicating parties;
- commonly understood and agreed definitions of the quality of service;
- means by which interconnected systems can guarantee the quality of service to their respective clients;
- means for determining the charges levied to a user or to an interconnected (CBMS) system for services provided.

(38) Cf. Vervest et al. (1986).
(39) $R = +.19$.
(40) Cf. Yankee Group (1984); Perry (1985); Frost & Sullivan 'Data Communications for Microcomputers', conference proceedings 17-18 September 1984.
(41) Cf. Yankee Group (1984).
(42) For an overview see Butler Cox Foundation (1984); Yankee Group (1983); Beesley (1981) p. 38-39.
(43) Licklider and Vezza (1978) p. 1331.
(44) Id.; Vervest and Wissema (1984) p. 35-38.
(45) Butler Cox Foundation (1984) p. 3-5.
(46) Keen (1978) p. 1-32; Alter (1980) p. 73-94.
(47) Cf. Yankee Group (1983); Vervest and Wissema (1984) p. 24-28.

CHAPTER 4.

THE IMPACT OF STANDARDS

4.1 MESSAGE HANDLING STANDARDIZATION

4.1.1 Protocol architecture

Standardization is defined as the development, implementation and successful acceptance of common rules for performing specific tasks. Standards are either voluntary or imposed: in both cases they require a certain agreement between those involved, including manufacturers, users, service providers, government and others. The development of communication and information systems standards has become increasingly more complicated. Moreover, the international structure for standards-making has come under pressure to deal with the variety of new possibilities. This chapter deals with the general framework of standards, in particular message-handling standards (section 4.1), the institutional structure of standardization (section 4.2), and the subtle relationship between standards and innovation (section 4.3).

The first detailed examination of the issues of internationally acceptable message-handling standards has been undertaken by the International Federation for Information Processing (IFIP) which established Working Group 6.5 on 'International Computer Message Systems' in 1978 (1). Working Group 6.5 developed from 1978-1982 a CBMS networking model which has been adopted as the basis for all significant standards on message-handling to date. It deals specifically with message transfer and cooperating message domains. Current issues of investigation include user-friendly naming and addressing conventions, directory service issues, and the standardization of document content architectures and interchange formats (2).

The work of IFIP Working Group 6.5 has been used by CCITT and ISO to design its OSI/MHS model. ISO TC97 developed a standard specifically for textual interchange: Message Oriented Text Interchange System (MOTIS) which is largely conforming to CCITT X.400 (3). As has been explained in section 2.3, the OSI model which was developed by ISO, and largely adopted by CCITT in the X.200 Recommendations, forms a general architecture for the development of standards aimed at the interconnection of information systems.

FIGURE 4.1 PROTOCOL ARCHITECTURE FOR STANDARDIZATION OF TELE-INFORMATION SERVICES

<table>
<tr><th colspan="16">OPEN SYSTEMS INTERCONNECTION – BASIC REFERENCE MODEL</th></tr>
<tr><td rowspan="2">X.200, X.210,
X.250,
IS 7498,
DP 8509</td><td colspan="14">Standardized applications</td><td rowspan="2">Private applications</td></tr>
<tr><td colspan="4">Telematics[2)]</td><td colspan="5">Office services</td><td colspan="5">Data processing</td></tr>
<tr><td rowspan="2">Layer 7

application layer</td><td rowspan="2">TELETEX F.200, F.201, T.60, T.63, T.90, T.91, X.430, DP 9063/2, DP 9064/2</td><td rowspan="2">FACSIMILE T.0, T.2, T.3, T.4, T.5 DP 9063/1, DP 9063/2</td><td rowspan="2">Mixed-mode teletex / facsimile T.62, T.72, T.73</td><td rowspan="2">VIDEOTEX F.300, T.100, T.101</td><td colspan="5">DOCUMENT STRUCTURE AND INTERCHANGE T.73 DP8613</td><td colspan="5">REMOTE DATA HANDLING</td><td>3)</td></tr>
<tr><td>OTHER</td><td>DIRECTORY, X.DS1, X.DS2 X.DS3, X.DS4, X.DS6, X.DS7</td><td>MAILING F.40, F.350, X. 400, X. 401, X. 408, X. 420</td><td>FILING DP 8571</td><td>PRINTING</td><td>OTHER DIS 8879</td><td>FILE TRANSFER, ACCESS AND MANAGEMENT DP 8571</td><td>JOB TRANSFER DP 8831, DP 8832</td><td>PROGRAMMING AND INTERPROGRAM COMMUNICATIONS IS 1538, IS 1539, IS 1989, IS 6160, IS 6373, DP 8485, DIS 8652, DP 8907, DP 9075</td><td>OTHER DP 8632, DP 8651, DP 9007, DP 9040, DP 9041</td><td></td></tr>
<tr><td>Layer 7a application sublayer</td><td colspan="14">X.410, X.411
DP 8505 (MOTIS), DP 8649, DP 8650</td><td></td></tr>
<tr><td>Layer 6 presentation layer</td><td colspan="14">T.50, T.51, T.61, T.73, T.100, X.409
IS 6937, DP 8822, DP 8823, DP 8824, DP 8825</td><td></td></tr>
<tr><td>Layer 5 session layer</td><td colspan="14">X.215, X.225, T.62
DIS 8326, DIS 8327</td><td></td></tr>
<tr><td>Layer 4 transport layer</td><td colspan="14">X.214, X.224, T.70
DIS 8072, DIS 8073, DIS 8602</td><td></td></tr>
<tr><td rowspan="2">Network oriented layers</td><td colspan="14">X.213, X.244, X.300, X.310, V.100, V.110, I.120, I.210, I.211, I.212, DIS 8348, DIS 8473, DP 8648, DIS 8802/1</td><td rowspan="2">Private Local Area Network (LAN) and/or Wide Area Network (WAN)</td></tr>
<tr><td colspan="3">PSTN</td><td colspan="3">CSPDN</td><td colspan="3">PSPDN</td><td colspan="3">ISDN</td><td colspan="2">LAN[4)]</td></tr>
<tr><td>Layer 3 Network layer</td><td colspan="3">telephone + X.25</td><td colspan="3">X.21</td><td colspan="3">X.25, X.3, X.28/ X.29, X.32 DIS 8208,DP 8878</td><td colspan="3">I.450, I.451, X.30, X.31</td><td colspan="2">DIS 8802/3, DIS 8802/4, DIS 8802/5, DIS 8802/6</td><td></td></tr>
<tr><td>Layer 2 Data link layer</td><td colspan="3">T.71 or X.25</td><td colspan="3"></td><td colspan="3">LAPB/X.25 DIS 7776</td><td colspan="3">I.440, I.441</td><td colspan="2" rowspan="2">DIS 8802/2</td><td></td></tr>
<tr><td>Layer 1 Physical layer</td><td colspan="3">e.g. V.24, V.25</td><td colspan="3">X.21, X.21 bis, X.22</td><td colspan="3">X.21, X.21 bis DIS 2110</td><td colspan="3">I.430, I.431</td><td></td></tr>
</table>

notes: 1. ISO standards are either International Standard (IS); Draft International Standard (DIS); or Draft Proposal (DP). CCITT Recommendations start with capital F., T., V., X., or I.
2. interworking with Telex (TWX) is foreseen, cf. F.201
3. examples are proprietary architectures such as SNA-DIA/DCA by International Business Machines (IBM) or specific application protocols such as MAP by General Motors
4. The following LAN technologies are standardized:
DP 8802/3 Carrier Sense Multiple Access/Collision Detection
DP 8802/4 token bus
DP 8802/5 token ring
DP 8802/6 slotted ring

Further information is given in the appendix.

It is also the basis for the standardization of tele-information services.

The resulting protocol structure has been laid down in Figure 4.1. It is composed of the following sets of standards (Recommendations):

- IS 7498 (ISO, 1983) on Information Processing Systems – Open Systems Interconnection – Basic Reference Model and specific layer standards (including DIS 8473, 8348, DP 8602 for connectionless transmission);
- CCITT Recommendations X.200, X.300 and X.400 Series;
- CCITT Recommendations on telematic services as well as on bearer services;
- local area network standards developed by the Institute for Electrical and Electronic Engineers (IEEE) and ISO (4).

A distinction is made between standardized applications and private applications. Private applications are based on proprietary architectures, developed independently of standardization institutes by manufacturers or user organizations. System Network Architecture (SNA) and Document Interchange Architecture (DIA)/Document Content Architecture (DCA) is an important proprietary architecture developed by International Business Machines corporation (IBM)(5). In general a proprietary architecture is not built for open systems interconnection and tends to exclude unlike systems from the environment. Communications across the boundaries necessitate gateway processors, which restrict inter-system communications to the lowest common denominator.

Another class of private applications is industry-sector specific applications. For instance, General Motors Manufacturing Automation Protocol (MAP) is an industry-specific application, but it is built and constructed as an application layer in OSI (6). Standards for industry-specific applications are aimed at inter-process communications, in order to enable cooperation among application processes within different systems. By using lower-level architectures from standardized applications, they can acquire the flexibility for interfacing with other applications.

The standardized applications have been defined particularly to cover tele-informational needs that are more or less uniform across industry sectors, e.g. office services, telematics and data processing. Office services and telematics are primarily text and document oriented services; office services aim to define message structures and to relate them to intra-organizational procedures for office information handling. Telematics are specifically concerned with terminal prescriptions and the definition of public services. The data processing applications enable remote data handling such as file transfer, job transfer, programming and inter-program communications.

4.1.2 Higher-level standardization

The more sophisticated inter-system applications are, the higher the level of standardization must be. In particular three types of standards become increasingly important: office document architectures, industry-generic transaction formats, and interprocess control standards.

Office document architectures

A document is an amount of information that can be manipulated as one unit, with the ultimate possibility of presenting the information to a human being in a way that allows the interpretation of the information. Document interchange formats define the data structures of the information for transmission in such a way that both sender and receiver can interpret this structure. Each document will be composed of different portions, with a specified relationship between them. This is called the document structure.

ISO has been working on an Office Document Architecture (ODA) with a complementary Office Document Interchange Format (ODIF) (7). A document is considered in two parts:

- a document profile includes the parameters used to handle, process and file the document;
- the content contains the information on how the document was created and the rules which were for making the document.

CCITT defines a Simple Formattable Document (SFD) in X.420 and a telematic documents interchange format in T.73 (the character set is defined in T.62).

Industry-generic transaction formats

Another set of important standards are those for business transactions. Much work for transaction standards has been performed by the Transportation Data Co-ordinating Committee (TDCC) in the USA (8). It has developed the Electronic Data Interchange (EDI) standard, with a generic software structure so that industries with similar data structures can adjust the standard to their specific requirements. EDI is composed of tables with respect to transaction set names, segments in each transaction set, segment names, data elements in each segment, and data element specifications.

Another important development has been by the American National Standards Institute (ANSI) which addressed the issue of multi-industry transaction standards. Important ANSI transaction standards define purchase order (ANSI X12.1), invoice (X12.2), data dictionary (X12.3), remittance/ pay advice (X12.4), and application control (X12.6).

Interprocess control

Increasingly information which is distributed over different systems must cooperate for a common task, such as for computer integrated manufacturing, data base enquiry, logistics and purchasing. Standards are needed that allow distributed information to be used as an integrated resource for certain tasks.

For this purpose the Manufacturing Automation Protocol (MAP) – discussed before – includes an eighth layer to OSI (9). This layer, called Manufacturing Message Format and Syntax defines the types and structures of the messages which may be sent among the various manufacturing systems. The MAP may eventually add a ninth layer for task repertoires and data input/output procedures of connected equipment.

4.1.3 Terminal standardization

The protocol architecture as given in Figure 4.1, supports explicitly telematic services which define both the terminal protocol and the external functionality of the user station with respect to the service. For instance, terminals for the Teletex service must comply both with protocol (T.51, T.61, T.62, T.70, T.73) as well as with service Recommendations (T.60, T.63, T.62, T.90, T.91).

FIGURE 4.2 PERSONAL COMPUTER COMMUNICATION MODEL

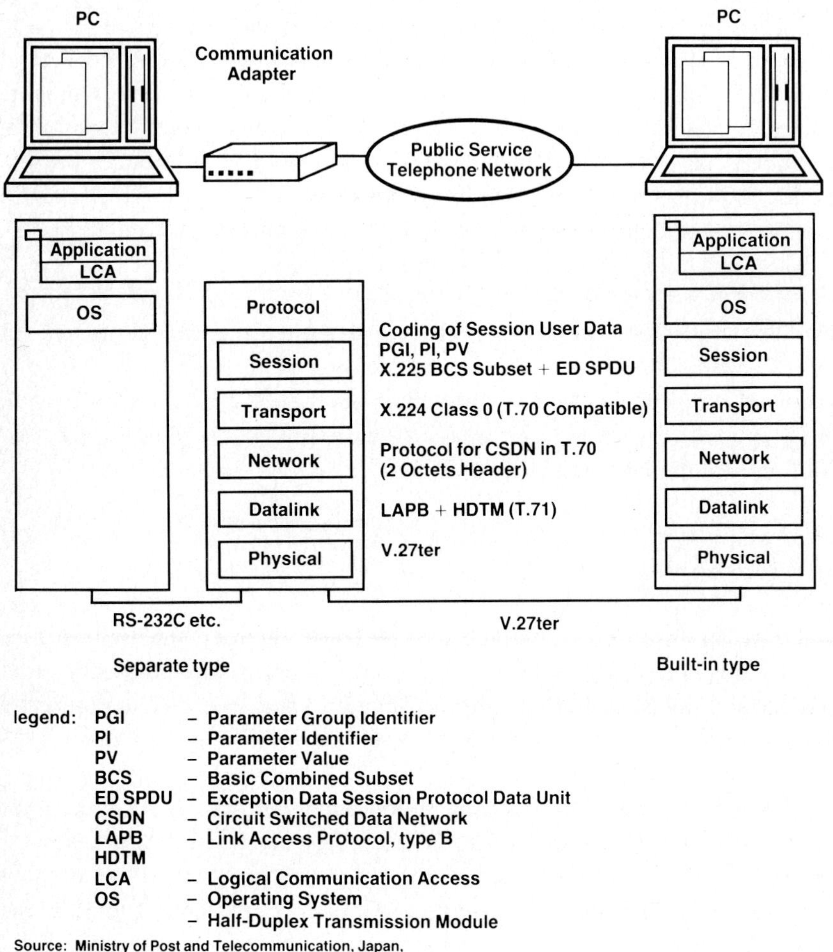

legend:
- PGI – Parameter Group Identifier
- PI – Parameter Identifier
- PV – Parameter Value
- BCS – Basic Combined Subset
- ED SPDU – Exception Data Session Protocol Data Unit
- CSDN – Circuit Switched Data Network
- LAPB – Link Access Protocol, type B
- HDTM
- LCA – Logical Communication Access
- OS – Operating System
- – Half-Duplex Transmission Module

Source: Ministry of Post and Telecommunication, Japan, February 1985

The growing number of personal computers and word processors with communication facilities necessitates similar specifications enabling:

- general communications between various types of personal computers and word processors;
- communications with telematic services;
- communications to message-handling systems, and other types of central computers.

Figure 4.2 shows two cases for PC communications, i.e. via a communication adapter and via an integrated module; the protocol definition on the basis of current standards is also given (10). The logical communication access (LCA) allows the application program to use both the communication facilities and the layer 1 to 5 protocols. The LCA is similar to the Reliable Transfer Server as defined in X.410. On session layer a subset of X.225 is used (Basic Combined Subset); on transport layer the simple class of X.224 with only functions for establishing connection, data transfer and protocol error reporting is applied. The network layers are based on T.70, T.71 and V.27ter.

An interesting feature of the protocol is the optional integrated access method that combines network connection and session connection in a single instruction. Moreover the use of V27ter (this modem type is generally used for Group 3 facsimile) will facilitate the connection of PC and Group 3 facsimile in the future (11).

4.2 THE PROMOTION OF STANDARDS

4.2.1 The international structure for the development of standards

A large number of organizations is involved in the development of standards in the area of communication and information systems. They can be classified in one or more of the following categories (12):

- national and international associations of technical experts such as IEEE and IFIP;
- national standardization organizations which are either voluntary or governmental;
- voluntary international organizations such as ISO and the International Electrotechnical Commission (IEC);
- international (treaty) organizations which are established by intergovernmental treaties, such as CCITT and the International Telecommunications Union (ITU);
- international user organizations such as the International Telecommunications User Group (INTUG);
- international manufacturers organizations such as the European Computer Manufacturers Association (ECMA).

The complexity of standardization in the areas of communication and information systems gives a specific role to the technical experts. Only experts are able to recognize and identify the standardization issues at an early stage of product development. The role of IFIP in initiating message-handling standardization has already been mentioned. IEEE had a pioneering role in the development of local area network standards. The fading boundaries between communication and information systems techologies, as well as the increasing number of applications, necessitate an economic use of scarce expertise; moreover it affects the cooperative structure and division of tasks between the international standardization bodies.

For instance, OSI/MHS is the result of close cooperation, on a voluntary basis, between technical experts active within CCITT and ISO. CCITT, formed in 1956, covers technical, operating and tariff aspects of international communications. The function of ISO, established in 1947, is to promote the development of international standards in all areas that are not covered by IEC. ISO TC97 has been very active in the development of standards for 'information processing systems'. The merging of communications and computers obscures the traditional boundaries between CCITT and ISO. It exemplifies the critical functions of those experts that hold positions in both organizations.

Another example of altered cooperation is the relationship between ISO and IEC. IEC – established in 1906 – is an authoritative body specialized in world standards in the area of electrical and electronic engineering. The more computers have become part of the appliance, entertainment and home equipment environments, the more conflicts and overlaps have arisen between ISO and IEC. This led to the establishment of a Joint Technical Programs Committee (JTPC) with the aim to develop 'joint logo' standards (13).

The scarcity of technical resources and the need to prevent conflicts and overlaps necessitates more detailed cooperation between the various standardization bodies. In particular, it promotes the contraction of standards-making efforts around the general framework of OSI.

At the same time there is a growing concern about the implementation of standards. As discussed in the ICA survey, users may view standards either as an a-priori requirement for the adoption of new technologies, or as the result of the success of a specific manufacturer's product. The availability of technical expertise may account for variations in innovative behavior and standardization can be seen as an alternative to having to acquire in-house technical expertise.

As a result users may have little effective influence on the processes of standards development itself, but will act as 'gatekeepers' to the diffusion if standards are not implemented. The promotion of standards seems largely a matter of industrial interests shared by governments, service providers (PTT's) and manufacturers. It leads Sirbu and Zwimpfer (1985)(14) to conclude that standards are needed more to create a market and to reduce variety, and not so much to ensure compatibility in the development of new technologies. They identify two reasons: first, the changes in technology and second, the deregulation of the telecommunications and computer industries. For instance, VLSI allows extremely complex devices to be manufactured at very low unit cost but at high initial costs: the challenge is to find a design needed in sufficient quantities to justify the front-end investments. Standards help to create and define such needs. A similar occurrence can be seen in complex software. This amounts to (15):

1. pressures to accelerate the standards process for commercial reasons;
2. definition of standards in parallel with R&D on the underlying technology;
3. increased risks of problems in the resultant standard due to hasty development;
4. the absence of market experience making difficult the resolution of controversies over the appropriate level of functionality to incorporate in the standard.

Deregulation is another factor that vastly increases the number of players, according to Sirbu and Zwimpfer (16). As telecommunication service providers lose their monopolistic control over the networks and the attachments to these networks, they are no longer in a position to impose the standards.

As a summary, the process of standardization in communication and information systems has changed the focus from the development of adequate standards to the timely implementation of newly developed standards within an industrial context. In this respect governments assume a different role in the various parts of the world. In particular the differences between USA, Japan and Western Europe are important.

4.2.2 Government promotion of standards

USA

While standardization in the USA is by and large the result of market factors (de-facto standardization), government agencies influence standards by procurement and regulatory policies. In this respect two organizations are important (17):

- National Telecommunications and Information Agency (NTIA), a part of the Department of Commerce, which has been delegated a broad authority for policy making and operations in telecommunications and information;
- Federal Communications Commission (FCC) reporting directly to the US Congress as a regulatory agency that is independent of the executive branch (the President's Office).

Important standardization bodies are the National Bureau of Standards (NBS) and the American National Standards Institute (ANSI). NBS designed a message format standard in 1982 ('Federal Information Processing Standard 98') that is significantly different from X.400, but since the formal approval of X.400 by CCITT in 1984 NBS has followed the latter standard (18). Note that ANSI and NBS deal largely with the development of standards and not so much their implementation programs.

Japan

Standardization in the area of telecommunication is specifically the responsibility of the Japanese Ministry of Post and Telecommunication (JMPT) and the Ministry of International Trade and Industry (MITI). Both ministries actively participate in international standardization but standards are allegedly a matter of national industry policy (19).

MITI has a Japanese Industry Standards Committee, supported by the Agency of Industrial Science and Technology. It is specifically dealing with the work of ISO and IEC, and has a regulatory committee for standards enforcement.

JMPT participates in CCITT and can issue a Computer Communication Network Protocol (CCNP) or a JMPT notification, which may result in a JUST standard (Japanese Unified Standard for Telecommunications). JMPT is assisted by a telecommunication council in which industry and universities participate.

In the area of message handling, important standardization is concentrated on PC communications and message-handling, Japanese Teletex, digital facsimile and interactive videotex (CAPTAIN).

Japanese standardization efforts are especially directed at implementation programmes by national manufacturers.

Western Europe

Early efforts at message-handling standardization from a Western European perspective have been made by ECMA by means of its Message Interchange Distributed Applications (MIDA) standard. It can be seen as an extension of X.400 for the particular case of a private system interconnecting either with a publicly managed system or with another private system (20). Particularly important is Technical Committee 32 on 'Communication, Networks and System Interconnection', which is responsible for the development of OSI service and protocol standards in relation with CCITT or PTT-defined services on telematics, message interchange and ISDN and for the connection with private networks.

Another important organization is the Conference of European Post and Telecommunications Administrations (CEPT) (21) which formulates joint administrative and technical programs between the European PTT's. CEPT is not an officially recognized intergovernmental body, but it harmonizes implementation programs of its member PTT's; in this way CEPT influences equipment procurement by its members.

An important agreement was made by CEPT in November 1985 in the Memorandum of Understanding on European Telecommunication Standards (22). It is open for adherence by CEPT members and lays down two important principles:

1. CEPT technical recommendations will be used to establish European Telecommunication Standards (NET's); CEPT will initiate the means to give these standards sufficient mandatory force, in particular to seek the establ-

ishment of a new EC Directive on such standards;
2. the standards will be used in the purchasing specifications of PTT's and for connection of terminal equipment to their networks.

Over the past years European governments have increasingly become aware of the necessity to concentrate their standardization efforts. This is not so much to develop new standards, but as a way to precipitate the implementation of standards and to facilitate the technological harmonization among the European nations. Mainly as result of the 'Round Table of European Industrialists', composed of representatives of twelve leading Western European information technology industries, the European Community (EC) has deployed a number of activities from 1983-1984 onwards. Two programs are specifically important:

1. European Strategic Program for R&D on Information Technology (ESPRIT), covering (23):

- advanced micro-electronics (submicron technology, computer-aided design, materials and opto-electronics);
- software technology (development methodology, production and maintenance, tools and management);
- advanced information processing (knowledge engineering, information and knowledge storage, external interfaces, computer architectures);
- office systems (office systems science and human factors, advanced workstations, communication systems, filing and retrieval, integrated office systems design);
- computer integrated manufacture (CAD/CAE/CAM, machine control systems, integrated system architectures and system applications).

Although R&D is its primary activity, ESPRIT also embraces demonstrator projects as well as projects for the ESPRIT infrastructure: these latter are to be used for the management and the implementation of the ESPRIT programs, such as EIES, i.e. ESPRIT Information Exchange System, which essentially uses MH technology for electronic mail and data base access.

2. R&D in Advanced Communications Technology in Europe (RACE), which is specifically aimed at R&D for integrated broadband communications.

Besides ESPRIT and RACE, the EC Inter-Institutional Information System

(INSIS) is a possible vehicle for the implementation of message-handling standards (24).

Other significant initiatives are undertaken by SPAG/CEN/CENELEC in order to secure European standardization. The Standards Promotion and Application Group (SPAG) is an interim organization of the Round Table of European Industrialists to coordinate their interests toward the EC initiatives (25). SPAG is active in three areas:

- technical coordination with standards-making bodies;
- validation and certification of standards;
- demonstration projects, of which MHS is the first to be realized.

CEN (Comité Européen de Normalisation) is the European association of national standardization institutes related to ISO; CENELEC is the equivalent for electrotechnical standardization related to IEC; it is composed of government representatives of 17 national electrotechnical committees (26). CEN and CENELEC have intensified their activities to harmonize information technology in Europe; in collaboration with CEPT they have established the Steering Committee for Information Technology (ITSTC) with an official mandate from the EC (27).

Figure 4.3 gives a schematic diagram of the European structure for implementing standards. The proposed procedures are as follows (28):

1. basic documents by CCITT, ISO, ECMA, and others are first converted into 'reference standards';
2. these form the basis for functional standards (European Norms) as rules for the application of specific functions, including rules for the use of the functional standards themselves;
3. specific European Norms are developed for certain aspects (safety, ergonomics, quality) and for certain hardware and software elements;
4. European Norms are also to be developed for test methods and conformity verification;
5. these norms lead to compulsory (EC) standards for specific equipment, including – among other things – compatibility requirements.

The recent European initiatives by the EC and the Roundtable of European Industrialists (29) show the need for standardization on a global scale in the area of communication and information technologies. Western Europe opts for

FIGURE 4.3 ORGANIZATIONAL STRUCTURE FOR STANDARDIZATION OF INFORMATION

TECHNOLOGY IN WESTERN EUROPE

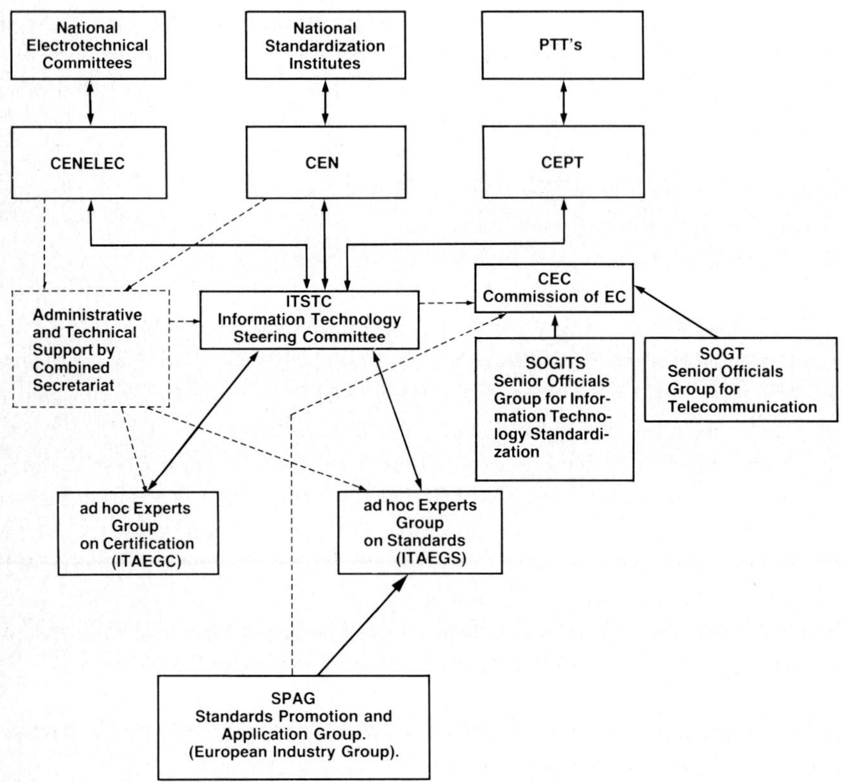

R&D cooperation and standardization in order to create both a technological and economic unity. The dominance of manufacturers and governments on the one hand, and the absence of user representation on the other hand, is remarkable.

4.3 STANDARDS AND INNOVATION

Technical complexity

The development of communication and information systems only seems possible after adequate standards have been developed. Because of the technical complexity involved, experts play a critical role. With respect to innovation in electronic mail, OSI/MHS forms a general architecture that makes it possible to separate the many standardization problems and to deal with them in isolation. In this way the standardization work can be divided while at the same time the overall compatibility can be maintained.

It must be emphasized that the OSI/MHS model is not an implementation nor does it specify the factual design for a system. Day and Zimmermann (1983) compare this with the term architecture in building: one cannot walk into Victorian architecture, but one can walk into a Victorian building (30). So OSI defines the type of open system but it does not define the implementation itself. The model is abstract by definition and has two main functions:

1. to allow a common understanding of intersystem communications and to provide a common terminology;
2. to group related problem areas together and to act as an organizational framework for defining constraints on factual system implementations.

The objective of building concrete products and services based on OSI/MHS demands special attention to the following issues:

- detail; although formal description techniques were employed (31), there remains much room for different interpretations of the model specifications;
- certification; the lack of adequate testing equipment makes the certification of systems very complicated. International arbitration of outstanding issues is either not organized or is not time effective (32);
- completeness; the descriptions leave a number of gaps, particularly with respect to the layers on top of layer 7. The most urgent issues are, according to White (1984) (33):

  - global directories and user-friendly terminology;
  - interworking with postal systems;

- operational procedures and tools (tariffing, exchange of charging and settlement information, message tracing, monitoring of resource usage, quality of service parameters)
- extensions such as mailbox services, portable User Agents and new interpersonal service elements (closed user groups, message circulation)
- document interchange formats and procedures
- message format prescriptions for business transactions
- support of voice mail

competing architectures; many manufacturers have their own architectures and protocols. SNA was announced by IBM in 1974 followed by DIA and DCA in 1983 (34). These three architectures provide a common basis for IBM and IBM-compatible products. Also other manufacturers develop or have developed proprietary architectures (35). This means that the building of systems in accordance with OSI/MHS will in most cases necessitate the development of the appropriate gateways to existing architectural designs. Particularly in this area little has been specified in OSI/MHS.

The economic-political dimension

As argued in section 4.2, the development of standards is largely a matter of service providers and manufacturers who can afford the necessary technical expertise and can persist with the long development cycles usually associated with standards-making. Users have a marginal role in the development process: standards have an informational and economic benefit for users in the sense that they reduce uncertainty with respect to product performance and lower the need for in-house expertise (36). Standards permit the interconnection of unlike systems, thereby removing constraints on the procurement of products and services and decreasing the dependence on certain suppliers. In this way standards also promote competition.

The manufacturers' interests in developing and complying with standards, however, are different from those of the user. As shown in the case of Western Europe, the promotion of standards by governments is mixed with the interests of large industrial firms. Standards are a way to create a market, say Sirbu and Zwimpfer (37). And this seems a particularly important argument in Western Europe. Standardization policy aims at a technological and economic unity within Western Europe with respect to communication and information systems.

The industrial orientation of standards is also seen in Japan.In the USA policy officials are worried about the politicization of standardization bodies; they see innovation as primarily generated by market demand (38). In summary, the impact of standards on innovation can be seen as follows:

1. by means of the early development of standards, scarce technical expertise can be shared in a pre-competitive environment, such as within international voluntary and intergovernmental standardization bodies; this will have a positive influence on directing R&D efforts;
2. standardization efforts remove informational barriers for users and decrease their dependence on certain suppliers; in this way standards can promote competition and facilitate the diffusion of innovations;
3. it seems possible for governments to have a deliberate policy for the development and implementation of standards as a method to promote the generation and diffusion of innovations; the endorsement of these policies by large industrial firms seems necessary.

NOTES CHAPTER 4
THE IMPACT OF STANDARDS

(1) Uhlig (1983) p. 399-401; cf. Vervest (1985) p. xv-xvii.
(2) Uhlig (1983) p. 405-409.
(3) ISO/TC97/SC18/WG4 No.59, 'The Message Oriented Text Interchange System (MOTIS)', DP 8505, DP 8506.
(4) Cf. The Institute of Electrical and Electronic Engineers, 'Project 802 on Local Area Network Standards' (1982).
(5) Cf. IBM (1982, 1983); see also Schick and Brockish (1982) and Vervest and Wissema (1984) p. 41-42.
(6) Cf. General Motors, 'Manufacturers Automation Protocol, MAP Version 2.1', GM Task Force on Automated Manufacturing, Detroit, March 1985.
(7) ISO/TC97/SC18/WG3 N 207 'Office Document Architecture', fourth working draft, September 1983; cf. for the concept of an office document architecture Applied Telematics Group (1984) p. 61-64.
(8) Cf. Yankee Group (1983).
(9) Cf. General Motors, 'Manufacturers Automation Protocol, MAP Version 2.1', GM Task Force on Automated Manufacturing, Detroit, March 1985.
(10) Cf. Vervest and Wissema (1985) p. 53-58.
(11) Id.
(12) Cf. International Chamber of Commerce (ICC, 1985).
(13) The joint committee between IEC and ISO, JTPC, was established in 1985. See also Sherr, S., A New International Structure for Information-Systems Standards, in: Computer, IEEE Computer Society, January 1986, p. 102-103.
(14) Sirbu and Zwimpfer (1985); cf. Bottaro (1981); Hemenway (1975) p. 21-29, p. 37-44.
(15) Sirbu and Zwimpfer (1985) p. 37.
(16) Id.
(17) NTIA (1983).
(18) NBS (1982); NBS has later on announced its support for the CCITT X.400 standards (EMA, 1984).
(19) Cf. Vervest and Wissema (1985) p. 51-62.
(20) Cf. Vervest (1985) p. 202-204; TC32 was a reorganization by ECMA of the former TC23, 24 and 25 at the end of 1984. Reference is made to the ECMA memo on TC32, January 1985.
(21) Cf. ICC (1985).
(22) Memorandum of Understanding on European Telecommunication Standards for Terminal Equipment (Accord sur les Normes Européennes de Télécommunication – NET – pour les Terminaux), agreed at the meeting of the Directors-General of CEPT Aministration (Copenhagen, 15 November, 1985).
(23) Cf. The Midterm Review of ESPRIT – Commission of the European Communities, Brussels, October 15th 1985, submitted by the ESPRIT Review Board, under chairmanship of A.E.Pannenborg.
(24) See for an interesting review on INSIS, 'INSIS Study – Office Automation & Communications 1985-1999' (INSIS 1985). RACE started in 1984 as part of the 'Action Line II' of the EC and is currently in a two-year definition phase.
(25) Current participants in SPAG are AEG, Bull (CII-Honeywell Bull), CGE (SIT/Alcatel/SESA), GEC, ICL, Nixdorf, Olivetti, Philips, Plessey, Siemens, STET (SGS/Itasiel/CERCI/CSELT, Thompson/EFCIS.
(26) ICC (1985).
(27) Note also the Senior Officials Group for Information Technology Standardization (SOGITS)

and the Senior Officials Group for Telecommunications (SOGT), which are advisory boards to the Commission of the EC, composed of senior officials of member countries.

(28) It should be emphasized that the revised structure is of recent date and still under discussion at various levels in CCITT, CEN, CENELEC, CEPT, EC, SPAG.

(29) Reference is also made to 'EUREKA', an initiative by the French government in 1985 (cf. Financieel Economisch Magazine, 30 November 1985, no.36, p. 29-35).

(30) Day and Zimmermann (1983) p. 1334-1335.

(31) The formal description technique has been laid down in X.409. See also Dickson and De Chazal (1983) and Vissers, Tenney and Bochmann (1983).

(32) Cf. with respect to the technical status, Linn and Nightingale (1983).

(33) White, lecture at the EMA conference (1984).

(34) Reference is made to section 4.1.

(35) For an overview see Meijer and Peeters (1982).

(36) Cf. Hemenway (1975).

(37) Sirbu and Zwimpfer (1985) p. 37, p. 39.

(38) Cf. NTIA (1983) p. 8-9.

CHAPTER 5.

REGULATION AND INNOVATION POLICY

5.1 CREATION OF AN 'EQUAL PLAYING FIELD'

The new developments in electronic mail concentrate on OSI/MHS. As discussed in Chapter 2., this is a systems approach to message communications with the potential to lead a new trajectory for technical change. In Chapter 3. I argued that the re-arrangement of networks, the integration of information-handling functions and the ability to add user value to message communications, are critical factors for the introduction of new mail systems. Standards development discussed in Chapter 4, is largely dependent upon manufacturers, service providers (PTT's), and government. Standardization has a vital impact on the generation of innovations as well as their diffusion. This chapter addresses the critical issues of government innovation policy and possible government actions for directing and promoting the innovation process.

Above all one should bear in mind that innovation is not an objective in itself nor can government innovation policy be isolated from overall social and economic objectives. Within the framework of the overall government policies, innovation policy is an intermediary for facilitating desirable change.

Particularly important are the constraints that exist in the current regulatory regimes for the provision of telecommunication services. Littlechild's cahier de charge pinpoints the vital elements (1983) (1). His tasks were to study and make recommendations in order to:

1. prevent British Telecommunications from using its dominant market position to exploit consumers;
2. encourage efficient and innovative telecommunication systems;
3. ensure the maximization of net proceeds from the sale of BT (on particular regulatory and profit assumptions);
4. facilitate the successful operation of BT as a commercial organization after flotation.

Littlechild argues specifically in favor of increasing competitive pressures (2): 'Without it (i.e. increasing competitive pressures) the regulators as well as the consumers are at the mercy of the dominant supplier'. The protection against monopoly, says Littlechild, is the prime purpose of de-regulation. Secondary objectives are higher efficiency and increased innovation, a lesser burden of regulation and the promotion of competition (3).

This restructuring of the traditional provision of telecommunications services is referred to as the 'creation of an equal playing field', which includes issues of 'fair competition' and data integrity.

Fair competition

Deregulation of traditional telecommunication service providers is a measure to open the market which they dominate, to new entrants. At the same time the traditional service provider is given the possibility to diversify into new markets, meaning that regulatory policy must aim at the creation of a new 'playing field' for parties who were previously not competitors (4).

An equal playing field raises the following important points (5):

1. what constitutes fair competition and how can the liberalization of the market be promoted? How can price skimming policies by service providers be prevented and in what way can service to all, independent of place or time, and for a fair price be safeguarded;
2. will certain services be subject to economies of scale, leading to a natural monopoly, and how do we discriminate such services from truly competitive services?
3. in what way must tariffs be regulated and to what extent shall service providers be allowed to cross-subsidize certain operations?
4. what ought to be the interconnect policy that forces market players to offer 'equal access' to all and that enables the resale of capacity and/or third-party traffic over leased circuits?

Perhaps the most critical issue for the creation of an equal playing field is regulating the setting of standards, type approval procedures and the verification of the compliance with standards. This is an area where actual market power and technical expertise can easily form a barrier for new entrants if it is not counter-balanced by the appropriate legal framework.

Data integrity

Increasingly important for regulatory regimes of telecommunication services are the provisions for 'data integrity'. These are defined as measures to protect data which is held in a computer system or in the process of being transmitted, from unauthorised use or undue loss, either by the service provider or any other party. Major issues include (6):

- the legal status of electronically transmitted information;
- security of computer installations and data protection;
- the protection of privacy;
- the liabilities for information transfer, fraud, mutilation and/or loss of information;
- the intellectual property rights of information;
- the valuation and taxation of information;
- the transborder flow of information.

The next section analyzes the changes in the regulation of telecommunication service provision, in particular with respect to the position of traditional service providers. The possible use of standardization policy as part of government innovation policy is discussed in section 5.3, leading to a recommendation for government actions in the Netherlands in section 5.4.

5.2 REGULATION OF TELECOMMUNICATION SERVICE PROVISION

5.2.1 Service provision in USA, Japan and Western Europe

The effects of technological changes and the emergence of new markets neccessitate a re-definition of the tasks, powers, organization, legal and regulatory structures of the traditional telecommunication service providers. The changes taken place are discussed below. The possible effects for traditional telecommunication and postal service providers such as PTT's and Recognized Private Operating Agents (RPOA's), are discussed in the next sections.

USA

The USA promotes an – international – unregulated environment. The NTIA (1983) (7) lays down the overall objective to:

'promote an – international – environment for the provision of telecommunications and information facilities, services, and equipment – and for the production and dissemination of information itself – in which maximum reliance is placed on free enterprise, open and competitive markets, and free trade and investment with minimum direct government involvement or regulation'.

The 1971 Specialized Common Carriers Decision of the FCC permitted entry into private line service in the USA, it being an almost exclusive monopoly for AT&T until 1968 ('Carterphone Decision'). Resisting the practical effectuation of this decision, AT&T was sued by the US Justice Department in 1974, which at second stage sought the divestiture from AT&T of the local exchange facilities. The suit was settled in 1982 and AT&T opted for divestiture, effected on January 1, 1984. In return, AT&T was released from the 1956 Consent Decree which precluded AT&T from competing in unregulated markets (8).

The AT&T case was a major change in telecommunications regimes. Pewitt and Selwyn (1984) list three underlying reasons to 'break up Bell' (9): the increasing competition in services ('a telephone is no longer a telephone'), the increasing number of possible competitors and the economies of scale in effecting equal access to telecommunication facilities.

However, in order to create an equal playing field, the dominant position of AT&T should be relinquished: alleviating regulatory control over AT&T should be in proportion to its relative market position, says a major competitor of AT&T (10).

In the USA an important distinction is maintained between 'basic' services and 'enhanced' services. This distinction is not similar with bearer and tele-services (11). Following the FCC Computer Inquiry II, services for processing information during end-to-end transmission (such as protocol, content and format conversion) are considered enhanced. Processing that does not occur during end-to-end communication, but facilitates calling or making use of the network (call setup, call routing, call termination, and communication with the network to control or obtain information about calls) are not considered to be enhanced, but are part of basic transmission services. Under Computer Inquiry

II it is not allowed to operate both a basic and enhanced service. This led to the proposal in the ongoing discussions on Computer Inquiry III, to establish a new category 'network processing'.

Japan

On 1 April 1985 the monopoly of NTT on telecommunication service provision was ended and the market for value-added services was opened to both Japanese and foreign companies. The essence of the reform of Japan's telecommunication legislation is as follows (12):

1. NTT was subjected to private management; a private joint stock company was formed in which the government will hold at least one-third of the voting rights while foreigners are not allowed to participate;
2. telecommunication business is categorized into Type 1 and Type 2; the first provide telecommunications service by establishing their own telecommunication circuit facilities. These are defined as 'machines, pieces of apparatus, wires and cables or any other electrical facilities for the operation of telecommunications'; all other service are Type 2;
3. there are two classes of Type 2 companies: Special Type 2 which 'provides for the use of communications by many and unspecified persons, telecommunications facilities which exceed in scale the standards stipulated in the applicable cabinet ordinance, or which provides telecommunications between Japan and foreign points for the use of communications of others'; all other services are called 'General Type 2', offering VAN services to particular geographic areas, industries, organizations, leagues of companies or individual computer users.

The Japanese Telecommunications Business Law (1985) entails the general principle of competition into telecommunication services, defining telecommunications as: 'transmitting, conveying or receiving codes, sound or images by wire, radio or any other electro-magnetic method'(13).

Type 1 telecommunication businesses must obtain permission from the Japanese Ministry of Post and Telecommunications (JMPT), must have their tariffs approved, and cannot refuse the provision of service within their territory; interconnection arrangements must be approved by JMPT, and can also be ordered by JMPT. Users can demand non-discrimatory connection of their facilities as long as they conform with the technical standards.

Special Type 2 business must obtain a registration by JMPT who can order the appropriate maintenance of the telecommunications facilities in accordance with the applicable standards (14).

The setting of standards and verification of compliance has been delegated to JMPT as concerns terminal connection to Type 1 telecommunication services (15).

Western Europe

United Kingdom

On 12 April 1984 UK enacted a new telecommunications law, transforming the state monopoly of BT into a licence run telecommunications service (22 June 1984) (16). In principle any person or organization can apply for a licence, to which certain conditions can be attached. These will be controlled by the Office of Telecommunications (OFTEL) (17).

Standards have become vested in independent institutes, in particular the British Approvals Board for Telecommunications (BABT) and the British Standards Institute (BSI) (18). Licenses granted to service providers may contain specific conditions for interconnection and network access (19).

France

In 1978 Nora and Minc delivered a spectacular report on the effects of information technology on the French society (20): Computerization, they say, is a key factor in the current French crisis and telematics will become just as common as electricity. From an international point of view France is far behind and therefore an active and daring government policy is needed to maintain the national sovereignty and international competitiveness.

The report has had a profound impact and, instead of liberalization, the French government has decided in favor of a nationwide and all-inclusive 'Telematique' program. One of the most significant developments is the 'Annuaire Electronique', stimulating terminal penetration in business and consumer environments and thereby leading to a great variety of new services (21).

Germany

The position of the Deutsche Bundespost (DBP) has remained remarkably stable as a state-owned company, effecting changes mainly with respect to (22):

1. networks access: the monopoly on PABX and non-traditional terminal equipment, such as Teletex, has been abandoned; the DBP will not supply non-traditional terminal equipment;
2. changed policy with respect to leased lines, aiming at traffic based pricing ('bit-tellers'), but still forbidding third-party traffic over leased lines (although storage and processing of user information for value-added services are generally allowed);
3. approval of terminals which are not supplied by the DBP has been delegated to an independent body ('Zentralamt fur Zulassungen im Fernmeldewesen').

DBP is engaged in extensive programs such as 'Bildschirmtext', office automation, and electronic mailbox services; there is only a gradual liberalization of the market with a leading role for a state-owned DBP (23).

The Netherlands

In January 1984 the Dutch government took the following decisions with respect to telecommunication service provision (24):

1. the Dutch PTT retains in principle an exclusive right to install, maintain and operate the telecommunication infrastructure;
2. both the Dutch PTT and others can supply terminal equipment to end-users; such equipment must comply with requirements set forth by the PTT; in the initial stage, traditional telephone and telex terminal equipment remain the monopoly of PTT;
3. PTT maintains a monopoly on public telegraph, telephone, telex and data communication services; all other services via switched PTT telecommunication infrastructure can be provided by both PTT and others;
4. competing services via CATV networks are forbidden except for trials and integration studies.

A new role of the PTT necessitates a clear distinction between its social task (telecommunications as a utility) and its entrepreneurial task (telecommunications as a business). The Steenbergen Committee (1985) (25) recommends establishing a public corporation for the Dutch PTT with three separate limited companies: Post, Telecom Utility and Telecom Entrepreneur.

Telecom Utility would be in charge of the telecommunications infrastructure and would provide all bearer services with the obligation to supply leased line services upon equal and fair conditions. In particular, resale of transmission capacity on leased lines, with respect to new tele-information services, must be allowed (26).

Regulatory tasks, including terminal approval, should be vested in a separate body of the government (27).

Conclusions

The need to change telecommunication regimes in order to meet the challenges of new tele-information services is obviously recognized in most countries of the world. Three different policy lines are followed:

1. privatization of public agencies such as in the United Kingdom and Japan;
2. liberalization of the market, i.e. increasing the degree of competition by opening certain segments of the tele-communication service markets to new entrants and also by allowing traditional telecommunication service providers access to new markets; examples are the USA, Japan and the Netherlands;
3. promoting nationwide innovation programs to be executed by the traditional telecommunication service providers as in France and Germany.

Increasing the level of competition is a policy that most countries follow to a certain degree. A distinction is made between terminals and public services. In almost all cases the provision of terminals and private systems has been liberalized – PTT's participate in this market on equal terms as private suppliers (28).

As concerns services, distinctions are made between traditional services such as telex and telephony, and other services; between bearer and telecommunication services; and between basic and enhanced services. Except for the United Kingdom, the Western European countries discussed above, do not allow competition in traditional services such as telex and telephony, nor is third-party traffic via private facilities allowed.

It is doubtful that the distinction between the types of public services based on the type of data (voice, text or other data) or the type of added-value (communications or information) can be maintained in practice. In particular, the recent Japanese reform does not apply this distinction on the grounds that it is technically and operationally not possible to control this difference (29). Japanese service operators are subjected to two different regimes; on the basis of their juridical ownership of telecommunication circuit facilities (Type I business) and on the type of subscribers (Special and General Type 2 business). Regulatory requirements, however, are irrespective of the type of service.

The liberalization of terminals and services necessitate a different method for establishing standards and for the verification of compliance with standards. For this purpose separate organizations are created, but it is often difficult to obtain the necessary technical expertise which is available in the traditional service companies.

Another important issue is the interconnect policy which refers to the conditions and terms for the interconnection of different private and/or public services. These newly created bodies for setting standards and the regulation of interconnection will need time before they can be effective. This may lead to a de-facto market power of traditional telecommunication service organizations.

5.2.2 The role of traditional telecommunication administrations in the provision of message-handling services

The provision of message-handling services is on the borderline of the different regimes of telecommunications and computers. The question arises which role telecommunication service providers (PTT's and RPOA's) can or should have, in particular whether the utility-argument, discussed in section 1.3, applies to some kind of package of message-handling services.

The analysis of the re-structuring of telecommunication regimes showed that there is a definite need to set appropriate standards, to verify compliance with these standards and to effect interconnection. Distinctions between various types of new telecommunication services are difficult from a practical point of view if they are based on the type of information or the type of added-value. Moreover, the definition of standards and the verification of compliance require resources, such as technical expertise, that are generally scarce.

Within this area, the traditional telecommunication service providers may be in a unique position to provide a generic OSI/MHS service. This is defined as the interconnect-service that makes the underlying telecommunications circuit facilities 'transparent' for message transfer and allows verification with access rules. An important facility is the provision of directory services that not only provide the information about ways to establish a connection, but also about the communication and information processing capabilities of the receiving party.

PTT's and RPOA's own, or have a factual control over the telecommunication networks; moreover they have the technical expertise. They can, therefore, provide a generic OSI/MHS service package, particularly with regard to:

1. standards definition and compliance verification services;
2. network and service access;
3. directory service;
4. 'reliable' message transfer service;
5. interworking and message conversion services.

The availability of a generic OSI/MHS service is a pre-requisite for the development of new tele-information services; PTT's and RPOA's can be given a mandate to provide a generic OSI/MHS service.

5.2.3 The future of the postal service

Because electronic mail cannot be a complete substitute for physical delivery of mail parcels, the new technology entangles the issue of postal service provision. Since postal service is highly labor intensive and the opportunities for productivity improvement through further mechanization and automation are limited, postal organizations are tempted to offer additional services. Engaging Generation 2 type of electronic mail services leads to the question of telecommunications between post offices. Moreover, electronic mail service providers (fully Generation 3) may want to offer physical delivery of electronic messages for their customers (30).

In 1982 the US Congress Office of Technology Assessment (OTA) delivered one of the first impact studies of electronic mail on traditional postal service (OTA, 1982) (31). It used two quantitative computer models: first to project the levels of electronic mail volumes under different sets of assumptions and the second to forecast the revenues and costs of the US Postal Service. Figure

FIGURE 5.1 MARKET PENETRATION FOR 'HIGH BUT PLAUSIBLE' GROWTH ALTERNATIVE (US Postal Service; assuming 2% growth in underlying mail-stream)

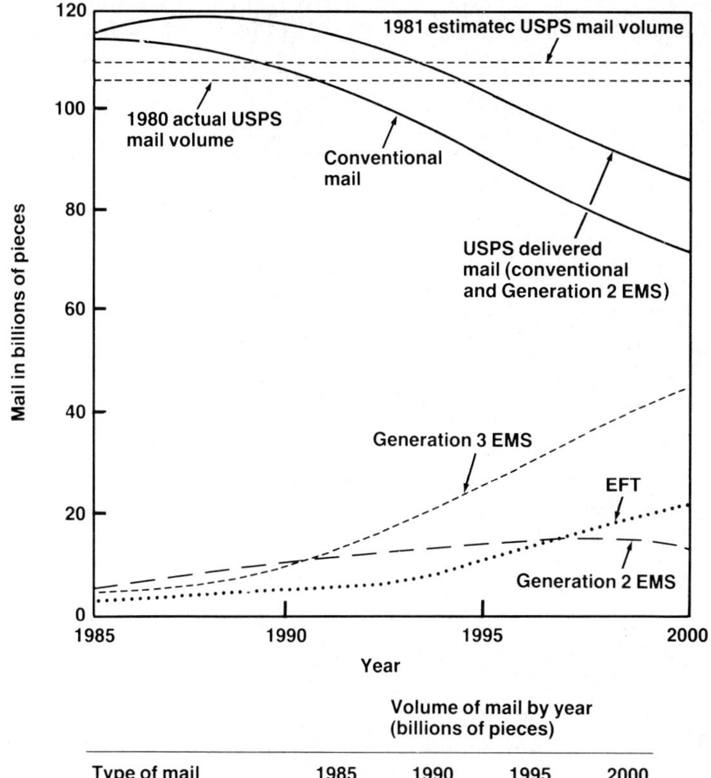

Type of mail	Volume of mail by year (billions of pieces) 1985	1990	1995	2000
Conventional	11316	10916	9073	7510
EFT (Electronic Funds Transfer)	178	492	1215	2463
Generation 2 EMS	251	905	1548	1343
Generation 3 EMS	244	934	2791	4833
Total	11989	13247	14626	16148
USPS delivered (conventional and Generation II EMS)	11577	11821	10620	8852

Source: US Congress Office of Technology Assessment (OTA, 1982)

5.1 shows the 'High But Plausible' Generation 2 EMS growth projection, based on a 2 % increase of the underlying flow of mail (32). According to this scenario, the total mail volume delivered by the US Postal Service by 1995 would be approximately the same as in 1980, but the amount of conventional mail would have declined from 94% in 1985 to as low as 62% in 1995. A sharp increase in Generation 3 EMS is projected, as high as 19% in 1995 (2% in 1985) (33).

The technological changes would result in significant losses of revenues between 1995 and 2000, assuming a successful Generation 2 EMS operation by US Postal Service. In the 21st century postal service could only maintain itself via reducing the level of service (number of delivery points, speed and frequency of delivery), or by engaging new business opportunities (34).

Blokland and Janssen (1984) (35) arrive at comparable conclusions for the Netherlands. Before 2000 the effects of substitution will be limited and mainly in the business area.

However, the long-term viability of postal service is at risk if it cannot innovate its traditional function. Moreover, traditional postal services can facilitate the acceptance of new mail technologies. Fleishman (1983) (36) says:

'If the (US) Postal Service is to survive and to be able to provide such services as the public demands of it, it must be given the freedom to compete in telecommunictions services. Given the Postal Service wide latitude to enter the telecommunications field, subject to its capacity to compete effectively, would enable the postal managers to defend it from some of the threat it faces from electronic diversion, whatever level that threat may ultimately prove to be. If the telecommunications activity is regulated by the Federal Communications Commission (FCC), the telecommunications competitors of the Postal Service will have as much opportunity to defend themselves as they do against American Telephone & Telegraph or any other of their competitors. The FCC would clearly provide an effective forum to challenge any attempt by the Postal Service either to cross-subsidize its telecommunications services with revenues from first class, or to take advantage of its tax exemption in formulating its telecommunications pricing'.

5.3 STANDARDIZATION AS A POLICY TOOL

Active government policy can overcome possible technological, institutional and cultural rigidities (37). Clearly such rigidities exist in the process of OSI/MHS innovations. Rigidities have been pointed out in the regulatory framework for telecommunication service provision (sections 5.1 and 5.2); in standardization (Chapter 4.); and in the development of intra- and inter-organizational applications of new OSI/MHS technologies (Chapter 3.). Standardization seems to have the specific role to induce innovation as well as to facilitate the transition from innovation to market diffusion. In particular, the revision of regulatory regimes for telecommunication service provision and also the user acceptance of new telecommunation systems is largely dependent on the development and enforcement of adequate standards.

Government can therefore stimulate and lead the innovation process by way of standardization policy. However, the way in which government can use standardization as a policy tool is more complicated than suggested by the distinction between business versus compliance innovation (38). In particular the availability of expertise and the industrial interests associated with standards determine the way in which standards policy can be constructed (39):

1. the availability of expertise is necessary to obtain consensus on standards; if expertise is available throughout a variety of categories, i.e. manufacturers and service providers as well as government and users, this will have a positive influence on the acceptance of innovations; in other words, standards that are accepted before diffusion of the innovation, will highly promote the innovation and diffusion processes;
2. industrial interests are another facilitator for the process of innovation; if manufacturers and service providers are the prime beneficiary of standards, they will promote the development of standards on their own account, for instance in order to to create new markets; if these interests are not that obvious, or if manufacturers and service providers will not take the lead in standards development, the user interests in forcing standardization are essentially left to government and/or a limited group of powerful users.

As shown in Figure 5.2 the above factors lead to four different scenarios for which government innovation policy should be constructed. In the liberal-technology scenario there is no agreement among technical experts, nor is there widespread technical expertise for the definition of necessary and acceptable standards; manufacturers and/or service providers take the lead in the definition and implementation of appropriate standards. Consensus on standards is also absent in the contrived-technology scenario, but in this case governments take the lead in the definition and the enforcement of standards.

FIGURE 5.2 STANDARDIZATION SCENARIOS

standardization initiator / consensus among manufacturers, service providers, users, and government	manufacturers and/or service providers	government
no consensus	liberal-technology scenario	contrived-technology scenario
consensus	market-led standards-promotion scenario	government-led standards-promotion scenario

There are two scenarios that assume consensus among manufacturers, services providers, users and government about the necessity and criteria for acceptability of standards. These assume that adequate technical expertise is available throughout industry, government and users. The market-led standards scenario leaves the market to initiate the factual development and implementation of standards; alternatively governments can take the initiative. The various scenarios lead to different government innovation policies.

Liberal-technology scenario

The basis of this scenario is the autonomy of technological developments and the 'logic' of the market to determine what it needs and to assimilate innovations as and when it is feasible.

Government policy is aimed at the generation of new technology and at the liberalization of the market, i.e. the creation of an equal playing field for the application and dissemination of technology into the market. Regulatory provisions are kept to a minimum and are intended to promote competition as an instrument for market innovation. An explicit standardization policy is not followed; moreover, standards are seen as the result of market forces (de-facto standards), not as a negotiated contract among stakeholders in the market.

As an 'equal' market player, the government will procure innovative products and services, but will not specifically favor new products. Subsidies to individual firms are granted for the generation of new technology, but not for the application of new products in the organization or for marketing.

There is a definite policy to stimulate the scientific and technological infrastructure, which is necessary for the generation of new technology; it is specifically directed toward a competitive knowledge infrastructure, which leads to a generosity of new product ideas. Science and technology policy also aims at lowering user barriers and creating a favourable attitude toward newness.

The liberal-technology scenario is completed by having a policy to encourage young starter companies, a flexible production infrastructure and a favorable financial climate.

The government will not promote public message-handling services in this scenario. Private enterprise will secure these services on a commercial basis. Antitrust law prevents market dominance while other regulations ensure fair pricing, equal access and terminal connection. A specific interconnect policy for networks will not be followed.

Contrived-technology scenario

The 'Leitmotiv' of this scenario is that innovation can be contrived, technology and market needs can be assessed, and governments can strategically manage the innovation process. Industrial and trade regulations are especially important. Monopoly positions of state-controlled firms can offer a technological base for innovation; monopolies of service providers make a controlled assessment of the innovation possible.

Technological development is stimulated as well as controlled via government procurement policies. This is also effected via subsidies to individual firms. Moreover, a specific science and technology policy supports the government strategic objectives. Small and medium size companies cater for the flexibility necessary to large companies, but are not a significant innovation factor.

Public message-handling services remain a government domain, but at the same time competition can be increased, being used as a policy to test new products or to import know-how from abroad. Interconnection of private domains will be regulated very strictly and government will approve terminals.

Consensus-standardization scenarios

Under assumption that there is common understanding of what the market needs and what technology can do, government policy aims at the standardization of new products prior to the factual market introduction. All involved parties, i.e. manufacturers, service operators, users, etc., are engaged in defining primarily functional standards. There are two alternative situations: either manufacturers and service providers agree upon the necessity of voluntary standards, or not. In the latter case government should take the lead in ensuring consensus standards. In both cases government interference is mainly the result of consulting the market players. Regulation is seen as a necessary instrument to enforce standards and can be used to cause the market to retaliate, if non-standard products are being introduced. While dominant market positions are not promoted, this need not harm innovation as long as the approval of standardized products is independent of the dominant player.

Government procurement policies follow standards rather than innovation and are applied to effect the generation of standardized new technology. Subsidies to develop standards by individual firms are given.

The scientific and technological infrastructure is very important in a consensus-standardization scenario, not so much as a means to create new ideas, but as

FIGURE 5.3 GOVERNMENT POLICIES

	liberal technology	contrived technology	consensus standardization
* regulation	minimal	all-important	follows the process
* procurement	neutral	industrial policy	standard equipment
* subsidies to individual firms	generation of new (basic) technology	generation of new (applied) technology	standards development
* science and technology infrastructure	competitive knowledge	trade-able knowledge	consensual architecture
* small and medium size companies	starter policy	flexibility for large organizations	lowering user barriers
* public message-handling service	competitive	monopoly/ supportive	government controls interconnection

a way to define overall and comprehensive architectures of technological pathways. Government policy aims at a rather uniform knowledge structure and interchangeability of ideas. The study of user functionality is promoted and users constraints are seen as a necessary evil to prevent non-standardized innovation. Policies for small and medium size companies are specifically to lower user barriers.

Government interference for the provision of a public message handling service is essential to this scenario as it provides the tool to prevent non-standard interconnection of private domains. Thus, only a limited number of public message-handling service operators will be allowed and government maintains supervision over network interconnection.

5.4 MESSAGE HANDLING POLICY IN THE NETHERLANDS

Having specialized in the traditional information-intensive industries, such as trade and transportation, the Netherlands may seek the challenge to innovate in electronic mail and message handling at an early point in time and in a way that increases its international position as information trader, and as information free-port (40).

In order to seize the opportunity, a specific policy should be adopted. This should aim at the early implementation of a public message-handling service and ensuring the branch-oriented interconnection of private domains and stand-alone terminals. In particular, the building of expertise throughout the involved market players, including users and user associations, can result in an international lead in message-handling, and should therefore have a high priority.

Three dimensions of public policy are distinguished as follows (41):

1. Generation of new technology

   - stimulate R&D on OSI/MHS, compliance test equipment and methods, message-handling facilities, complicated network arrangements, network security systems and workstations, in particular communication modules for compound document workstations;
   - promote the development of international standards and a common architecture for value-added services;

- promote a message-handling 'center of excellence' and the education and training of students in message handling technology, applications and management;

2. Market policy

- ensure the early availability of public message-handling services on the basis of government approved standards;
- stimulate the marketing of data base and other value-added services via public message-handling networks;
- issue a general information program on message-handling;
- start demonstrator projects;
- promote the use of standardized equipment for applications within the government;
- implement a governmental network for use between government agencies that can be also accessed publicly;
- promote the use by small and medium size companies via value-added services to be offered by professional associations, cooperative leagues, etc., and via subsidies for communication devices on local workstations;

3. Non-market policy

- increase competition in value-added services, ensuring that public message-handling services are being offered at a favourable and equal price;
- implement a new regulatory regime for the provision of public message-handling services and interconnect facilities as well as standards approval procedures;
- establish a regulatory regime to ensure security, reliability, integrity and privacy of message communications.

A government policy that is specifically aimed at the development and implementation of public message-handling services, can be highly rewarding if it manages to breakthrough the stalemate of networks, terminals and value-added services. Examples of possible application fields of message-handling in the Netherlands are (42):

- academic and educational networks, such as SURF (43);
- transportation networks, such as INTIS (44);
- agricultural networks;
- retail and transactional/financial networks.

Above all the Dutch policy should be international and see in a generic OSI/MHS service a challenge for the international trade of information comparable with commodity trading. The EC programs on information technology, in particular ESPRIT, can form a starting point for the building and internationalization of Dutch expertise. Western European networks, such as RARE, EARN, EC networks (INSEM, INSIS), are possible areas of message-handling interest (45).

NOTES CHAPTER 5
REGULATION AND INNOVATION POLICY

(1) Littlechild (1983) p.v.
(2) Id. p. 38.
(3) Id. p. 10-11.
(4) Cf. Vervest and Wissema (1984) p. 73-81.
(5) Id. See also Littlechild (1983) p. 6-10; Beesley (1981) p. 21-36.
(6) Cf. Uhlig (1983) p. 399-409; Lee (1982) p. 153-172; Scott (1984); see also Vervest and Wissema (1984) p. 73-77.
(7) NTIA (1983) p. 12. The first objective is: 'enhance the free (without restriction or control) flow of information across national borders, with limited exceptions condoned only for the most compelling reasons' (NTIA, op cit.).
(8) Evans (1983) p. 2-3.
(9) Vervest and Wissema (1984) p. 79-80.
(10) Id.; see also Brock, W.A., Evans, D.S., Predation: A Critique of the Government's Case in US v. AT&T, in Evans (1983) p. 41-60.
(11) Vervest and Wissema (1984) p. 77-78; cf. Vestal 'Special Report on computer Enquiry III', Telecommunications, p. 30-34, September 1985.
(12) Cf. Vervest and Wissema, p. 63-65.
(13) Telecommunications Business Law, article 2; Communications Study Group (1984).
(14) Id. articles 9, 31, 34, 38, 39; most of the regulations as given under note (64) also apply to Special Type 2.
(15) Id. article 68.
(16) Telecommunications Act (1984) articles 2, 5 and 60-69; the license was granted on 22 June 1984 in 'License Granted by the Secretary of State for Trade and Industry to British Telecommunications under Section 7 of the Telecommunications Act 1984' Department of Trade and Industry, London (1984).
(17) OFTEL has been set up under the Telecommunications Act 1984 in effect by 5 August 1984, with the following functions (cf. 'An Introduction to OFTEL', London, 1984):
- to ensure that holders of telecommunications licenses comply with their license conditions;
- to maintain and promote effective competition in telecommunications;
- to promote, in respect of prices, quality and variety the interests of consumers, purchasers and other users of telecommunication services and apparatus.

(18) Cf. Telecommunications Act 1984, article 25.
(19) Cf. 'License Granted by the Sectretary of State for Trade and Industry to Britsh Telecommunications' (22 June 1984), Part 2, article 13-14.
(20) Nora and Minc (1980, 1978).
(21) Cf. Texier, A.,'Télétel after Two Years of Commercial Service' in Online (1984) p. 33-44.
(22) Cf. DBP (1984); Schön (1984).
(23) Cf. 'Staatsvertrag uber Bildschirmtext', 23 June 1983, in Werner (1985) p. 130.
(24) Scherpenhuizen 'Taak en Functie van de PTT met betrekking tot Informatie- en Telecommunicatietechnologie' ('Task and Function of the PTT with respect to information and Telecommunication technology') (1984).
(25) Commissie Steenbergen 'Signalen voor Straks – een Nieuwe Richting voor de PTT' ('Signals for Later – a New Direction for the PTT') (1985) p. 33-38, p. 41-44.
(26) Id. p. 32.
(27) Id. p. 38-41.
(28) Cf. Appendix C of the report by the Commissie Steenbergen (note 25); Bordewijk and Arnbak

(1983) p. 5.1-5.13; Littlechild (1981) p. 40-42.
(29) Cf. Vervest and Wissema (1985) p. 64.
(30) Some of the general issues can be found in Sherman (1980) 'Perspectives on Postal Service Issues' and Fleishmann (1983) 'The Future of the Postal Service'. Note that these are American textbooks.
(31) OTA (1982); see also the related study on 'Selected Electronic Transfer Issues' (OTA, 1982a).
(32) OTA (1982) p. 38.
(33) Id.
(34) Id. p. 81-83.
(35) Blokland and Jansen (1984) p. 400-401; similar conclusions are made by Huber 'Die Folgen moderner Telekommunikationsdienste fur die Post- und Postbankdienste'.
(36) Fleishman (1983) p. 38.
(37) Cf. Rothwell and Zegveld (1985) p. 38-44.
(38) Cf. section 1.2.3.
(39) Cf. sections 3.2.3 and 3.3; cf. Vervest et al. (1986).
(40) The concept of an 'information freeport' can be compared with tax freeports: because of international competitiveness in respect of tariffs, transborder data regulations or facilities, the information freeport attracts message traffic for communications, processing of messages, or storage.
(41) Cf. section 1.3.
(42) Most of these are branch-specific and aimed at cooperation in newly-formed interorganizational networks; this necessitates a policy toward consensual standards making.
(43) Cf. SUR 'Samenwerking...Reken Maar', the provision of computer-services by scientifc research and education, 1986-1990, September 1985.
(44) 'Internationaal Transport Informatie Systeem' ('International Transport Information System').
(45) RARE 'Réseaux Associés pour la Recherche Européenne; EARN 'European Academic Research Network'.

CHAPTER 6.

TOWARDS OPEN INFORMATION NETWORKS

6.1 SUMMARY: THE MYRIAD OF INTERCONNECTIONS

The growth of computer installations and the need to exchange information among distributed computer systems, diverts communication needs from human beings toward computer systems. Electronic mail becomes not so much an aid for interpersonal (textual) information exchange, as an access method to computer processing facilities (in order to access data bases, fill-in forms, effect transactions, etc.)

The variety in computer systems, communication procedures, and networking facilities, lead to a great diversification of interconnection possibilities. One of the major changes in telecommunications is this re-orientation from human communications toward machine communications. The growth in telecommunications is in the number of computers which will be connected and not in the number of human end-users. Telecommunications will have to deal with an enormous variety of 'users', while not knowing in great detail which specific applications they support.

Sophistication of applications

Large user organizations anticipate substantial use of new mail technologies. This development must be seen as part of their office automation plans on the one side, and the construction of company wide area networks on the other side. Office automation and company wide area networks will make information available to each member of the organization, at the proper time and place, and to the extent it is needed for the correct fulfillment of organizational tasks. It will be an indispensable tool to compete and to perform in modern business.

Moreover, applications of computers in such areas as design, manufacturing, logistics, marketing and administration, necessitate access to information which may be scattered over different departments and locations of the organization. A message handling network can provide the communication capabilities for this type of inter-process control.

Increasing sophistication is also pre-eminent in inter-organizational applications. The kernel of value-added services lies in message handling technologies which support distributed applications, enabling information exchange, resource sharing and transactions. Increasingly applications become dependent on highly specific information, that must be collected and compiled from many different sources, at different locations, and which is subject to different organizational and juridical regimes.

Non-growth and additive substitution

As indicated in the ICA survey, significant changes in usage patterns of current mail technologies are expected in the coming 10 years. Traditional mail technologies exhibit almost no growth (post) or are declining (telex/TWX, analog facsimile). As a proportion of total mail volume, a significant substitution can be seen but overall, the application of new mail technologies is complementary or supplementary to current use.

Interworking between old and new mail technologies seems mandatory in order to obtain a critical user mass for the new technology, and to ignite the substitution process. However, this process will be more complicated than the present one-to-one relation: some message volume will be transferred to the newer technology, while at the same time, the latter creates new messages for the conventional technology.

Limited acceptance of new technology

A number of bottlenecks exist in market acceptance: office automation at the departmental and intra-site level has only just begun to spread through the large organizations. Company wide area networks for traditional messaging services (post, telex/TWX, analog facsimile) and for connecting large EDP centers, are often in place. However with regard to the company wide support of office automation and interprocess information handling, only the first steps have been made. Cost justification is generally difficult. Moreover, technology is still in a development stage.

Acceptance of new technology at the user level is another bottleneck. Communications capabilities of workstations, e.g. word processor, personal computer, are 'user-unfriendly', impeding the widespread use by individuals in both large and smaller organizations. Training and education of users is necessary; more intelligent interfaces between man and machine need to be built.

With regard to small and medium size companies, the use of personal computers for communications with outside resources seems a definite opportunity. It requires, however, that the appropriate networks and services are in place.

The interdependence of availability of networks and services on the one side, and the penetration of workstations on the other, is highly complicating the development of the market.

Standards-making and regulatory regimes

A major change has been effected in telecommunication standardization. On the one hand the demand for increased variety in communication leads to destandardization of products and services. On the other hand, the myriad of interconnection possibilities makes standards increasingly more desirable. From being technical standards for the quality of service, standards have become oriented toward external functionality. As the number of parties involved in the standardization process increased, the enforcement of standards became more important.

Liberalization of the telecommunications service market increases the number of service providers; at the same time, traditional service providers are challenged to enter new markets. As a result, the organizational and juridical aspects of interconnection and standardization become more complicated and less uniform across different countries in the world. New regulatory regimes are being created for telecommunication service provision, because of which aspects of data integrity are gradually becoming more pressing.

Critical objectives for innovation policy

In summary the most critical objectives for successful innovation in electronic mail are:

- the continued development of OSI/MHS and its broad acceptance by scientists, policy makers, manufacturers, and users;
- the development and implementation of network equipment and network arrangements complying with OSI/MHS;
- simple-to-operate communication capabilities for workstations and private systems;
- the widespread use of office automation in large organizations and the construction of company-wide area networks;
- the evolution of a new industry of value-added network services for facility sharing, access to information and transactions;
- the lowering of users inhibitions at the individual and organizational level, with special emphasis for the small and medium size company;
- the promotion of standards, both with respect to the speed of the standards-making processes, and to the implementation and enforcement of such standards;
- the creation of a new regulatory regime with respect to the provision of new telecommunication services, the position of traditional telecommunication service providers, and aspects of data integrity.

With the advent of OSI/MHS, a new technological trajectory has been advanced to deal with the variety in computer communications. The fundamental characteristic of this innovation can be summarized as follows:

> OSI/MHS induces the development of a systems technology that shields the variety of telecommunication networks from the application processes. This is done in such a way that distributed, formalized information systems can cooperate in order to perform a common task by 'meaningful' message exchange.

OSI/MHS constitutes the architectural design for the provision of tele-information services allowing the inter-operability of these services. As an architectural design, OSI/MHS makes a critical distinction between communication and application-oriented functions. It does so through a common boundary embodied in message handling. Via this architecture the pathway has been laid for the evolution of electronic mail toward worldwide computer-mediated message communications. Base technologies i.e. network processors, computers, workstations, operating systems and programming tools, which are generally available, will have to be applied to the OSI/MHS architecture, whereas proprietary designs should be divested as concerns their communications with the outside world ('gateway policy').

FIGURE 6.1 COMMON MESSAGE-HANDLING BOUNDARY

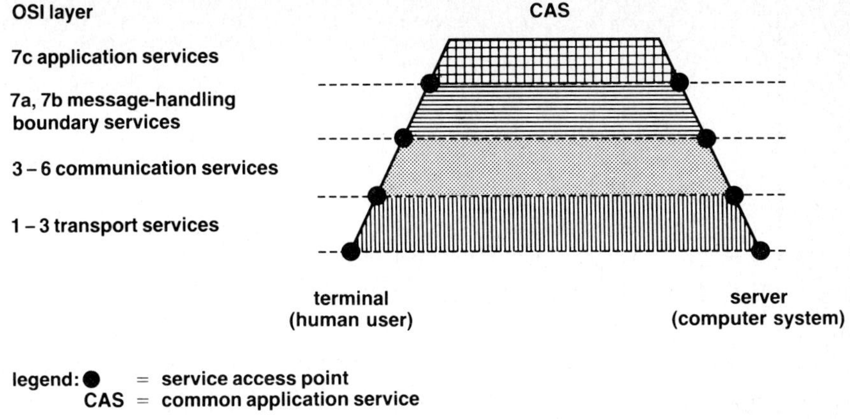

For the interconnection of distributed (computer) systems in the public area, OSI/MHS seems an unavoidable choice. Whether it will materialize itself in concrete products and services, largely depends on the future feedbacks from the market and production centers.

A winning technology?

Message-handling technology can become the leading development toward a generic value-added network. The various technologies that are currently performing the mailing functions will undergo a rapid change induced by the concept of a generic value-added network. Figure 6.2 shows a possible development path of mailing in Japan toward what has been named a 'message-handling highway' (1).

As concerns Western Europe the following trends have been forecast (2):

- telex as the leading form of electronic mail during this decade will gradually flatten off and decline in absolute numbers;
- teletex gradually taking over, in particular gaining acceptance during the beginning stages in multi-site organizations;
- facsimile increasing in use due to falling cost of equipment and developing as part of a mixed-mode, modular terminal;
- a non-significant demand for communicating wordprocessors, mailbox and store-and-forward message switching.

FIGURE 6.2 MESSAGE HANDLING DEVELOPMENT IN JAPAN

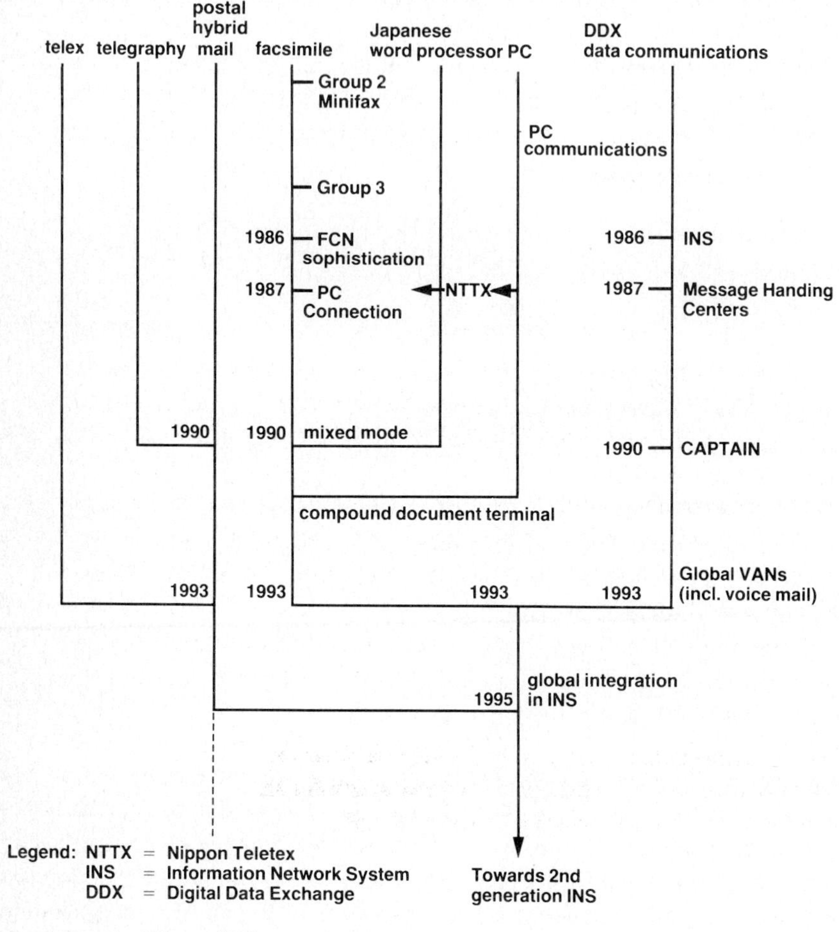

Source: Vervest and Wissema (1985)

The foregoing study exemplified the importance of electronic mail beyond the simple transport of textual messages over telecommunication networks. Message-handling technology as the kernel of the innovation process in electronic mail, will achieve the interconnection of many networks for a variety of terminal systems and document formats and can lead the way toward an integrated information network. This leads to the following requirements for new electronic mail services:

- they should be relatively independent of the network that is used;
- all kinds of terminals must be accommodated with little restrictions on the document structure capabilities;
- there should be access to a variety of resources, residing on computer systems distributed across the message-handling system;
- messages should be captured, processed and delivered according to the requirements and capabilities of the sender and recipient systems.

6.2 INNOVATION, REGULATION AND STANDARDIZATION

Since the early application of computers to message communications during the 1970s, the directions for innovation in electronic mail have been laid down along the lines of OSI/MHS. The innovation has only just begun and the interrelatedness of technological innovation and diffusion forms a complicated methodological problem.

Diffusion is not a once-for-all phenomenon, says Dosi (1984) (3). In a truly dynamic account, technological imitation within an industry is coupled with further technological innovation along a specified trajectory of technical change. There is a dynamic relation of both inter-firm diffusion of innovations (Dosi calls these the diffusion of production) and diffusion in demand, and the two are strongly interdependent (4). This strong technological inter-dependence between those industry sectors for which the new products are not final goods, is comparable with the French filiere (5). As a consequence of the industrial interrelations, a radical change in technology can transform the industrial structures: technical progress is partly endogenous, directed by the economic system, but long-run advances stem from exogenous and radical digressions of the prevailing technological paths. New companies can evolve and disrupt the entrenched oligopolistic positions of present industrial structures (6).

In the opinion of Nelson and Winter (1982) (7), technical change is primarily the result of the active searching of present firms to improve on their current technology. Economic growth is a pure selection process between competing technologies, similar to the notion of survival-of-the-fittest in biology. Firms are adaptive to changes in technology, even when it changes the industrial structure, and regardless of the source of the new technology (8).

The methodological puzzle of autonomous technology on the one side and the interdependence of technology and market on the other, is a formidable obstacle for contemporary innovation research (9). How can one be certain a new trajectory is presenting itself? And given this uncertainty, how can markets be defined that will be affected? And how can the possible influences of the new technology on the industry structure be determined? If one cannot assess the factors of change, how can one predict or recommend actions? Ultimately the forecasting and impact analysis of new technologies, and the analysis of market acceptance is a normative study of our views on the ability to change our environment and our human capabilities to do so (10).

The belief that technology has an 'inner logic' independent of anticipated user needs is a specifically dangerous one: technology is then seen as the externalization of human functions (Mumford, 1963; Van Dongen, 1982) (11), that starts having a 'phantom objectivity', a reality of itself. Reification of technology leads to alienation and problems in having technology accepted. Alternatively, the widespread adoption and diffusion of technology requires its social embodiment, the de-reification of technological changes and coherence with current social and cultural norms (12).

One particular aspect of the autonomy of technology is its science base. Modern technology requires formal scientific techniques as opposed to the crafts in the agricultural times (Freeman, 1982) (13). Rapid scientific advance is indispensable to sustain the technical progress necessary to satisfy increasingly complex human needs. Moreover, science has become highly capital intensive and demands a sophisticated educational system throughout society (14).

The marriage of science and technology has been successful in the production of new technologies, but not in facilitating the acceptance of technology. Gershuny and Miles (1983) (15) introduce the notion of 'social innovation': change that takes place in the non-formal economy because of the transformations in the means for satisfying certain households needs. In particular the new information technology, says Gershuny (16), makes it possible for consumers to add value to semi-finished products that they buy from the formal economy. In most cases this is imperative for the product's viability, e.g. the programming of a home computer. Not only technical innovation, but increasingly social innovation is needed for human progress.

The impact of standardization

If the path of development of technology is without reference to market needs, then the fate of new technologies can be compared with the proliferation and extinction of species in Darwin's theory. As a result, standardization is of little value in the early stages of development. Standards would emerge as a de-facto result of technological developments.

In the case of electronic mail, the trajectory of conventional technologies is affected by applying computer systems for mediating communications. The emphasis by telecommunications industries on consensus-standardization relates exactly to this crossing point of traditional technology on the one side, and computers on the other side. Standardization allows them to conceptualize the impacts of the changing technology on their business. This should not deny the contributions of the telecommunications industries to new developments and inventions, but rather stress that the telecommunications industries have not been able to keep up with the rapid developments in computers, either by short-sightedness or by regulatory restrictions. The new technologies will have a profound impact on the industrial structure of the telecommunications industry; standards-development processes may give time to adapt to this changing environment.

Standardization can be seen as the discriminating factor between the autonomy of technology versus the autonomy of the market. It is the borderline where all involved in the innovation process will meet. Prospective users, vested suppliers and innovators will each have different interests in making standards. For the users, standards mean the interchangeability of technology and the reduction of variety. For the traditional suppliers (or the endangered species) standards are a protection against the threatening innovation of their market. Moreover, standards allow them to manage the currently installed base of equipment and also their clientele; standards should allow the 'graceful degradation' of new technology for the installed base (17).

There are two specific circumstances that will induce the entrepreneurial innovator to opt for standardization in stead of creating an exclusive market position. First, the standardization of technology can give economic benefits. This could be because the standard increases the applicability of the new technology; establishes an international market; lets the supplier operate outside the traditional customer base; or makes production more efficient. Second, standardization can diminish development risks. It allows sharing of technical know-how; the early verification of user needs; or it supports the creation of new industrial structures to wrestle with the traditional establishment.

Although standards will benefit the prospective users of new technology, the effects of standards on their innovative behavior are little known. Standardization can block early adoption processes or endanger the adaptive capabilities of user organizations. The pace and direction of technical change may be so uncertain that standards are practically impossible. However, standards from the user point of view can be a substitute for developing in-house expertise.

On the one hand it does not seem tenable to rely on the user for guiding technology into the market. On the other hand, the conflicting interests of the entrepreneurial innovator and the industrial establishment do not ensure stable market introduction of new technology. In essence, this leaves governments to pursue a policy aimed at standards making and early implementation. This policy requires:

- adequate expertise at government level to judge the practicability and market acceptance of standards for new technology;
- the timing of functional standards before entrepreneurial or leading manufacturers have obtained a dominant position in the market;
- absence of leading-edge technologies that outdate possible standards even before prototypes could be manufactured;
- a national and international standards enforcement mechanism;
- obvious benefits to all involved for jointly agreeing to a standard.

The main benefit of an active government policy for standards-making must lie in improving the technology-market interface. Policy aimed at standards making as a means to improve technological innovation and market acceptance can be highly rewarding. Moreover, a technology-standards policy can be a means for government to monitor its prevailing industrial structures and to dam possible side effects of new technology at an early stage (18).

Technology innovation policy and regulation

A public policy with respect to standards will become of increasing importance for government to stimulate and direct technological innovation. It requires, however, a delicate and subtle balance between persuasion and coercion. Standards can only stimulate innovation if they are based on attainable goals for technical development and market change; the definition of these goals should be primarily the responsibility of the producers and consumers of technology. At the same time governments must have the ability to overcome technical, industrial and cultural rigidities. If regulatory means are used to direct technical change, one should be aware that the effects of regulation on innovation are far from clear.

Regulations can stifle innovation or mislead the active search of firms for new possibilities. Regulations impede change since the process of regulatory reform is slow and leads to uncertainty. However, it is not proven that regulations always have this negative impact (Nelson, 1982; Rothwell and Zegveld, 1981, 1985). According to Rothwell and Zegveld (1985) (19) the negative impact of regulations has been more often due to the uncertainties associated with the regulatory formulation and the implementation system rather than with the actual regulations themselves.

The regulatory framework should aim to control the external factors when using technology (i.e. safety, environmental protection, ergonomics) and provide the basis for creating industrial structures for technology to prosper, such as security, privacy and anti-trust legislation. Standards policy provides a means to involve industry and users in directing the regulatory framework at an early stage.

6.3 AN OPEN INFORMATION NETWORK

OSI/MHS is a way toward an 'open information network' which provides access to information, as much as possible independent of the physical location, technical and operational facilities which maintain the information. Accepting that information is increasingly more important for modern life (20), access to information wherever available and whenever needed is critical for human progress. Although initially conceived for interpersonal communications, electronic mail can constitute the basis for this global information access. In particular, OSI/MHS is a new paradigm for the provision of a variety of new tele-information services which allows the inter-operability of services and the mutual exchange of information between such services.

The fundamental transition toward an open information network is the use of formalized information-processing systems which act on behalf of the human being. Vallee (1982) (21) refers to this development as the 'network revolution'. At the same time standards themselves start having a reality, in that common rules for message transfer as well as for message content determine the degree in which the inter-operability between tele-information services can be achieved. Standards are definitely an inherent part of the innovation process before diffusion can take place.

The traditional telecommunication service providers will undergo the resulting changes (22) as 'de-regulation', 'de-monopolization', and 'liberalization' take place. This change can be compared with the transition in transportation systems from train to automobile (23). The railway system developed well before the road system; it provided a service directly for the human being on the basis of a time-table. The road system, however, provided a service for cars (i.e. safe roads and crossings at the interconnect points) rather than for human end-users. The human user drives the car himself, guided by direction posts. Moreover he became flexible not only with respect to time and direction, but also with respect to the goods to be transported in his vehicle.

Message-handling can give a similar flexibility for telecommunication networks as cars did for transportation. It results in fundamentally different concepts for 'service provision': the terminal need no longer be part of the service, nor need constraints on the use of the system be related with the information to be transported as was the case for traditional services such as telephony. Utility services are needed, however, with respect to the actual 'transport' (bearer services), to arrange 'crossings' (interconnect facilities), and to make road direction posts (directory services). Traditional telecommunication service providers can have an important role in making these facilities available. These are referred to in my study as the 'generic value-added network' services. OSI/MHS serves as the principle for the construction of such a network.

Analogous to the road system, the separation of the terminal (car) from the operation of the technical facilities (the road system), necessitates a body for approving and monitoring safe and available transportation service, which is independent and separate from both car manufacturers and road operators. Finally, a tariff structure is needed to guarantee return on long-term investments in infrastructural provisions.

Let me capture the kernel of my thesis as follows:

1. new developments in electronic mail are progressing along OSI/MHS, which is fundamentally a new paradigm for the design, development and organization of the technical infrastructure for message transfer (in the broadest sense of the term 'message'); at present OSI/MHS does not cover

the management of associations between distributed, formalized information-processing systems; this will become increasingly more important;

2. standardization plays a particular role in the transition from the conventional way for the provision of tele-communication services to new arrangements made necessary due to the growth of computer communications; standardization determines both user-acceptance and the possible inter-operability of new tele-information services;

3. technical expertise is a critical factor affecting both innovation and diffusion processes; the critical role of standards may be an alibi for proprietary expertise;

4. public facilities are needed for factual message transfer, for interconnection, and for directories; traditional telecommunication service providers can play a leading role in providing these services; however, an independent institution should ensure the definition, development and compliance of standards on a consensus basis;

5. government policy is an important factor, determining to a great extent the speed and direction of the innovation and diffusion processes; the existing rigidities in regulatory regimes are particular bottlenecks.

Governments can -and should- actively engage in creating international forums to develop standards; by promoting the increase of expertise in user organizations, standards can have a more positive influence on diffusion processes. This will lead manufacturers to a better understanding of user needs and aid the development of better product concepts at an early stage.

NOTES CHAPTER 6
TOWARDS OPEN INFORMATION NETWORKS

(1) Vervest and Wissema (1985) p. 11-12.
(2) Logica 'Eurodata Foundation Text & Facsimile Study – Summary of Results' (June, 1983).
(3) Dosi (1984) p. 284-295.
(4) Id.
(5) Id. p. 288.
(6) Id. p. 292-301.
(7) Nelson and Winter (1982) p. 171-172, p. 279-280, p. 400-404; see also Nelson and Winter (1977).
(8) The idea of an analytic break between the generation of innovation and the 'fate' of innovation, implies that firms will try to take advantage of any innovation that presents itself to the market place. This is similar to what Schumpeter describes as the effects of imitation; cf. Nelson and Winter (1982) p. 275-281.
(9) Cf. Mowery and Rosenberg 'The Influence of Market Demand Upon Innovation – A Critical Review of Some Recent Empirical Studies' (1979).
(10) Cf. Wissema 'Zeg Mij, Wat voor een Ding is Technologie?' ('Tell Me, What Kind of Thing is Technology?') (1982). Wissema (id. p. 22) argues in favor of a technological planning office in order:
- to search and collect signals of possible technological changes;
- to propose projects for the development and application of technical knowledge;
- to propose the elimination of bottlenecks for the creation of new branches of industry;
- to conduct an annual research of technological strengths and weaknesses, a survey of the nature and degree of availability and the application of technical knowledge in the Netherlands, compared with the international situation;
- to determine the social limiting conditions for the development and application of technical knowledge and to propose the formalization in this respect.

(11) Van Dongen 'De Invloed van Nieuwe Technologieën op Sociale Verandering' ('The Influence of New Technologies on Social Change') in Huppes and Berting (1982) p. 89-106.
(12) Cf. Keat and Urry (1975) p. 180-195.
(13) Freeman (1982) p. 15-18.
(14) Rothwell and Zegveld (1981) p. 147-174. Cf. for the impact of the science-technology infrastructure on the progress in semiconductors: Levin 'The Semiconductor Industry' in Nelson (1981) p. 9-100; ditto for computers: Goody Katz and Phillips 'The Computer Industry' id. p. 162-232.
(15) Gershuny and Miles (1983) p. 83-94, p. 121-130; cf. Gershuny (1983).
(16) Gershuny and Miles (1983) p. 173-177, p. 243-245; Gershuny (1983) p. 24-31.
(17) The compatibility of the innovation has generally been recognized as a user requirement (cf. Rogers 1983, p. 223-227), but not for the vested industry.
(18) In the ICA Questionnaire Survey we found contradictory relations between innovativeness and the use of non-standardized mail technology, but were unable to detect a consistent pattern. Cf. Vervest et al. (1986).
(19) Rothwell and Zegveld (1985) p. 43.
(20) Cf. Toffler (1980).
(21) Vallee (1982).
(22) Cf. Toffler (1985).
(23) Introduction, p. 12-13.

APPENDIX A

OPEN SYSTEMS INTERCONNECTION/ MESSAGE HANDLING SYSTEMS

A.1 INTRODUCTION

Electronic mail systems provide services to transfer electronic messages in the broadest sense of that term. As a result of the efforts of the International Federation for Information Processing (IFIP), the International Organization for Standardization (ISO) and the International Telegraph and Telephone Consultative Committee (CCITT), architectural rules and conventions have been developed for future computer-mediated message systems (1). This model for Message Handling Systems (MHS) is based on another model, i.e. the Open Systems Interconnection Basic Reference Model (OSI); collectively they form the basis for future developments in electronic mail. An understanding of this approach is necessary for evaluating the direction and possible impacts of message handling; the OSI/MHS model is reviewed in this Appendix.

Message handling facilities

A basic electronic mail system has been shown in Figure 2.1. The function of electronic mail is provided via a telecommunication system, which to this end can have a number of message handling facilities for intermediate message manipulation. Because of the application of modern computer processing, message manipulation can become increasingly more sophisticated (2). First the types of message handling facilities are explained; the second section discusses the OSI model and its relation with message handling. Finally the message-handling functional model is reviewed.

Message-handling facilities can be distinguished as follows (see Figure A.1):

1. Access, interworking and conversion facilities

Access provides the adaptation to a communications domain (defined as a communications system with limited connectivity with its environment) (3).

Network access concerns the adaptation to a specific communications network, covering:

- public switched telephone network (PSTN);
- circuit (CSPDN)- or packet (PSPDN)-switched public data network;
- the future integrated services digital network (ISDN);
- private networks, such as based on private automatic branch exchange (PABX), local area network (LAN), and global or wide area networks (WAN);
- broadband and broadcast networks, maritime and other nets.

Service access provides the necessary functions for access to a telecommunications service. CCITT distinguishes B and T-Services (Study Group XVIII, 1984) (4): a B or bearer service will transport binary information only without any further assumption on the semantics of their bitstring. For T or tele-service the semantics of the bitstring are relevant and form part of the service offered. Service access for bearer- and tele-services are quite distinct (5).

Interworking enables communication between distinct communication domains that are compatible among themselves. Compatibility refers to the commonality in functions between two or more systems. The level of incompatibility determines the scope of cooperation between the involved systems. ISO identified a broad range of cooperation subjects such as information exchange, com-

FIGURE A.1 MESSAGE HANDLING FACILITIES

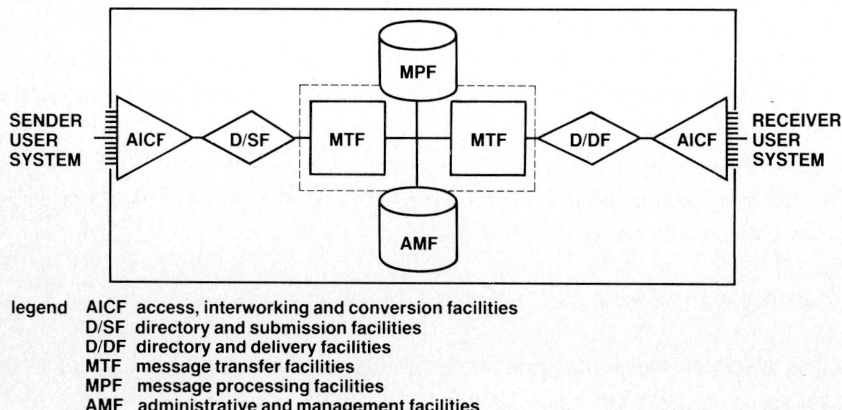

munication capabilities, data representation, data storage, process and resource management, integrity and security and program support (6).

CCITT defines in X.300 two classes of interworking: transmission-orientated interworking adapts different communication networks – note that the difference can be both from a technical, an operational or juridical point of view (7). The adaptation is restricted to the transmission capabilities of each network.

Communication-oriented interworking involves the adaptation of the datatype (the semantics of the bitstring) and is related to the complete functionality of the tele-service.

Conversion is defined as the translation and reformatting of user-designated information. It is either communications-oriented or application-oriented. Conversion of user information for the purpose of communications is needed in order to adapt the binary representation and the semantics of the data for transmission. This primarily affects the presentation of data as user-designated information.

Application data conversion is needed to adapt data for the purpose of information processing; this is very much dependent upon the meaning of the data for the connected systems.

2. Directory and submission/ delivery facilities

There are two types of directories: directories for identifying communication entities (the latter term is used by the present CCITT Study Group on directories) and directories for classifying messages.

The first directory is a tool to identify the communication entities (8) and to define their communication capabilities. It is mandatory that each communication entity can be uniquely identified by the mailing system; naming is the common method for this identification, but there are many different and often incompatible naming conventions (9).

The directory also gives information about the capabilities or properties of the communication entities. Important types of properties include:

- network or bearer service access numbers;

- tele-service access numbers;
- user and application service numbers.

The message type directory is needed to identify the message which is transported and to define the properties of the message (10). Messages can be named and their properties could be uniquely assigned, such as:

- requested message forwarding facilities;
- content and data structure types;
- conversion facilities and content processing.

For each message handling transaction, the message directory and the communication entity directory form a unique combination. A message handling transaction (MHT) is defined as: the actual submission, transfer and delivery of a message between the sending and the receiving communication entity via message handling facilities. After message submission, the message directory and the communication entity directory uniquely define which services are to be performed by the mailing system and which message handling facilities are needed. This defines among other things addressing and routing.

Submission and delivery facilities define the methods and procedures used for communication entities to fold and unfold user-messages. The submission facilities enable a sender to package application data into a message and to submit it for message transfer. Usually an envelope structure is used.

Delivery facilities enable the receiving of a message by the receiver and the unpacking of the data (user-designated information) for the application processes.

The directory in conjunction with submission/ delivery facilities controls the access by a communication entity to the facilities and authenticates the communication entities.

3. Message transfer facilities

The facilities for message transfer enable the transport of the message via telecommunication networks. It includes:

- message acceptance from sending communication entities;

- identification of sender and receiver, and of message types;
- routing to intermediate message handling facilities for message transfer, message processing or message administration/ management;
- message storage and forwarding at various points inside MHS;
- message delivery to the receiver.

4. Message processing facilities

As concerns message transfer, the contents of the message itself are irrelevant, once it has been classified by an appropriate directory labelling. Message processing provides those facilities that can add 'value' to the message itself from the point of view of the application; the contents are not neutral and can be manipulated, including:

- data-type conversion;
- interpersonal messaging support;
- format processing;
- user-information management;
- programming;
- filing and data base management.

An important notion is that of the 'active message' (11): the contents of an active message are computer instructions to activate certain application processes. Active messages are facilitators for human-to-computer and computer-to-computer message communications. Via an active message a sender may request certain application data that should be collected at another communication entity.

5. Administrative and management facilities

The control over message-handling facilities is grouped in a number of 'management domains': the set of facilities managed by an organizational or juridical entity that includes at least one message transfer facility (12). Each management domain is responsible for the administration and management of own its facilities. The functions include:

- communication entity access management and certification;
- maintenance and operational control;

- security and integrity management;
- interconnection management with other management domains;
- configuration and capacity management;
- accounting, logistics and cost allocation.

A.2 OSI/MHS ARCHITECTURE

A.2.1 OSI and layering

ISO defines the term Open Systems Interconnection as the exchange of information among systems that are 'open' to one another for this purpose by virtue of their mutual use of the applicable standards (13). System is defined as: 'a set of one or more computers, the associated software, peripherals, terminals, human operators, physical processes, information transfer means, etc., that form an autonomous whole capable of performing information processing and/or information transfer' (14).

An 'open system' should obey OSI standards in its communication with other systems: this will allow not only the transfer of information between systems but also the capability for interworking, that is to achieve a common (distributed) task (15).

The OSI architecture is an abstract model for systems interconnection. Each system is viewed as an hierarchical division of a number of subsystems. Subsystems of the same order, but belonging to different overall systems constitute a layer. Thus, the (*n*)-subsystem of system A is on the same level as the (*n*)-subsystem of system B; in this way, the (*n*)-subsystems of A and B collectively constitute a peer layer. Except for the highest layer, which represents the systems's application, each layer provides services for the next higher layer. The OSI architecture distinguishes seven layers as given in Figure A.2.

The OSI principles for layering are the following (16):

1. layers are defined so as to group similar functional entities together;
2. each layer adds to the services provided by the layer below, except for the lowest layer;
3. each layer has one or more peer protocols for the interaction among its

FIGURE A.2 THE ISO SEVEN-LAYER REFERENCE MODEL

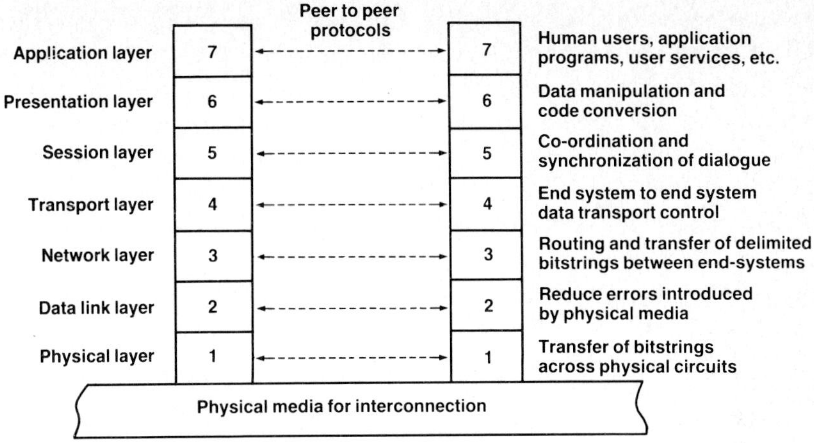

functional entities;

4. different protocols may be used within the same layer without affecting the layer service definition;
5. interactions across layer boundaries are minimized;
6. the number of layers is kept to the minimum consistent with the above principles.

An (*n*)-layer service, or (*n*)-service is defined by the service elements which are provided to the ($n+1$)-layer. For this purpose the services of the next lower layer, the (*n*-1)-layer are used. This cascade of lower layer services is viewed as an abstract machine (17).

The (*n*)-protocol defines how functional entities in an (*n*)-layer cooperate to constitute an (*n*)-service on top of an (*n*-1)-service. A relay is an intermediary function to forward data between layer-entities of different systems.

A.2.2 The application layer

All lower layer services support the cooperation among application-processes of different systems at the highest layer, i.e. the application layer. OSI defines application-process as: 'the information processing for a particular application' (18), which can be a human operator, a computer program, or anything that yields 'OSI transferrable data'.

The application layer is responsible for the transfer of information between application processes. The presentation layer is responsible for the presentation of the information to the application layer. The distinction can be thought of as one between the semantics (meaning of the information to be exchanged) versus the concrete syntax (external representation of the information being exchanged) (19). The application layer ultimately defines the meaningfulness of information, while the lower layers are dealing with the technical aspects of communications: layers 1 to 5 provide the application layer the freedom to ignore the details of the underlying communications mechanisms (20).

As said, interconnection enables open systems to cooperate and to achieve a common task. This cooperation among open systems involves the following range of activities, according to ISO (21):

1. interprocess communication, which concerns the exchange of information and activity synchronization between application-processes;
2. data representation, which concerns all aspects of the creation and maintenance of data descriptions, and data transformations for reformatting data exchanged between open systems;
3. data storage, which concerns the storage media, and the file and data base systems for managing and providing access to data stored on the media;
4. process and resource management, which concerns the means by which OSI application-processes are declared, initiated and controlled, and the means by which they acquire OSI resources;
5. integrity and security, which concern information processing constraints that must be preserved or assured during the operation of open systems;
6. program support, which is the definition, compilation, linking, testing, storage, transfer, and access to the programs executed by OSI application-processes.

The cooperation is a function at the application layer and will in most cases necessitate the access of other systems via OSI lower layer services. Common application layer services are (22):

- identification of communication entities;
- authorization to communicate;
- determining availability and authentification;
- privacy settling between communication entities;
- cost and resource allocation;
- determining acceptable quality of service;

- associate application-processes and synchronization;
- selection of dialogue discipline;
- agreements on integrity of data transfer;
- identification of constraints on data syntax.

A.2.3 Message-handling support in the application layer

Following OSI, the MHS functionality has been defined as two sub-layers of the application layer: the Message Transfer Layer (MTL), which is the lowest sublayer and which provides the Reliable Transfer Service (RTS); and the interpersonal messaging sublayer, or Cooperating User Agent Layer (UAL), providing the Interpersonal Messaging service (IPM). The latter is an optional layer on top of MTS and supports message exchange between human beings.

Figure A.3 shows the message-handling protocol structure (23). The Message Transfer Layer contains two types of entities. The first is the Submission/Delivery Entity (SDE): it performs the functions that can be directly associated with an individual user of MH facilities. The second entity type is the Message Transfer Agent Entity (MTAE) which performs the functions associated with the message transfer itself. Related to this layer are two protocols:

* P1 is a relay protocol for the exchange of messages between MTAE's
* P3 is an access protocol for submission and delivery of messages.

The second sublayer (UAL) provides inter-personal messaging services. User Agent is defined as an application process in a device that supports an individual user in preparing, storing, sending and receiving messages. The User Agent Entity (UAE) embodies those aspects that concern the content of the message and the cooperation with other UA's (24). Related to this layer are the following protocols:

* P2 defines the cooperation between UAE's and enables the interpersonal messaging service
* Pt defines the cooperation between the device embodying the UA and the UAE. Pt can be seen as the terminal protocol by which a user accesses the UA.

Note that P2 /Pt can be seen as one of a class of services which can be provided on top of the MTL. Other sets of protocols can be defined (so called Pc protocols) for message based information transfer other than inter-person.

FIGURE A.3 MESSAGE HANDLING PROTOCOL STRUCTURE FOLLOWING OSI/MHS

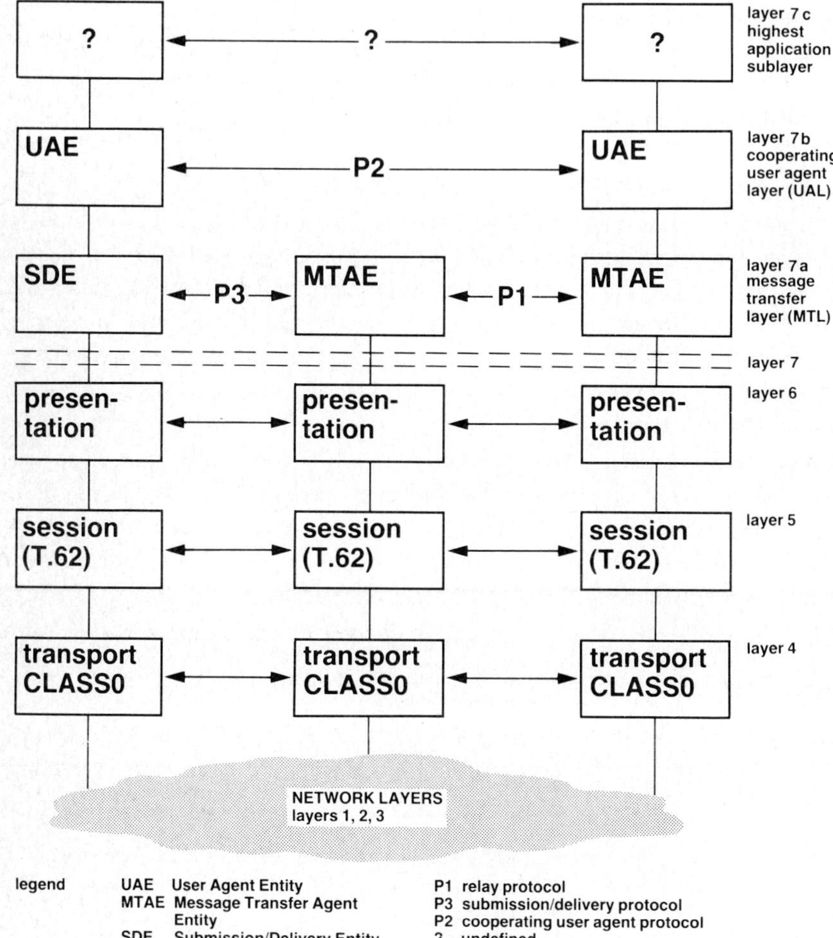

A.3 MESSAGE HANDLING MODEL OF CCITT

A.3.1 Functional model

The following 1984 Recommendations of CCITT describe the OSI/MHS model (25):

OSI

X.200	Reference model of open systems interconnection for CCITT applications
X.210	OSI layer service definition conventions
X.213	Network service definition (for OSI for CCITT applications)
X.214	Transport service definition
X.215	Session service definition
X.224	Transport protocol specification
X.225	Session protocol specification

MHS

X.400	Systems model-service elements
X.401	Basic service elements and optional user facilities
X.408	Encoded information-type conversion rules
X.409	Presentation transfer syntax and notation
X.410	Remote operations and reliable transfer service
X.411	Message transfer layer
X.420	Interpersonal messaging user-agent layer
X.430	Access protocol for teletex terminals

The objective of the CCITT message handling model is to enable subscribers to exchange messages on a store-and-forward basis. Two MH services are defined: Interpersonal Messaging (IPM) which supports interpersonal communications, including communication with existing CCITT telex and telematic services. Message Transfer (MT) service which supports general, application-independent message transfer. MT and IPM services can act as the interconnection services for CBMS and other proprietary mail systems.

The functional model is as given in Figure A.4 (X.400). A user can be any type of application-process, either a human being or a computer process. The five basic elements in this model are: message origination, submission, relaying, delivery and reception.

Relaying is typically the function between a number of MTA's. Submission and delivery are located inside an application-process, the UA. A user interacts with the UA for both sending processes and for receiving processes. The UA on its behalf interacts with the MTA. The UA functions for Inter Personal Messaging (IPM-UA) are (X.400) (26):

1. provide the functions for message preparation;

FIGURE A.4 FUNCTIONAL VIEW OF THE MHS MODEL

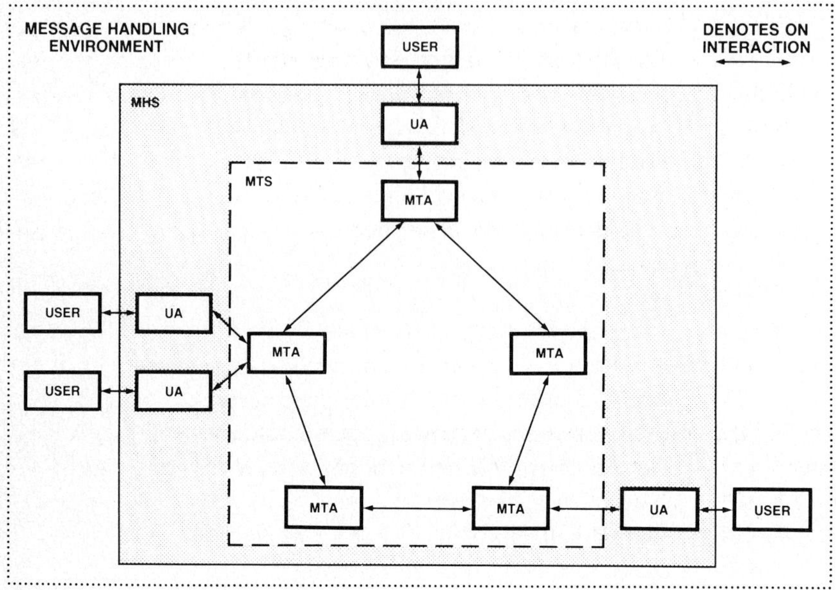

2. interact with the MTS for submission;
3. interact with the MTS for delivery;
4. present messages to the user;
5. cooperate with other IPM UA's;
6. perform additional message preparation and manipulation functions.

The complexities around the above simple model are basically the following (see Figure A.5):

- various physical implementations may be used. These have all to be defined and the interconnections must be associated.
- message data types will vary and the relation and possible conversion between data types has to be defined. The system can be used for all sorts of message communications; the syntax and semantics of such communication has to be defined. At present only Inter Personal Messaging (IPM) has been defined with P2 as the first of the Pc class of protocols.

- existing and new messaging services, such as telex and telematic services must be able to communicate with the users of the MHS.
- different organizational and juridical owners may be involved. X.400 (27) defines three classes: user-to-Administration supplied UA, private UA-to-Administration MTA, and private MTA-to-Administration MTA. There is also a private MTA-to-private MTA class, although not covered by Series X.400 (28). For the purpose of interconnection, the term Management Domain is used: a system of at least one MTA and zero or more UA's owned by an Administration or other organizational/ juridical entity is called Management Domain (MD).

A.3.2 The IP-message

The MTS transfers messages that should have an envelope, representing the control information for the MTS- and a content, which is 'transparent' user information and/or status report information. Each message is assigned a unique number upon submission by the UA.

The envelope identifies the originator and recipient names (O/R names, X.400); the O/R names are given to the UA's and as a minimum they should unambiguously identify the MD of the recipient UA. This is called the base attribute set (29). The development of directory system capabilities will enable the routing information to be derived for other base attribute sets; the objective is a universal support of naming conventions, eliminating dependence on hierarchical naming structures (30).

In general the contents of the message are undefined except for Inter-Personal (IP) messages. The IP message consists of:

- a single envelope with the O/R names
- one or more content parts separated via headings
- one or more body parts that belong to a specific heading

The recognized body part types are (31): IA5, telex, digitally encoded voice, Group 3 facsimile (T.4), Text Interchange Format 0 (TIF0, T.73), Teletex (T.61), Videotex (T.100, T.101), encrypted, nationally defined, forwarded IP-message, Simple Formattable Document (SFD), Text Interchange Format 1 (TIF1, T.73).

FIGURE A.5 EXAMPLE OF A COMPLEX MESSAGE HANDLING ENVIRONMENT

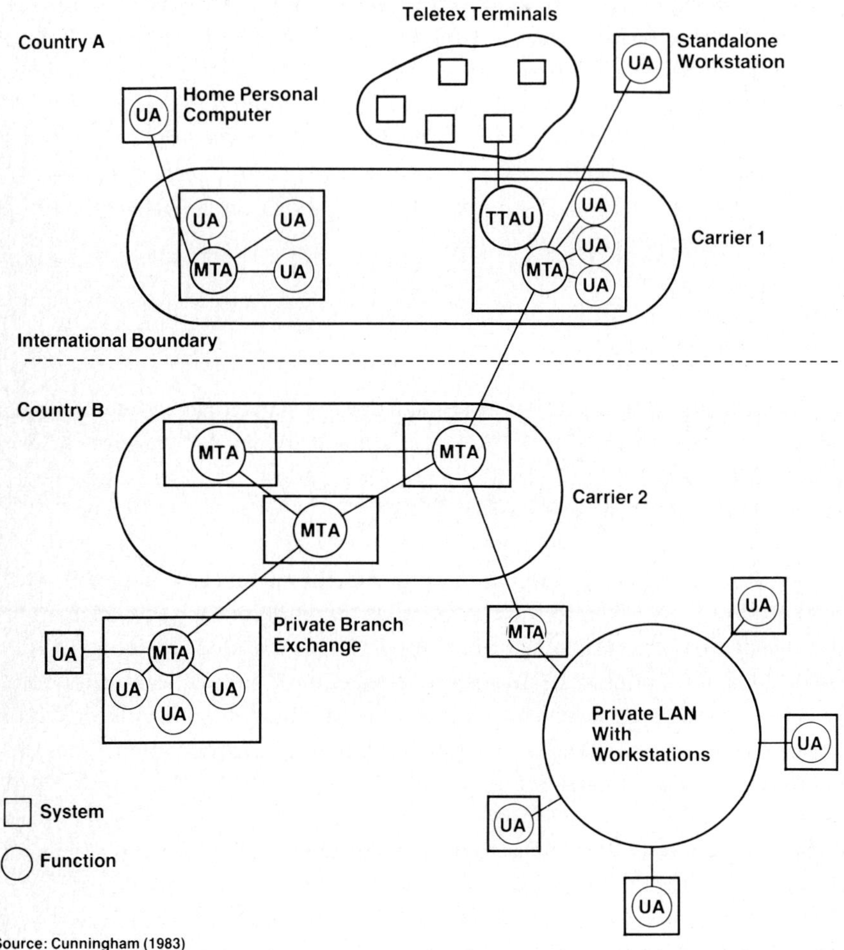

Source: Cunningham (1983)

The nature and attributes, or type of each body part can be defined independently. In this way IP services can be distinguished among various body parts of the same message; it also enables data type conversion, see Figure A.6 (32).

FIGURE A.6 ENCODED INFORMATION-TYPE CONVERSION

To / From	TLX	IA5 Text	TTX	G3 Fax	TIF-0	TIF-1	VTX	Voice	SFD
TLX	–	a	a	a	a	a	b	a	a
IA5 Text	b	–	b	a	a	b	b	b	a
TTX	b	b	–	a	a	a	a	b	b
G3 Fax	c	c	c	–	a	a	c	c	c
TIF-0	c	c	c	a	–	a	c	c	c
TIF-1	b	b	b	a	a	–	b	b	b
VTX	b	b	b	a	a	FS	FS	FS	FS
Voice	c	c	c	c	c	c	c	FS	c
SFD	b	b	a	a	a	a	b	FS	–

LEGEND

–	NO CONVERSION
a	POSSIBLE WITHOUT LOSS OF INFORMATION
b	POSSIBLE WITH LOSS OF INFORMATION
c	IMPRACTICAL
FS	FOR FURTHER STUDY
TLX	TELEX
IA5	INTERNATIONAL ALPHABET 5
TTX	TELETEX
G3 FAX	GROUP 3 FACSIMILE
TIF 0 1	TEXT INTERCHANGE FORMAT-0 1
VTX	VIDEOTEX
SFD	SIMPLE FORMATTABLE DOCUMENT

Source: X.408

A.3.3 Message Handling System service elements

Two sets of MH service elements have been defined in X.401: message transfer service elements (see Table A.1) and inter-personal messaging service elements (see Table A.2).

A.3.4 P5 protocol

One of CCITT's design requirements is the accommodation of telex and telematic messaging services in the IPM services, as shown in Figure A.7. The IPM system comprises the MTS, a specific class of cooperating UA's, and access to telex and CCITT Telematic services; its users are typically people and not com-

TABLE A.1 MESSAGE TRANSFER SERVICE ELEMENTS

Service group	Service Elements	Categorization
Basic service	Access management (UA-MTA)	Basic
	Content type indication	"
	Converted indication	"
	Delivery time stamp indication	"
	Message identification	"
	Non-delivery identification	"
	Original encoded information types indication	"
	Registered encoded information types	"
	Submission time stamp indication	"
Submission and delivery options	Alternate recipient allowed	E-PM
	Deferred delivery	"
	Deferred delivery cancellation	"
	Delivery notification	"
	Disclosure of other recipients	"
	Grade of delivery selection (three priorities)	"
	Multi-destination delivery	"
	Prevention of non-delivery notification	A-PM
	Return of contents	"
Conversion options	Conversion prohibition	E-PM
	Explicit conversion	A-PM
	Implicit conversion	A-CPT
Query options	Probe	E-PM
Status and inform options	Alternate recipient assignment	A-CPT
	Hold for delivery	"

legend
- E essential optional user facility
- A additional optional user facility
- PM selectable on a per-message basis
- CPT agreed for a contractual period of time

Source: X.400, X.401

puter systems (33). P5 has been specified for this purpose (laid down in X.430). Protocols for other services such as telex, interactive videotex and facsimile have been left for further study. Note that videotex is viewed within CCITT

TABLE A.2 INTERPERSONAL MESSAGING SERVICE ELEMENTS

Service group	Service elements	Categorization CES	CER
Basic IPM service	Basic MT service elements:		
	Access management (UA-MTA)	Basic	Basic
	Content type indication	”	”
	Converted indication: P2	”	”
	Delivery time stamp indication	”	”
	Message identification	”	”
	Non-delivery notification	”	”
	Original encoded information types indication	”	”
	Registered encoded information types	”	”
	Submission time stamp indication	”	”
	Specific IPM service elements:		
	IP-message identification	Basic	Basic
	Typed body	”	”
Submission and delivery options	MT submission and delivery options:		
	Alternate recipient allowed	A-PM	A-PM
	Deferred delivery	E-PM	N/A
	Deferred delivery cancellation	A-PM	”
	Delivery notification	E-PM	”
	Disclosure of other recipients	IXA-PM	E-PM
	Grade of delivery selection	E-PM	N/A
	Multi-destination delivery	”	”
	Prevention of non-delivery notification	A-PM	N/A
	Return of contents	”	”
Conversion options	MT conversion options:		
	Conversion prohibition	E-PM	E-PM
	Explicit conversion	A-PM	N/A
	Implicit conversion	A-CPT	A-CPT
Query option	MT option: Probe	A-PM	N/A
Status and inform	MT status and inform options:		
	Alternate recipient indication	A-CPT	A-CPT
	Hold for delivery	”	”
Cooperating IPM UA action options	Blind copy recipient indication	A-PM	E-PM
	Non-receipt notification	A-PM	A-PM
	Receipt notification	”	”
	Auto-forwarded indication	”	E-PM

TABLE A.2 INTERPERSONAL MESSAGING SERVICE ELEMENTS

Service group	Service elements	Categorization CES	CER
Cooperating IPM UA information conveying options	Originator indication	E-PM	E-PM
	Authorizing users indication	A-PM	”
	Primary and copy recipients indication	E-PM	”
	Expiry date indication	A-PM	”
	Cross-referencing indication	”	”
	Importance indication	”	”
	Obsoleting indication	”	”
	Sensitivity indication	”	”
	Subject indication	E-PM	”
	Replying IP-message indication	”	”
	Reply request indication	A-PM	”
	Forwarded IP-message indication	”	”
	Body part encryption indication	”	”
	Multi-part body indication	”	”

legend
E essential optional user facility
A additional optional user facility
PM selectable on a per-message basis
CPT agreed for a contractual period of time

Source: X.400, X.401

as an interactive, rather than a messaging terminal. As such, it is seen as an input/output device for interacting with a UA but not as the UA itself (34).

The P5 protocol defines the access of a Teletex terminal to the MTS via a Teletex Access Unit (TTXAU). (See Figure A.8). It is a Pt-type protocol, specifying the interaction between user and UA (the Teletex terminal); it also defines P1 and P2 elements for the interaction between TTXAU and the MTAE and UAE. Due to the specific Recommendations for basic Teletex terminals, control information able to be read by human beings is needed for message submission and delivery (35).

The TTXAU can have a Document Storage to provide simple mailbox facilities for its users. It caters for a ‘hold for delivery’ function. The Teletex terminal can receive delivery-status notifications and exception reports via the TTXAU IP-messages from other UA’s.

FIGURE A.7 INTERPERSONAL MESSAGING SYSTEM – TELEX AND TELEMATIC SERVICES

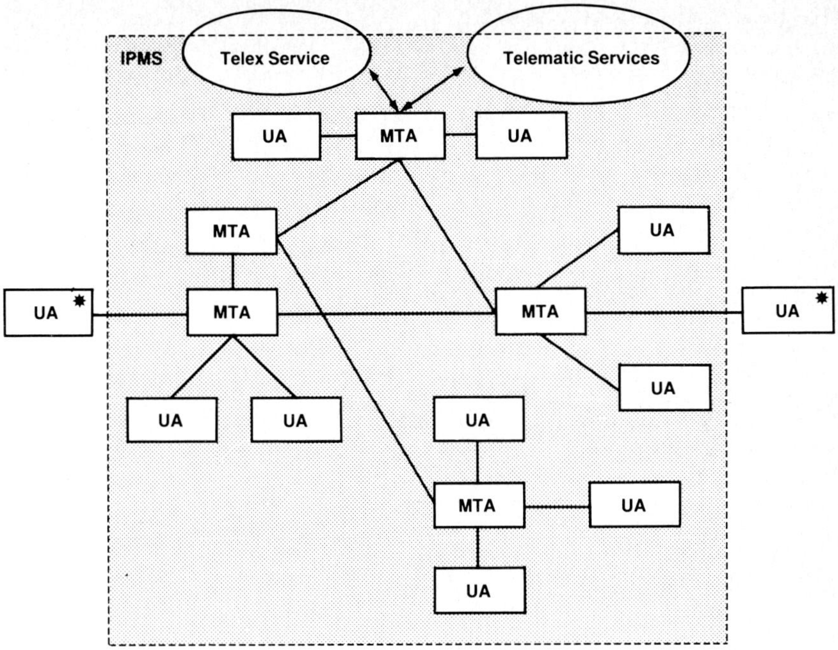

Source: X.400 ✱ NON-P_2 UA

FIGURE A.8 TELETEX ACCESS PROTOCOL ENVIRONMENT

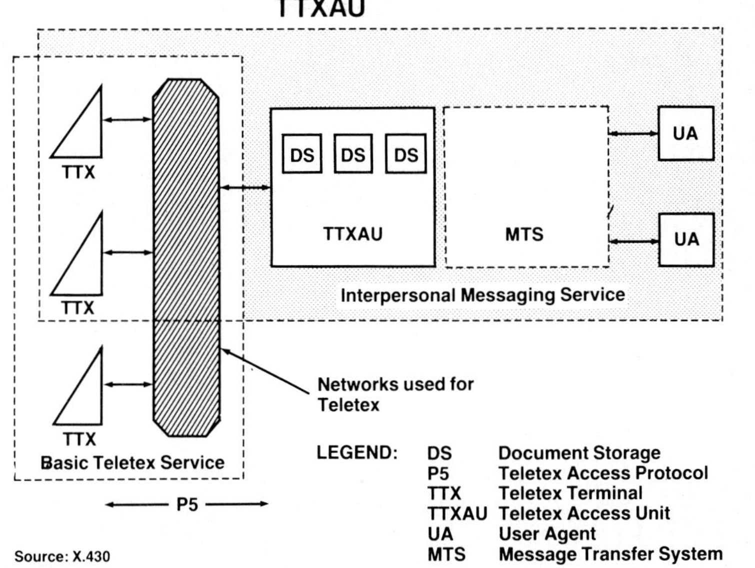

Source: X.430

The only mandatory type of message that a Teletex terminal should be able to send is a 'send document'. Optional send messages are probe, registration, and receipt acknowledgement (36).

NOTES APPENDIX A

(1) Cf. Uhlig (1983) p. 399-400; Vervest (1985); also the work of the ECMA and NBS have contributed to the design and the development of OSI/MHS.
(2) Vallee (1984) p. 137-149; Licklider and Vezza, 'The Utility of Electronic Message Systems' in Kahn, Vezza and Roth (1981) p. 11-32.
(3) Vervest (1985) p. 190.
(4) Id. p. 90-93.
(5) Id. p. 155-158.
(6) IS 7498 (ISO, 1983) p. 2-6.
(7) Vervest (1985) p. 194-195.
(8) Steedman, D., CCITT Study Group VII, Draft Recommendations X.ds0 – X.ds6, Directory Systems, May 1985, define directory services and structure.
(9) Cf. Vervest (1985) p. 166-167.
(10) This type of directory has not been included in the Draft Recommendations on directories, but they are implicitly needed because of encoded information-type identification (X.408).
(11) Vittal, J., Active Message Processing: Messages as Messengers' in Uhlig (1981) p. 175-195. Cf. McQuillan (1984) p. 4.14-4.23.
(12) X.400 p. 9-14.
(13) ISO (1983) p. 2; cf. Day and Zimmermann (1983).
(14) ISO (1983) p. 4.
(15) Id. p. 6.
(16) Id. p. 9-12, p. 39-40; Day and Zimmermann (1983) p. 1335-1338; Vervest (1985) p. 149-152.
(17) Id.
(18) ISO (1983) p. 4-6; cf. Bartoli (1983) p. 1404-1408.
(19) Vervest (1985) p. 150.
(20) Cf. Meijer and Peeters (1982) p. 14-28.
(21) ISO (1985) p. 6.
(22) Id. p. 42-43; cf. Tanenbaum (1981) p. 440-482.
(23) Cf. Cunningham (1983) p. 1427.
(24) Id. p. 1426; cf. Myer (1983) and the proceedings 'The Future of Electronic Mail and Messaging' 13-15 November 1984, Electronic Mail Association (EMA 1984).
(25) Approved by the CCITT Plenary Assembly, October 1984; for an overview see Vervest (1985) p. 163-186, p. 207-212.
(26) X.400 p. 7-8.
(27) X.400 p. 9-13.
(28) Id.
(29) X.400 p. 15-19.
(30) Cf. Steedman, D., CCITT Study Group VII, Draft Recommendations X.ds0 – X.ds6, Directory Systems, May 1985.
(31) X.400 p. 27-33.
(32) X.408 p. 62-69.
(33) X.400 p. 7-8, X.430.
(34) Id.
(35) Cf. X.430.
(36) Id.

APPENDIX B

APPLICABLE CCITT AND ISO DOCUMENTS
(with reference to Figure 4.1)

INTERNATIONAL TELEGRAPH AND TELEPHONE CONSULTATIVE COMMITTEE (CCITT) RECOMMENDATIONS

F. and T. Series

F.40x,4,2	Message Handling System Services (Draft Recommendations)
F.200	Teletex service
F.201	Interworking between the Teletex service and the telex service
F.300	Videotex service
F.350	Provisions applying to the operation of an international public automatic message switching service for equipment utilizing the International Telegraph Alphabet No.1
T.0	Classification of facsimile apparatus for document transmission over the public networks
T.2	Standardization of Group 1 facsimile apparatus for document transmission
T.3	Standardization of Group 2 facsimile apparatus for document transmission
T.4	Standardization of Group 3 facsimile apparatus for document transmission
T.5	General aspects on Group 4 facsimile apparatus
T.50	International Alphabet No.5
T.51	Coded character sets for Telematic services
T.60	Terminal equipment for use in the Teletex service
T.61	Character repertoire and coded character set for the international Teletex service
T.62	Control procedures for Teletex and Group 4 facsimile services
T.63	Provisions for verification of Teletex terminal compliance
T.70	Network-independent basic transport service for the Telematic services
T.71	LAPB extended for half-duplex physical level service
T.72	Terminal capabilities for mixed-mode of operation
T.73	Document interchange protocol for the Telematic services

T.90	Teletex requirements for interworking with the telex service
T.91	Teletex requirements for real-time interworking with the telex service in a packet switching network environment
T.100	International information exchange for interactive videotex
T.101	International interworking for videotex services

V. Series

V.21	300 bits per second duplex modem standardized for use in the general switched telephone network
V.22	1200 bits per second duplex modem standardized for use in the general switched telephone network and on point-to-point 2-wire leased telephone-type circuits
V.22bis	2400 bits per second duplex modem using the frequency division technique standardized for use in the general switched telephone network and on point-to-point 2-wire leased telephone-type circuits
V.23	600/1200 baud modem standardized for use in the general switched telephone network
V.24	List of definitions for interchange circuits between data terminal equipment and data circuit-terminating equipment
V.25	Automatic answering equipment and/or parallel automatic calling equipment on the general switched telephone network including procedures for disabling of echo control devices for both manually and automatically established calls
V.25bis	Automatic calling and/or answering equipment on the general switched telephone network (GSTN) using the 100-series interchange circuits
V.26bis	2400/1200 bits per second modem standardized for use in the general switched telephone network
V.26ter	2400 bits per second duplex modem using the echo cancellation technique standardized for use on the general switched telephone network and on point-to-point 2-wire leased telephone-type circuits
V.27ter	4800/2400 bits per second modem standardized for use in the general switched telephone network
V.32	A family of 2-wire, duplex modems operating at data signalling rates of up to 9600 bit/s for use on the general switched telephone networks and on leased telephone-type circuits
V.100	Interconnection between public data networks (PDNs) and the

	public switched telephone network (PSTN)
V.110	Support of data terminal equipments (DTEs) with V-series type interfaces by an integrated services digital network (ISDN)

X. Series

X.3	Packet assembly/disassembly facility (PAD) in a public data network
X.21	Interface between the data terminal equipment (DTE) and the data circuit-terminating equipment (DCE) for synchronous operation on public data networks
X.21bis	Use on public data networks of data terminal equipment (DTE) which is designed for interfacing to synchronous V-Series modems
X.22	Multiplex DTE/DCE interface for user classes 3-6
X.25	Interface between the data terminal equipment (DTE) and data circuit-terminating equipment (DCE) for terminals operating in the packet mode and connected to public data networks by dedicated circuit
X.28	DTE/DCE interface for a start-stop mode data terminal equipment accessing the packet assembly/disassembly facility (PAD) in a public data network situated in the same country
X.29	Procedures for the exchange of control information and user data between a packet assembly/disassembly (PAD) facility and a packet mode DTE or another PAD
X.30	Support of X.21 and X.21bis based data terminal equipments (DTEs) by an integrated services digital network (ISDN)
X.31	Support of packet mode terminal equipment by an ISDN
X.32	Interface between data terminal equipment (DTE) and data circuit-terminating equipment (DCE) for terminals operating in the packet mode and accessing a packet switched public data network through a public switched telephone network or a circuit switched public data network
X.71	Decentralized terminal and transit control signalling system on international circuits between synchronous data networks
X.75	Terminal and transit call control procedures and data transfer system on international circuits between packet-switched data networks
X.200	Reference Model for Open Systems Interconnection for CCITT Applications

X.210	Open Systems Interconnection (OSI) Layer Service Definition Conventions
X.213	Network Service Definition for Open Systems Interconnection (OSI) for CCITT Applications
X.214	Transport Service Definition for Open Systems Interconnection (OSI) for CCITT Applications
X.215	Session Service Definition for Open Systems Interconnection (OSI) for CCITT Applications
X.224	Transport Protocol Specification for Open Systems Interconnection (OSI) for CCITT Applications
X.225	Session Protocol Specification for Open Systems Interconnection (OSI) for CCITT Applications
X.244	Procedure for the exchange of protocol identification during virtual Call Establishment on Packet Switched Public Data Networks
X.250	Formal description techniques for data communications protocols and services
X.300	General principles and arrangements for interworking between public data networks and other public networks
X.310	Procedures and arrangements for data terminal equipments accessing circuit switched digital data services through analogue telephone networks
X.400	Message handling systems: system model-service elements
X.401	Message handling systems basic service elements and optional user facilities
X.408	Message handling systems: encoded information type conversion rules
X.409	Message handling systems: presentation transfer syntax and notation
X.410	Message handling systems: remote operations and reliable transfer service
X.411	Message handling systems: message transfer layer
X.420	Message handling systems: interpersonal messaging user agent layer
X.430	Message handling systems: access protocol for Teletex terminals
X.ds1	Directory systems: model and service elements (Draft Recommendation January 1986)

X.ds2	Directory systems: information framework (Draft Recommendation January 1986)
X.ds3	Directory systems: protocols (Draft Recommendation January 1986)
X.ds4	Directory systems: standard attribute types (Draft Recommendation January 1986)
X.ds6	Directory systems: suggested naming practices (Draft Recommendation January 1986)
X.ds7	Directory systems: authentication framework (Draft Recommendation January 1986)

I. Series

I.120	Integrated Service Digital Networks (ISDNs)
I.210	Principles of Telecommunication services supported by an ISDN
I.211	Bearer services supported by an ISDN
I.212	Teleservices supported by an ISDN
I.310	ISDN – Network functional principles
I.430	Basic user-network interface – Layer 1 specification
I.431	Primary rate user-network interface – Layer 1 specification
I.440	ISDN user-network interface data link layer – General aspects
I.441	ISDN user-network interface data link layer specification
I.450	ISDN user-network interface layer 3 – General aspects
I.451	ISDN user-network interface layer 3 specification

INTERNATIONAL ORGANIZATION FOR STANDARDIZATION (ISO) INTERNATIONAL STANDARDS (IS), DRAFT INTERNATIONAL STANDARDS (DIS) AND DRAFT PROPOSALS (DP)

IS 7498	Information processing systems – Open Systems Interconnection – Basic Reference Model (1984)
IS 1538	Programming languages – Algol 60 (1984)
IS 1539	Programming languages – Fortran (1980)
IS 1989	Programming languages – Cobol (1985)
IS 6160	Programming languages – PL/1 (1979)
IS 6373	Programming languages – Basic (1984)
IS 6937	Information processing – Coded character sets for text communication (1983)

DIS 2110 Data communication – 25-pin DTE/DCE interface connector and pin assignment
DIS 7776 Information processing systems – Data communications – High-level data link control procedures – Description of the X.25 LAPB compatible DTE data link procedures
DIS 8072 Information processing systems – Open Systems Interconnection – Transport service definition
DIS 8073 Information processing systems – Open Systems Interconnection – Connection oriented transport protocol specification
DIS 8208 Data communication – X.25 packet level protocol for data terminal equipment
DIS 8326 Information processing systems – Open Systems Interconnection – Basic connection oriented session service definition
DIS 8327 Information processing systems – Open Systems Interconnection – Basic connection oriented session protocol specification
DIS 8348 Information processing systems – Data communications – Network service definition
DIS 8473 Information processing systems – Data communications protocol for providing the connectionless-mode network service
DP 8485 Programming languages – APL
DP 8505 Information processing systems – Text communication – Functional description and service specification for message oriented text interchange system (MOTIS)
DP 8509 Information processing systems – Open Systems Interconnection – Service conventions
DP 8571 Open Systems Interconnection – File transfer, access and management (Parts 1, 2, 3, 4)
DIS 8602 Information processing systems – Open Systems Interconnection – Protocol for providing the connectionless-mode transport service
DP 8613 Information processing systems – Text preparation and interchange – Document structures (Parts 1, 2, 3, 4)
DP 8632 Information processing systems – Computer graphics metafile for transfer and storage of picture description information (Parts 1, 2, 3, 4)
DP 8648 Information processing systems – Data communications – Internal organization of the network layer
DP 8649 Information processing – Open Systems Interconnection – Definition of common application service elements (Parts 1, 2, 3)
DP 8650 Information processing – Open Systems Interconnection – Specifi-

	cation of protocols for common application service elements (Parts 1, 2, 3)
DP 8651	Graphical Kernel System (GKS) language bindings (Part 1 – Fortran; part 2 – Pascal; part 3 – Ada)
DIS 8652	Programming languages – Ada
DP 8802/1	Local area networks – Part 1: General introduction
DP 8802/2	Information processing systems – Local area networks – Part 2: Logical link control
DP 8802/3	Information processing systems – Local area networks – Part 3: Carrier sense multiple access with collision detection
DP 8802/4	Information processing systems – Local area networks – Part 4: Token-passing bus access method and physical layer specification
DP 8802/5	Information processing systems – Local area networks – Part 5: Token ring access method and physical layer specification
DP 8802/6	Information processing systems – Local area networks – Part 6: Slotted ring access method and physical layer specification
DP 8822	Open Systems Interconnection – Presentation service definition
DP 8823	Open Systems Interconnection – Presentation protocol specification
DP 8824	Information processing – Open Systems Interconnection – Specification of abstract syntax notation one (ASN.1)
DP 8825	Information processing – Open Systems Interconnection – Specification of basic encoding rules for abstract syntax notation one (ASN.1)
DP 8831	Open Systems Interconnection – Job transfer and manipulation concepts and services
DP 8832	Open Systems Interconnection – Specification of the basic class protocol for job transfer and manipulation
DP 8878	Information processing systems – Data communications – Use of the X.25 to provide the open systems interconnection connection-oriented network service
DIS 8879	Information processing – Text and office systems – Standard Generalized Markup Language (SGML)
DP 8886	Information processing systems – Data communications – Data link service definition for OSI
DP 8907	Information processing systems – Database languages – Network database language
DP 9007	Information processing systems – Concepts and terminology for the conceptual schema and the information base
DP 9040	Information processing – Open Systems Interconnection – OSI

virtual terminal service

DP 9041 Information processing – Open Systems Interconnection – OSI virtual terminal protocol

DP 9063/1 Information processing – Text preparation and interchange equipment – Text charts and text patterns – Part 1: Facsimile equipment

DP 9063/2 Information processing – Text preparation and interchange equipment – Text charts and text patterns – Part 2: Teletex equipment

DP 9064/1 Information processing – Text and office systems – Minimum information to be included in specification sheets – Part 1: Facsimile equipment

DP 9064/2 Information processing – Text and office systems – Minimum information to be included in specification sheets – Part 2: Character coded text and office systems including equipment suitable for participating in the CCITT telex and Teletex services

DP 9075 Information processing systems – Programming languages – Relational database language

BIBLIOGRAPHY

Abramowitz, M., Stegun, I.A., (editors), *Handbook of Mathematical Functions*, Dover Publications Inc, New York, 1970

Ackoff, R.L., Toward a Behavioral Theory of Communication, *Management Science*, p. 218-234, Vol.4, 1958

Ackoff, R.L., Systems Organizations and Interdisciplinary Research, *General Systems Handbook*, Society for General Systems Research, p. 1-8, Vol.5, 1960

Ackoff, R.L., Emery, F.E., *On Purposeful Systems*, Aldine-Atherton, New York, 1972

Alter, S.L., *Decision Support Systems – Current Practice and Continuing Challenges*, Addison-Wesley Publishing Company, Reading, MA, 1980

Applied Telematics Group, *Integrated Message Systems – Developments and Opportunities*, Applied Telematics Group/ British Telecommunications, Tunbridge Wells, 1984

Bartoli, P.D., The Application Layer of the Reference Model of Open Systems Interconnection, *Proceedings of the IEEE*, p. 1404-1408, Vol.72, No.12, December 1983

Bass, F.M., A New Product Growth Model for Consumer Durables, *Management Science*, p. 215-277, Vol.15, January 1969

BECOM, *Digitale Telecommunicatie Stelsels voor de Negentiger Jaren* (DTS-90) (Digital Telecommunication Structures for the Nineties), BECOM Working Group, Dr. Neher Laboratorium, Leidschendam, November 1985

Beesley, M.E., *Liberalisation of the Use of British Telecommunications Network, Report to the Secretary of State*, Department of Industry, London, January 1981

Blokland, L.J., Jansen, J.P.G., Het Postverkeer in de Informatiemaatschappij (Postal Traffic in the Information Society), *Economische en Statistische Berichten* (ESB), p. 396-401, May 1984

Bocker, P., Gerke, P.R., The Integrated Services Digital Network (ISDN) and its Use for Text and Data Communication, in: Uhlig, R.P., *Computer Message Systems, Proceedings of the IFIP TC-6 International Symposium on Computer Message Systems*, Ottawa, Canada, 6-8 April 1981, North-Holland Publishing Company, New York, 1981

Bomers, G.B.J., Ontwikkelingen in de Bedrijfskunde (Developments in Management Science), *Bedrijfskunde*, p. 84-94, Vol.55, No.1, 1983

Bordewijk, J.L., Arnbak, J.C., *Basis voor een Tele-Informatie Beleid* (Foundation for a Tele-Information Policy), Projectgroep Beleid Informatie Toepassingen (BIT), The Hague, December 1983

Bordewijk, J.L., Kaam, B. Van, *Allocutie – Enkele Gedachten Over Communicatie Vrijheid in een Bekabeld Land* (Allocution – Some Thoughts About Freedom of Communications in a Wired Country), Bosch & Keuning NV, Baarn, 1982

Bottaro, D., *Analysis of Factors Affecting the Demand for and the Supply of Voluntary Consensus Standards*, Tech. Report No.MIT-EL82-0003WP, MIT Energy Laboratory, MA, 1981

Butler Cox Foundation, *Value-Added Network Services*, The Butler Cox Foundation, Report Series No.42, August 1984

Cantraine, G., Destine, J., (editors), New Systems and Services in Telecommunications, *Proceedings of the International Conference on New Systems and Services in Telecommunications*, Liege, Belgium, November 24-26, 1980, North-Holland Publishing Company, Amsterdam, 1981

CCITT, *Recommendation X.400, Message Handling Systems: System Model – Service Elements*, Study Group VII, International Telegraph and Telephone Consultative Committee, International Telecommunications Union, Geneva, 1984

CCITT, *Recommendation X.401, Message Handling Systems: Basic Service Elements and Optional User Facilities,* Study Group VII, International Telegraph and Telephone Consultative Committee, International Telecommunications Union, Geneva, 1984

CCITT, *Recommendation X.408, Message Handling Systems: Encoded Information Type Conversion Rules,* Study Group VII, International Telegraph and Telephone Consultative Committee, International Telecommunications Union, Geneva, 1984

CCITT, *Recommendation X.409, Message Handling Systems: Presentation Transfer Syntax and Notation,* Study Group VII, International Telegraph and Telephone Consultative Committee, International Telecommunications Union, Geneva, 1984

CCITT, *Recommendation X.410, Message Handling Systems: Remote Operations and Reliable Tranfer Server,* Study Group VII, International Telegraph and Telephone Consultative Committee, International Telecommunications Union, Geneva, 1984

CCITT, *Recommendation X.411, Message Handling Systems: Message Transfer Layer,* Study Group VII, International Telegraph and Telephone Consultative Committee, International Telecommunications Union, Geneva, 1984

CCITT, *Recommendation X.420, Message Handling Systems: Interpersonal Messaging User Agent Layer,* Study Group VII, International Telegraph and Telephone Consultative Committee, International Telecommunications Union, Geneva, 1984

CCITT, *Recommendation X.430, Message Handling Systems: Access Protocol for Teletex Terminals,* Study Group VII, International Telegraph and Telephone Consultative Committee, International Telecommunications Union, Geneva, 1984

Chapin, A. Lyman, Connections and Connectionless Data Transmission, *Proceedings of the IEEE,* p. 1365-1371, Vol.71, No.12, December 1983

Communications Study Group, *Japanese Legislation of Telecommunications*-Vol.1, Telecommunications Business Law, Communications Study Group, Tokyo, December 1984

Compaine, B.M., (editor), *Understanding New Media – Trends and Issues in Electronic Distribution of Information*, Ballinger Publishing Company, Cambridge, MA, 1984

Connell, S., Galbraith, I.A., *The Electronic Mail Handbook – A Revolution in Business Communications*, Century Publishing Co., London, 1982

Cunningham, I., Electronic Mail Standards to Get Rubber-Stamped and Go Worldwide, *Data Communications*, p. 159-168, May 1984

Cunningham, I., Message-Handling Systems and Protocols, *Proceedings of the IEEE*, p. 1425-1430, Vol.71, No.12, December 1983

Datapro, *Electronic Mail – A Management Overview*, Datapro Research Corporation, Delran, New Jersey, December 1983

Daumas, M., *A History of Technology and Invention*, Crown Publishers Inc, New York, 1969

Davies, D.W., Communication Networks to Serve Rapid Response Computers, *Proceedings of the IFIP Congress*, 72, 650, August 1968

Davies, D.W., Barber, D.L., Price, W.L., Solomonides, C.M., *Computer Networks and Their Protocols*, John Wiley & Sons Ltd, Chichester, 1979 (reprint 1983)

Davies, D.W., Price, W.L., *Security for Computer Networks*, John Wiley & Sons, Chichester, 1984

Day, J.D., Zimmermann, H., The OSI Reference Model, *Proceedings of the IEEE*, p. 1334-1345, ,Vol.71, No.12, December 1983

DBP, *Konzept fur den Deutschen Bundes Post zur Weiterentwicklung der Fernmeldeinfrastruktur* (Concept for the German PTT for the Continued Development of its Communications Infrastructure), Der Bundesminister fur das Post und Fernmeldewesen, Stab 202, Bonn, 1984

Dickson, G.J., Chazal, P.E. De, Status of CCITT Description Techniques and Application to Protocol Specification, *Proceedings of the IEEE*, p. 1346-1355, Vol.71, No.12, December 1983

Diebold, *Voice Communications in the Office*, Document No. 225S, The Diebold Group inc, May 1984

Dosi, G., *Technical Change and Survival – Europe's Semiconductor Industry*, European Research Centre, University of Sussex, Brighton, 1981

Dosi, G., *Technical Change and Industrial Transformation*, The MacMillan Press Ltd, London, 1984

Drucker, P.F., *Toward the Next Economics*, Harper & Row Publishers, New York, 1970

Duijn, J.J. van, *De Lange Golf in de Economie* (The Long Wave in Economy), Van Gorcum, Assen, 1979

Duuren, J. Van, The Common ICAO Interchange Network (CIDIN) Procedures, *Philips Telecommunication Review*, p. 201-210, Vol.39, No.4, 1969

Evans, D.S., (editor), *Breaking Up Bell – Essays on Industrial Organization and Regulation*, Elsevier Science Publishing Co. Inc, New York, 1983

EMA, *The Future of Electronic Mail and Messaging – A New Look in Light of the X.400 International Standards*, 13-15 November 1984, Boulder, Colorado, Electronic Mail Association, Washington, DC, 1984

Emery, F.E., (editor), *Systems Thinking*, Penguin Books Ltd, Harmondsworth, 1969.

EMMS, Cost Comparison of Leading Computer Mailbox Systems, Caswell, S., *EMMS (Electronic Mail and Message Systems)*, International Resource Development Inc, p. 1-5, Vol.8, No.6, 15 March 1984

Feigenbaum, F.A., Barr, A., Cohen, P.R., *The Handbook of Artificial Intelligence*, 3 Vol., William Kaufmann Inc, Los Altos, CA, 1981

Fisher, J.C., Pry, R.H., A Simple Model of Technological Change, *Technological Forecasting and Social Change*, p. 75-88, Vol.3, 1971

Fleishmann, J.L., (editor), *The Future of the Postal Service*, Praeger Publishers, New York, 1983

Foley, J.S., The Status and Direction of Open Systems Interconnection, *Data Communications*, p. 177-193, February 1985

Folts, H.C., desJardins, R., Scanning the Issue – The Special Issue on Open Systems Interconnection (OSI) – New International Standards Architecture and Protocols for Distributed Information Systems, *Proceedings of the IEEE*, p. 1331-1452, Vol.71, No.12, December 1983

Freeman, Ch., *The Economics of Industrial Innovation*, Frances Pinter (Publishers) Ltd, London, 1982 (2nd edition)

Freebody, J.W., *Telegraphy*, Pitman and Sons Ltd, London, 1958

Friedrich, K., Der Weg zum internationalen Fernschreib-Teilnehmersverkehr (The Route to International Telegraph Subscriber Traffic), *Siemens Zeitschrift*, p. 301-318, Vol.14, 1934

Frost & Sullivan, *The European Market for Electronic Mail Equipment and Services*, Frost & Sullivan Ltd, London, 1983

Frost & Sullivan, Data Communications for Microcomputers, *Proceedings of the 17-18 September 1984 Seminar*, International Management Services inc, Framingham, MA, 1983a

Galbraith, I.A., Teletex and Electronic Mail – The Shape of Things to Come, *Telephony*, p. 36-54, June 1984

Galjaard, J.H., *Informatisering – Paradox van Organisatie Technologie* (Informatization – Paradox of Organization Theory), Delftse Universitaire Pers, Delft, 1979

Ganley, O.H., Ganley, G.D., *To Inform or To control – The New Communication Networks*, McGraw-Hill, New York, 1982

GAS5, *Determination of the Economic Impact of New Servcices on Telecommunication Undertakings*, GAS5, Economic Studies No.9, International Telegraph and Telephone Consultative Committee, International Telecommunications Union, Geneva, 1984

Gershuny, J., *Social Innovation and the Division of Labour*, Oxford University Press, Oxford, 1983

Gershuny, J., Miles, I., *The New Service Economy*, Frances Pinter (Publishers) Ltd, London, 1983

Goldstein, R.C., Database – Technology and Management, John Wiley & Sons, New York, 1985

Goody Katz, B., Phillips, A., The Computer Industry, p. 162-232, in: Nelson, R.R., *Government and Technical Progress – A Cross Industry Analysis*, Pergamon Press Inc, New York, 1982

Gould, I.H., IFIP – *Guide to Concepts and Terms in Data Processing*, North-Holland Publishing Company, Amsterdam-London, 1971

Hayes-Roth, F., The Knowledge-based Expert System – A Tutorial, *Computer*, p. 11-28, September 1984

Hemenway, D., *Industrywide Voluntary Product Standards*, Ballinger Publishing Company, Cambridge, MA, 1975

Hill, C.T., Utterback, J.M., *Technological Innovation for a Dynamic Economy*, Pergamon Press, New York, 1979

Huppes, T., Berting, J., *Op Weg Naar de Informatiemaatschappij – Maatschappelijke Gevolgen en Determinanten van de Technologische Ontwikkeling* (Toward the Information Society – Social Consequences and Determinants of the Technological Development), Stenfert Kroese, Leiden, 1982

IBM, *Office Information Architectures – Concepts*, GC23-0765-0, International Business Machines Corporation, Austin, TX, March 1983

IBM, *Systems Network Architecture – Concepts and Products*, GC-30-3072, International Business Machines Corporation, Austin, TX, March 1983

ICC, *Corporate Handbook to International Telecommunications Organizations*, International Chamber of Commerce, Document No.373/29, Paris, 1985

IDC, *Strategies for Office Systems – Electronic Mail and Voice Mail*, Report ""2465, International Data Corporation, Framingham, January 1984

INSIS, INSIS Study – *Office Automation & Communications 1985 to 1995*, Communications & Information Systems (C/IS), The Yankee Group, Watford Herts, 1984

Irmer, T., The International Approach to ISDN – Facts and Trends, *Inter-national Switching Symposium*, paper 41-B2, Montreal, 1981

ISO, *Information Processing Systems – Open Systems Interconnection - Basic Reference Model*, International Organisation for Standardisation, ISO/IS 7498, ISO/TC97/SC16 (Rev), Geneva, 1983

Johnston, S.C., Jones, C., How to Organize for New Products, *Harvard Business Review*, p. 49-62, May-June 1957

Kahn, R.E., Vezza, A., Roth, A.D., Electronic Mail and Message Systems - Technical and Policy Perspectives, *Proceedings of the AFIPS Workshop on Technical and Policy Issues in Electronic Mail and Message Systems*, American Federation for Information Processing Societies (AFIPS) Inc, Arlington, VA, 1981

Kampen, H. Van, The Type DS714 Computer-Based Message and Data Switching System, *Philips Telecommunication Review*, p. 135-146, Vol.28, No.3, 1969

Keat, R., Urry, J., *Social Theory as Science*, Routledge & Kegan Paul Ltd, London, 1975

Keen, P.G.W., *Decision Support Systems – An Organizational Perspective*, Addison-Wesley Publishing Company, Reading, MA, 1978

Kitahara, Y., *Information Network System – Telecommunications in the Twenty-First Century*, Heinemann Educational Books, London, 1983

Kotler, Ph., *Marketing Management – Analysis, Planning and Control*, Prentice-Hall International Inc., London, fourth edition, 1980

Kramer, N.J.T.A., De Smit, J., *Systeemdenken* (Systems Thinking), Stenfert Kroese BV, Leiden, 1974

Kuhn, T.S., *The Structure of Scientific Revolutions*, The University of Chicago Press Ltd, London, 1962, 2nd edition 1970

Lee, A.M., *Electronic Message Transfer and its Implications*, Lexington Books, D.C.Heath and Company, Lexington, MA, 1983

Lee, D.L., Lochovski, F.H., Voice Response Systems, *Computing Surveys*, p. 351-374, Vol.15, No,4, December 1983

Levitt, T., *Innovation in Marketing – New Perspectives for Profit and Growth*, McGraw-Hill Book Company, New York, 1962

Levitt, T., Exploit the PLC, *Harvard Business Review*, p. 81-94, November-December 1965

Licklider, J.C.R., Vezza, A., The Utility of Electronic Message Systems, p. 11-32 in: Kahn, R.E., Vezza, A., Roth, A.D., Electronic Mail and Message Systems – Technical and Policy Perspectives, *Proceedings of the AFIPS Workshop on Technical and Policy Issues in Electronic Mail and Message Systems*, American Federation for Information Processing Societies (AFIPS) Inc, Arlington, VA, 1981

Licklider, J.C.R., Vezza, A., Applications of Information Networks, *Proceedings of the IEEE*, p. 1330-1346, Vol.66, No.11, November 1978

Link, *Electronic Mail Services – A Comparative Analysis*, Report ""0011, Link Resources Corporation, New York, August 1982

Link, *Value-Added Network Systems and Services*, Report ""0044, Link Resources Corporation, New York, May 1983

Linn, R.J., Nightingale, J.S., Testing OSI Protocols at the National Bureau of Standards, *Proceed-*

ings of the IEEE, p. 1431-1434, Vol.71, No.12, December 1983

Lipsey, R.G., Steiner, P.O., *Economics*, Harper & Row Publishers, New York, 1972

Littlechild, S.C., *Regulation of British Telecommunications' Profitability*, Report to the Secretary of State, Department of Trade, London, February 1983

Logica, *Data Communications in Western Europe in the 1980s*, The Eurodata Reports, prepared by Logica Ltd for the Eurodata Foundation, London, 1980

Logica, *Successful Word Processing*, Logica Holdings Ltd, London, 1980

Mackintosh, *Electronic Mail in Western Europe and North America 1978-1987*, multi-client study by Mackintosh Consultants Company Ltd, London, 1978

Mackintosh, *The Strategic Impact of Teletex on Text, Image and Data Communications Markets*, multi-client study by Mackintosh Consultants Company Ltd, London, 1983

Mansfield, E., *Industrial Research and Technological Innovation*, W.W. Norton & Company Inc, New York, 1968

Mansfield, E., Technical Change and the Rate of Innovation, *Econometrica*, p. 741-766, Vol.29, 1961

Martin, J., *The Wired Society – A Challenge for Tomorrow*, Prentice-Hall Inc, Englewood Cliffs, New Jersey, 1978

Maurice, Ph., Le Teletex Mode-Mixte – Le Courrier Electronique de Demain, *L'Echo des Recherches*, p. 41-50, No.116, 2e trimestre 1984

McFarlan, E.W., McKenney, J.L., Pyburn, Ph., The Information Archipelago - Plotting a Course, *Harvard Business Review*, p. 145-156, January-February 1983

McFarlan, E.W., McKenney, J.L., The Information Archipelago – Governing the New World, *Harvard Business Review*, p. 91-99, July-August 1983

McLaughlin, J.F., Birinyi, A.E., *Mapping the Information Business, Program on Information Resources Policy*, Harvard University, Cambridge, MA, 1980

McQuillan, J.M., *Electronic Mail*, Conference Lectures 10-11 December 1984, CGS Institute, London, 1984

Meijer, A., Peeters, P., *Computer Network Architectures*, Pitman Publishing Ltd, London, 1982

Mensch, G., *Das technologische Patt* (The Technological Path), Umschau Verlag, Berlin, 1975

Mintzberg, H., Patterns in Strategy Formulation, *Management Science*, p. 24-29, May 1978

Mowery, D., Rosenberg, N., The Influence of Market Demand Upon Innovation – A Critical Review of Some Recent Empirical Studies, *Research Policy*, p. 102-153, Vol.8, 1979

Mumford, L., *Technics and Civilization*, Harcourt Brace Yovanovitz, New York, 1963

Myer, Th.H., Standards for Global Messaging – A Progress Report, *Journal of Telecommunication Networks*, p. 413-433, Vol.2, No.4, Winter 1983

NBS, *Specification for Message Format for Computer Based Message Systems*, proposed Federal Information Processing Standard 98, Gaithersburg, Maryland, 1982

NCC, *Handbook of Data Communications*, The National Computing Centre Ltd, NCC Publications, Oxford, 1982

Nelson, R.R., *Government and Technical Progress – A Cross Industry Analysis*, Pergamon Press Inc, New York, 1982

Nelson, R.R., Winter, S.G., *An Evolutionary Theory of Economic Change*, The Belknap Press of Harvard University Press, Cambridge, MA, 1982

Nelson, R.R., Winter, S.G., In Search of Useful Theory of Innovation, *Research Policy*, p. 36-76, No.6, 1977

Nora, S., Minc, A., *The Computerization of Society*, The MIT Press, Cambridge, MA, 1980 – original publication: L'Informatisation de la Société, La Documentation Francaise, Paris, 1978

Nothhaft, H.R., Making a Case for Using Electronic Mail, *Data Communications*, p. 85-93, May 1983

NRC, *Electronic Message Systems for the US Postal Service*, US Postal Service Support Panel, National Research Council, National Academy Press, Washington, DC, 1976

NTIA, *Long-Range Goals in International Telecommunications and Information – An Outline for United States Policy*, Committee on Commerce, Science and Education, US Senate, National

Telecommunications and Information Administration (NTIA), US Government Printing Office, Washington, DC, 1983

Online, *Videotex International, Proceedings of Videotex '84 International*, held in Amsterdam, November 1984, Online Conferences Ltd, Pinner, Middlesex, 1984

OTA, *Computer-based National Information Systems – Technology and Policy Issues*, US Congress Office of Technology Assessment, Publication 81-600144, US Government Printing Office, Washington, DC, 1981

OTA, *Implications of Electronic Mail and Message Systems for the US Postal Service*, US Congress Office of Technology Assessment, Publication 82-600599, US Government Printing Office, Washington, DC, 1982

OTA, *Selected Electronic Funds Transfer Issues – Privacy, Security, and Equity*, US Congress Office of Technology Assessment, Publication 82-600524, US Government Printing Office, Washington, DC, 1982a

Perry, W.E., *The Micro-Mainframe Link*, John Wiley & Sons, New York, 1985

Renton, R.N., *Telex Service*, The Institution of Post Office Electrical Engineers, Publication no.207, London, 1954

Roebuck, C., *The World of Ancient Times*, Charles Scribner & Sons, New York, 1966

Rogers, E.M., *Diffusion of Innovations*, 3rd edition, The Free Press, New York, 1983

Rosenberg, N., *Inside the Black Box: Technology and Economics*, Cambridge University Press, Cambridge, London, 1982

Rosenberg, N., *Technology and American Economic Growth*, Harper Torch Books Inc, New York, 1972

Rothwell, R., Zegveld, W., *Industrial Innovation and Public Policy – Preparing for the 1980s and the 1990s*, Frances Pinter (Publishers) Ltd, London, 1981

Rothwell, R., Zegveld, W., *Reindustrialization and Technology*, Longman Group Ltd, Harlow, 1985

Roukens, J., Renuart, J.F., (editors), *ESPRIT '84 – Status Report of Ongoing Work*, Elsevier Science Publishers BV, North-Holland, Commission of the European Communities, 1985

Samuelson, P.A., *Economics*, McGraw-Hill Inc, New York, 1970, Het Spectrum, Utrecht, 1972

Schenke, K., Ruggeberg, R., Otto, J., *Teletex – A New International Telecommunication Service for Text Communication*, Deutsche Bundes Post, Fernmelde-Technisches Zentralamt, Bonn-Darmstadt, 1982

Scherpenhuijzen, J.F., *Taak en Funktie van de PTT met betrekking tot Informatie- en Telecommunicatietechnologie* (Task and Function of the PTT with respect to Information- and Telecommunication Technology), Tweede Kamer, 1983-1984, Document No. 17 370, The Hague, 19 January 1984

Sherman, R., (editor), *Perspectives on Postal Service Issues*, American Enterprise Institute for Public Policy Research, Washington, Dc, 1980

Schick, T., Brockish, R.F., The Document Interchange Architecture – A Member of a Family of Architectures in the SNA Environment, *IBM Systems Journal*, p. 220-245, Vol.21, No.2, 1982

Schicker, P., The Computer-Based Mail Environment – An Overview, *Computer Networks*, p. 435-443, Vol.5, 1981

Schön, Die Deutsche Bundespost auf ihrem Weg zum ISDN (The German PTT towards ISDN), *ZPF*, p. 21-30, Vol.6, 1984

Scott, M.D., *Computer Law*, Wiley Law Publications, John Wiley & Sons, New York, 1984

Shannon, C.E., Weaver, W., *The Mathematical Theory of Communication*, University of Illinois Press, Chicago, 1963

Siegel, J., Moving Data Between PC's and Mainframes, *Byte*, p. 248-255, Fall 1984

Siegman, J., *Electronic Mail Services – A Report to Help the Prospective User Select an Electronic Message System*, Seybold Publications Inc, Pennsylvania, 1983

Sirbu, M.A., A Survey of Electronic Mail Technology, p. 57-80 in: Kahn, R.E., Vezza, A., Roth, A.D., Electronic Mail and Message Systems – Technical and Policy Perspectives, *Proceedings of the AFIPS Workshop on Technical and Policy Issues in Electronic Mail and Message Sys-*

tems, American Federation for Information Processing Societies (AFIPS) Inc, Arlington, VA, 1981

Sirbu, M.A., Zwimpfer, L.E., Standards Setting for Computer Communications – The Case of X.25, IEEE *Communications Magazine*, p. 35-44, Vol.23, No.3, March 1985

Sjöström, O., Strindlund, E., Nordic Public Data Network with AXB 30, *Ericsson Review*, p. 22-30, Vol.1, 1982

Solomon, J., The Future Role of International Telecommunications Institutions, *Telecommunications Policy*, p. 213-221, Vol.8, No.3, September 1984

Stamps, G.M., *The Future for Electronic Document Distribution*, Institute for Graphic Communications, MA, USA, 1982

Steenbergen, Th.S., *Signalen voor Straks – Een Nieuwe Richting voor de PTT* (Signals for Later – A New Direction for the PTT), Commissie Steenbergen, ordered by the Secretary of State, Department of Trade, Distributiecentrum Overheidspublikaties (DOP), The Hague, July 1985

Stern, N., *From ENIAC to UNIVAC – A Case Study in the History of Technology*, Digital Press, Bedford, MA, 1981

Tanenbaum, A.S., *Computer Networks*, Prentice-Hall inc, Englewood Cliffs, New Jersey, 1981

Technology Analysis Group, *Value-Added Network Services in the United States*, Technology Analysis Group inc, Washington, DC, March 1984

Telecommunication Act 1984, Chapter 12, Her Majesty's Stationery Office, 12 April 1984

Toffler, A., *The Third Wave*, Bantam Books inc, New York, 1980

Toffler, A., *The Adaptive Corporation*, McGraw-Hill Book Company Ltd, London, 1985

Trebing, H.M., Issues in Public Utility Regulation, *Proceedings of the Institute of Public Utilities Tenth Annual Conference*, Michigan State University, 1979

Uhlig, R.P., International Computer Message Services, *Journal of Telecommunication Networks*, p. 399-409, Vol.2, No.4, Winter 1983

Uhlig, R.P., Computer Message Systems, *Proceedings of the IFIP TC-6 International Symposium on Computer Message Systems*6, Ottawa, Canada, 6-8 April 1981, North-Holland Publishing Company, New York, 1981

Uhlig, R.P., Farber, D.J., Bair, J.H., *The Office of the Future*, The International Council for Computer Communications, North-Holland Publishing Company, New York, 1979

Vallee, J., *The Network Revolution*, Penguin Books, New York, 1982

Vallee, J., *Computer Messaging Systems*, McGraw-Hill, New York, 1984

Vervest, P.H.M., Research Proposal – *The Management of Public Electronic Mail Service: An Assessment of Technological Change and Market Acceptance,* unpublished working paper, Graduate School of Management, Delft, August 1983

Vervest, P.H.M., Wissema, J.G., *Electronic Mail and Message Handling in the USA – Results of the May 1984 Study Tour*, Erasmus University Rotterdam, October 1984

Vervest, P.H.M., Wissema, J.G., *Electronic Mail and Message Handling in Japan – Results of the February, March 1985 Study Tour*, Erasmus University Rotterdam, April 1985

Vervest, P.H.M., *Electronic Mail and Message Handling*, Frances Pinter (Publishers) Ltd, London, 1985

Vervest, P.H.M., Visser, M., Van Aller, J., Wissema, J.G., *The Introduction of Electronic Mail – Perspectives for Telecommunication Managers – Results of the April/ May 1985 Questionnaire for the International Communications Association (ICA), Dallas*, Eburon, Delft 1986

Vezza, J.C.R., Licklider, A., Applications of Information Networks, *Proceedings of the IEEE*, Vol.66, No. 11, p. 1330-1346, November 1978

Vissers, C.A., Tenney, R.L., Bochmann, G.V., Formal Description Techniques, *Proceedings of the IEEE*, p. 1356-1364, Vol.71, No.12, December 1983

Vittal, J., Active Message Processing – Messages as Messengers, p. 175-195 in: Uhlig, R.P., Computer Message Systems, *Proceedings of the IFIP TC-6 International Symposium on Computer Message Systems*, Ottawa, Canada, 6-8 April 1981, North-Holland Publishing Company, New York, 1981

Von Hippel, E., Successful Industrial Products from Customer Ideas, *Journal of Marketing*, p. 39-49, Vol.42, January 1978

Von Hippel, E., Transferring Process Equipment Innovations from User-Innovators to Equipment Manufacturing Firms, *R&D Management*, October 1977

Waterman, D.A., *A Guide to Expert Systems*, Addison-Wesley Publishing Company, Reading, MA, 1985

Watzlawick, P., Beavin, J.H., Jackson, D.D., *Pragmatics of Human Communications*, W.W. Norton & Company Inc, New York, 1967, Van Loghum Slaterus' Uitgeversmaatschappij NV, Deventer, 1983

Webster, F.E., Wind, Y., *Organizational Buying Behavior*, Prentice-Hall Inc, Englewood Cliffs, New Jersey, 1972

Werner, K., *Das Bildschirm-Recht Entwickelt sich* (Videotex Law is Developing), Bildschirmtext-Anbieter Vereinigung, VDE-Verlag, Berlin, 1985

Wiener, N., *Cybernetics: Or Control and Communication in the Animal and the Machine*, The MIT Press, Cambridge, MA, 1948, 1961; third printing July 1982

Williams, M.B., (editor), *Pathways to the Information Society, Proceedings of the Sixth International Conference on Computer Communications, London, 7-10 September 1982*, North-Holland Publishing Company, Amsterdam, 1982

Wilson, P.A., *Introducing the Electronic Mailbox*, The National Computing Centre Ltd, NCC Publications, Oxford, 1984

Wilson, P.A., *Commercial Electronic Mailbox Systems*, The National Computing Centre Ltd, NCC Publications, Manchester, 1983

Wind, Y., *Product Policy: Concepts, Methods and Strategy*, Addison-Wesley Publishing Company, Reading, MA, 1982

Wissema, J.G., *De Kunst van het Strategisch Management – Invoering, Toepassing, Trends* (The Art of Strategic Management – Introduction, Application, Trends), NIVE-Kluwer, Deventer, 1986

Wissema, J.G., *Zeg mij – Wat Voor een Ding Is Technologie?* (Tell me – What Kind of Thing is Technology?), Kluwer, Deventer, 1982

Yankee Group, *Electronic Messaging and Facsimile*, Industry Research Report, The Yankee Group, Boston, MA, 1982

Yankee Group, *Electronic Transactions*, The Report on Electronic Mail, The Yankee Group, Boston, MA, 1983

Yankee Group, *The Network Resource Report*, The Yankee Group, Boston, MA, May 1984

Zaltman, G., Wallendorf, M., *Consumer Behavior*, John Wiley & Sons, New York, 1979

INDEX